# THE
# • 50 •
# HEALTHIEST PLACES
# TO LIVE AND RETIRE IN
# THE UNITED STATES

## Norman D. Ford

Mills & Sanderson, Publishers

1991

**Published by Mills & Sanderson, Publishers**
Box 665, Bedford, MA 01730
Copyright © 1991 Norman D. Ford

**Library of Congress Cataloging-in-Publication Data**

Ford, Norman D., 1921-
 The 50 healthiest places to live and retire in the United States /
Norman D. Ford.
  p.  cm.
 Includes bibliographical references and index.
 ISBN 0-938179-25-X : $12.95
 1. Retirement, Places of--United States.  I. Title. II. Title:
Fifty healthiest places to live and retire in the United States.
HQ1063.F67 1991
646.7'9--dc20                                                                90-49964
                                                                                      CIP

Printed and manufactured by Capital City Press, Inc.
Cover design by Lyrl Ahern.


**Printed and Bound in the United States of America**

*To my wife Shirley who shares the low-risk lifestyle with me in one of America's most healthful cities*

# Other Books by Norman D. Ford

*Best Rated Retirement Cities and Towns*
*Where to Retire on a Small Income*
*Norman Ford's Florida Retirement Guide*
*Retiring in Mexico*
*Retirement Paradises of the World*
*Formula for Long Life*
*Lifestyle for Longevity*
*Minding Your Body*
*Sleep Well, Live Well*
*Good Health Without Drugs*
*Natural Ways to Relieve Pain*
*How to Travel Without Being Rich*
*America by Car*
*How to Beat the Common Cold*

# ABOUT THE AUTHOR

Norman D. Ford brings to this book a background of 40 years of experience in researching and writing guidebooks to the geography of retirement. Starting in 1951, his *Where to Retire on a Small Income* immediately achieved best-seller status and eventually ran through 26 revised editions. In the ensuing years, Ford authored almost two dozen other books on retirement and health including the million copy best seller *Norman Ford's Florida Retirement Guide; Retiring in Mexico; Retirement Paradises of the World; and Best Rated Retirement Cities and Towns,* now one of the Consumer Guide series.

As a member of the American Medical Writers Association, Ford has also authored a variety of books dealing with the low-risk lifestyle, ranging from *Formula for Long Life* and *Lifestyle for Longevity* to *Good Health Without Drugs; Sleep Well, Live Well;* and *Keep on Pedaling--the complete guide to adult bicycling.*

Ford lives in the hill country of Texas with his wife Shirley. Aged 70 and an active bicyclist, hiker and swimmer, Norman Ford credits his excellent health to having strictly followed the low-risk lifestyle for over 30 years.

# CONTENTS

# AMERICA'S MOST HEALTHFUL CITIES—From A to Z

| | |
|---|---|
| Alamogordo, NM | La Crosse, WI |
| Albuquerque, NM | Las Cruces, NM |
| Ann Arbor, MI | Los Alamos, NM |
| Austin, TX | Madison, WI |
| Birmingham, AL | Melbourne, FL |
| Bloomington, IN | Minneapolis-St. Paul, MN |
| Boulder, CO | Missoula, MT |
| Boulder City, NV | Moab, UT |
| Bozeman, MT | Mount Dora, FL |
| Bradenton-Sarasota, FL | Paradise, CA |
| Cedar City, UT | Pensacola, FL |
| Chapel Hill, NC | Portland, OR |
| Clearwater, FL | Prescott, AZ |
| Colorado Springs, CO | Providence, RI |
| Columbus, OH | Redding, CA |
| Corvallis, OR | St. Petersburg, FL |
| Davis, CA | San Antonio, TX |
| Durango, CO | San Diego, CA |
| Eau Claire, WI | Santa Fe, NM |
| Eugene, OR | Seattle, WA |
| Fayetteville, AR | Silver City, NM |
| Gainesville, FL | Sun Cities, AZ |
| Green Valley, AZ | Tallahassee, FL |
| Huntsville, AL | Tucson, AZ |
| Kerrville, TX | West Palm Beach, FL |

# ACKNOWLEDGEMENTS

So many direct and indirect sources were consulted in researching this book that it is impractical to acknowledge every one. Nonetheless, my deepest appreciation goes to these people:

Jennifer Merrill. Communications Assistant, Zero Population Growth for permission to quote from Zero Population Growth's 1988 *Urban Stress Test* study; Nick Naymark, Assistant Vice President, Northwest National Life Insurance Company for providing access to the company's 1990 report, *The NWNL State Health Ratings*; Paul Hoffman, Editor-in-Chief, *Discover* magazine for permission to quote from the article "Dawn of the Human Race" by Jared Diamond (professor of physiology, UCLA School of Medicine) published in *Discover* magazine, May 1989; Martha Moyer, Assistant Director, Public and Community Relations, Del Webb Corporation for a penetrating analysis of changing exercise trends in retirement communities; Linda L. Van Orden, Coordinator of Communications and Business Data, Eugene Area Chamber of Commerce, Oregon for invaluable guidance to community sources of health and fitness information; and to Gregory W. Heath, D.H. Sc., M.P.H., Exercise Physiologist, Centers for Disease Control, Atlanta.

I would also like to acknowledge the outstanding help and cooperation of the staff of the Chambers of Commerce and Convention and Visitors Bureaus of each of our healthful cities, not only for supplying hard-to-find statistical data and quality of life profiles but also for providing a wealth of leads to other city departments, many of which gave me exclusive information on a wide range of health and fitness aspects in their cities.

I must also acknowledge the unstinting help and assistance provided by personnel in the parks and recreation (or leisure) departments in each of our healthful cities. Frequently, they were the only knowledgeable source of guidance to fitness facilities, and to opportunities for staying fit and healthy.

Everyone who contributed facts and information to this book has helped make it infinitely better than I could have ever done without their help.

Norman D. Ford
Kerrville, TX

# KEY TO THE 50
# HEALTHIEST CITIES

| City # | City/State | Healthfulness Score | City # | City/State | Healthfulness Score |
|---|---|---|---|---|---|
| 1 | Boulder, CO | 63 | 26 | Minneapolis-St. Paul, MN | 52 |
| 2 | Eugene, OR | 61 | 27 | Silver City, NM | 51 |
| 3 | Ann Arbor, MI | 61 | 28 | Missoula, MT | 51 |
| 4 | Madison, WI | 60 | 29 | Green Valley, AZ | 50 |
| 5 | Chapel Hill, NC | 59 | 30 | Eau Claire, WI | 50 |
| 6 | Santa Fe, NM | 59 | 31 | Pensacola, FL | 50 |
| 7 | Colorado Springs, CO | 59 | 32 | Austin, TX | 50 |
| 8 | Davis, CA | 58 | 33 | Portland, OR | 50 |
| 9 | Gainesville, FL | 57 | 34 | Kerrville, TX | 49 |
| 10 | San Diego, CA | 57 | 35 | Fayetteville, AR | 49 |
| 11 | Durango, CO | 56 | 36 | Tucson, AZ | 49 |
| 12 | Bloomington, IN | 56 | 37 | San Antonio, TX | 49 |
| 13 | Prescott, AZ | 55 | 38 | Redding, CA | 48 |
| 14 | La Crosse, WI | 55 | 39 | Clearwater, FL | 48 |
| 15 | Albuquerque, NM | 55 | 40 | West Palm Beach, FL | 48 |
| 16 | Corvallis, OR | 54 | 41 | Mount Dora, FL | 47 |
| 17 | Bradenton-Sarasota, FL | 54 | 42 | Cedar City, UT | 47 |
| 18 | Bozeman, MT | 53 | 43 | Las Cruces, NM | 46 |
| 19 | Huntsville, AL | 53 | 44 | Tallahassee, FL | 46 |
| 20 | Columbus, OH | 53 | 45 | Birmingham, AL | 46 |
| 21 | Seattle, WA | 53 | 46 | Paradise, CA | 45 |
| 22 | Los Alamos, NM | 52 | 47 | Providence, RI | 45 |
| 23 | Alamogordo, NM | 52 | 48 | Moab, UT | 43 |
| 24 | Sun Cities, AZ | 52 | 49 | Melbourne, FL | 43 |
| 25 | St. Petersburgh, FL | 52 | 50 | Boulder City, NV | 41 |

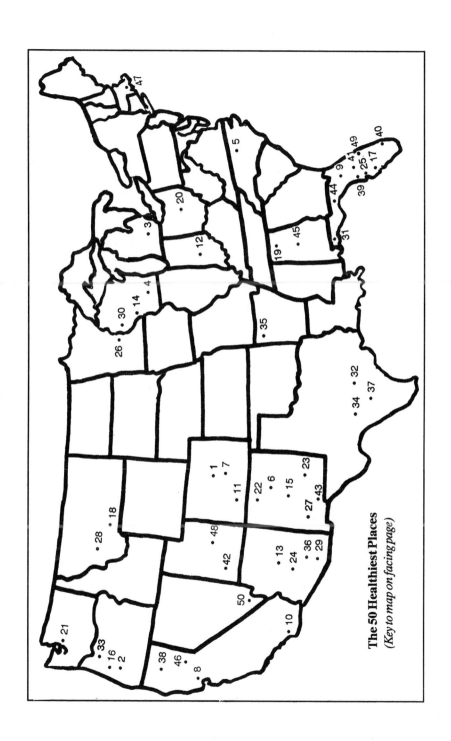

**The 50 Healthiest Places**
(Key to map on facing page)

# 1
# Citadels of Health and Long Life

Earlier in this century, it was a popular pursuit for medical journals to select a locale and brand it, "the healthiest place in the United States." Among places chosen at various times were St. Petersburg, Florida; Kerrville, Texas; and a peninsula in Washington state.

In those days, tuberculosis, pneumonia, and appendicitis ranked among the leading causes of death in the United States. And a place was defined as *healthy* on the basis of climate; beauty of setting; elevation and purity of air; and apparent freedom from congestion and urban stress.

Issues like these, which are built into, or arise out of, the very fabric of a city and its environment, are regarded today as *inherent* factors that influence health. Fifty years ago, it was assumed that if you moved to a *healthful* city and went on living as usual, somehow these inherent factors would help you to become healthier and live longer.

Today we know better.

A man who smokes two packs of cigarettes and downs three cans of beer a day, eats a high-fat diet, is overweight, and doesn't exercise is unlikely to achieve any significant health benefit by moving to a *healthful* city and continuing these habits. Even relocating to our top-ranking city might net him only an extra month or two of life.

So how do we measure the healthfulness of a city today?

## New Dimensions of Healthfulness

First, we must accept a different definition of "healthfulness." T.B. and appendicitis are no longer feared killer diseases. Among mature Americans, the leading causes of death today are heart disease, stroke, cancer, Type II diabetes, emphysema, osteoporosis, and renal disease.

Secondly, we must realize that the greatest triumph of modern medical science has not been to produce powerful drugs and hi-tech treatments for those already sick. It has been the thoroughly validated and documented discovery that, by simply upgrading our personal lifestyle habits, we can significantly reduce the risk of ever becoming sick in the first place.

The greatest medical discovery in recent decades is that most of the diseases that kill Americans are brought on by the vicissitudes of our own lifestyles. Thousands of studies from all over the world have confirmed, beyond any question of doubt or debate, that when we replace our health-destroying habits with health-building behaviors we can statistically reduce our risk of getting cancer, heart disease, and most other common killer diseases by as much as 90 percent, and in some cases more.

Scientifically validated studies have already demonstrated that many cases of hypertension and Type II diabetes are readily reversible by beneficial lifestyle changes alone. Using sophisticated medical tests, Dean Ornish, M.D., and other researchers have proved that progress of angina and coronary artery disease can also be halted—and in many cases gradually reversed—by replacing our typical high-fat, high-stress lifestyle with a safer way of living and eating.

A way of living that eliminates all health-destroying habits and replaces them with health-promoting habits is known as a low-risk lifestyle.

2

## *The Wellness Lifestyle*

Nowadays, we know that merely sitting in a place with the purest of air and water, and with a mild, sunny climate, isn't going to make us healthy if we avoid all exercise, eat nothing but junk food, are 50 pounds overweight, feel lonely and depressed, and are filled with worry and anxiety.

Today, the key factor that determines a city's healthfulness is the extent to which it provides facilities and support for living a low-risk lifestyle.

Virtually every major health-advisory agency in America has publicly endorsed at least some of the steps in the low-risk lifestyle. Nowadays, the most prestigious health authorities in America are urging us to eat more fruits, vegetables, and whole grains, and fewer fats and foods of animal origin. The American Heart Association, the National Cancer Institute, the National Academy of Sciences, and the Surgeon General himself have all recommended eating this low-fat, high-fiber diet. They have also urged that we exercise more, avoid loneliness, and minimize stress. Other top researchers recommend keeping the mind active, expressing altruism through volunteer work, and having faith in a higher power.

When we incorporate all these health-restoring habits into our lifestyle, results can be dramatic. That's because a low-risk lifestyle effectively prevents most of the diseases commonly associated with growing old. Study after study has demonstrated that most of the diseases that kill older Americans are not due to aging at all but to a lifetime of health-destroying habits. By replacing these lethal habits with health-enriching habits, we can become biologically younger and add many years of creative, productive living to our statistical life expectancy.

Thus the main thrust of progress in medical science is on how to prevent disease rather than to cure it. Even after indulging in health-destroying habits for years, provided no irreparable damage is done, it is usually possible to shift gears and regain a fairly high level of wellness. That's because all our lifestyle habits are under our direct personal control and we are perfectly free to change any of our habits whenever we choose.

Yet in practice, lifestyle habits are so deeply entrenched in our society that changing them is something most people would rather avoid. Doctors are accustomed to hearing pleas such as: "Drug me! Cut me open! Do a by-pass operation! But don't ask me to change my diet or to begin an exercise program."

Knowing this helps explain why any attempt to upgrade our lifestyle habits is much more likely to succeed when we have the full support and approval of the community. This same rationale explains why so few Americans are able to stay with a low-risk lifestyle in a city that is uncaring and unreceptive to the health and fitness movement, and where they feel isolated and ignored.

By way of example, a recent study by the Centers for Disease Control in Atlanta showed that, nationwide, only 7.6 percent of adults exercise sufficiently to provide any benefit to their hearts and lungs. Yet in such health-oriented cities as Eugene, Oregon or Boulder, Colorado, the figure is at least three to four times as high. In these cities, approximately one of every three adults owns a high-performance bicycle and everyone who seeks to follow a low-risk lifestyle experiences total acceptance and a high level of community support.

### How a Type-A City Stresses Your Health

Does your city's attitude encourage becoming healthier and fitter? Or is it a Type-A city with a level of urban stress so high that residents regard lifestyle improvement with hostility and cynicism?

Just as hostility and cynicism make a Type-A person prone to heart disease, so the fast pace of life in a Type-A city leads to a distinctly higher rate of stress-related disease. America is filled with Type-A cities that are more interested in promoting jobs, growth, and more cars than in preserving the health and well-being of their residents. Almost three out of every four Americans—150 million altogether—are already breathing air that is polluted far beyond allowable EPA standards. In some cities, to exercise outdoors during a health alert is to risk bouts of coughing and chest discomfort that can persist for hours.

Toxins from overloaded garbage landfills are contaminating drinking water in hundreds of U.S. cities. And many of these cities are facing a garbage disposal crisis as property available for new landfills is rapidly running out.

Meanwhile, driving to and from work through ferocious freeway traffic has become a twice daily trauma for millions of people. So destructive to health and well-being is the crime, overcrowding, and noise in many large American cities that the top priority of millions of residents is to get out and move to a more health-nurturing environment.

While highly motivated individuals may still manage to follow a low-risk lifestyle in a Type-A city, it is obviously much easier and more pleasant to do so in a low-stress city with a health-oriented attitude.

## Requirements of a Healthful City

A healthful city is primarily a place in which both the community and one's peers are strongly supportive of a low-risk lifestyle. Ideally, a healthful city offers us the perfect environment and it provides all the resources and encouragement we need to launch into a low-risk lifestyle and to make it a permanent part of our lives. In the process, we can minimize our risk of ever getting heart disease, stroke, cancer, Type II diabetes, emphysema, osteoporosis, or renal disease—at least, until very late in life.

Typically, most larger healthful cities have an ample supply of natatoriums and swimming clubs, walking and bicycling trails, heart exercise trails, and tennis complexes, plus at least one large supermarket dedicated exclusively to natural foods. You'll find vegetarian restaurants and singles clubs for all ages, while opportunities abound for personal and intellectual growth and social contacts. Acupuncturists, naturopaths, and other alternative health professionals are taken for granted while M.D.'s who offer holistic, non-drug healing approaches practice next to others offering sports medicine and mainstream allopathy.

By comparison, all too many Type-A cities do little or nothing to encourage residents to exercise or to stay with a healthful diet. City fathers regard bicyclists as a problem, and the need for bicycle paths or exercise trails is often totally ignored. Year around lapswimming is unavailable to most Americans. And in all too many cities, residents are programmed by the community attitude, and by their peers, to grow old rapidly and to accept the idea that chronic disease is inevitable and unavoidable.

In stark contrast, most healthful cities offer powerful incentives for continuing to live in optimal health. Most residents view health and longevity as a great opportunity to lead a life brimming with activity, adventure, and creativity. Instead of being addicted to alcohol, cigarettes, or prescription drugs, residents become addicted to life itself. Those following a low-risk lifestyle typically wake up with such zeal and enthusiasm they can hardly wait to get out of bed and begin another exciting day. Life is too exhilarating and filled with challenge and interest to allow time to contemplate senility, sickness, or suicide.

Although all this may sound exaggerated, it is taken for granted by anyone who is actively following and practicing the low-risk lifestyle.

## *The Geography of Healthfulness*

Whether you're able to move now or must wait until you retire, if you're seeking a healthful and less stressful city to live in, then this is your book. In these pages, we have tried to select and to rank the 50 most healthful cities in the United States in which to live and retire.

Rating the United States' best places to live is a popular pastime indulged in each year by several major magazines and by half a dozen annually-revised guidebooks. Most base their rankings and choices on an array of statistical data. But statistics are subject to so many disparities that selecting a locale on the basis of statistics alone can often be disappointing. For instance, some cities measure air pollution levels in the heart of downtown while others quote levels taken as far away as possible from the center. Crime and other factors are frequently taken from county statistics and applied to a city that may occupy only a small part of the county. And many authors tend to read too much into their figures.

Since we believe that this is the first effort made in recent times to select and rank the United States' healthiest cities, we must admit that our methodology is still somewhat inexact, rather experimental and not infallible. But we do believe it's the most thorough assessment that anyone has made to date.

## *Assessing Health Requires a Whole Person Approach*

Right from the beginning it was evident that to measure the healthfulness of a city, we must address every issue that influences wellness and well-being. To find out whether a city will contribute to your health—or possibly ruin it instead—requires taking a holistic or Whole Person approach. That means evaluating not merely hard facts and statistics but more elusive and unquantifiable factors such as a city's basic attitude to health.

Does a city's attitude encourage the health and fitness culture or does the couch potato lifestyle still rule? In a health-conscious city, residents are usually dedicated to preserving the environment, eliminating pollution, promoting recycling instead of larger landfills, and spending funds on facilities for physical fitness rather than on new roads and highways for more automobiles. Bicycles are encouraged for transportation, and everything possible is done to maintain and enhance the quality of life. Obviously, factors like these are not readily translatable into statistics. So rather than pretend to offer a definitive and sophisticated statistical analysis, we have combined those statistics which do bear on health with our own written evaluation of other issues which are more intangible and subjective. Finally, we have given a ranking number for each of thirteen key factors that most affect a city as a healthful place to live. We then total these to arrive at a Total Healthfulness Score.

### How a City Influences Your Health

All factors which affect a city's healthfulness fall into a natural dichotomy.

1. *Inherent influences*—climate, elevation, scenic beauty, hardness of water, size, growth rate, levels of air and water purity, crime, extent of hazardous waste and sewage problems, education, crowding, and economics, each of which is a by-product of the city and its environment.

2. *Lifestyle influences*—facilities and programs for physical fitness, the awareness of the population regarding health and nutrition, availability of stress management programs, opportunities to exercise the mind through intellectual and cultural activities, opportunities to interact with others through social contacts, opportunities to volunteer, and opportunities for spiritual growth.

8

Each of these lifestyle factors plays an essential role in a low-risk lifestyle, and each exerts a powerful influence on a person's overall wellness. Opportunities to avoid loneliness by socializing with other people, and to express altruism through volunteer work, can be as important to health as eating a low-fat diet and exercising regularly.

## *In Search of a Healthful City*

John and Sally Reid learned about the low-risk lifestyle through a prevention-type health program offered to employees by John's corporation. Through adopting just two lifestyle steps—eating a low-fat diet and exercising regularly—the Reids saw their cholesterol levels drop 40 percent in just a few weeks. As part of the program, they also took up a variety of fitness recreations that included regular lapswimming, tennis, brisk walking, and bicycling. Again, in just a few weeks, they achieved such robust energy that they could easily walk or bicycle for hours without feeling tired.

But Sally and John lived in a typical Type-A city. And they soon encountered peer pressure that hindered their new lifestyle. Some friends and relatives ridiculed their diet, while others joked about their tennis whites and "funny" bicycling clothes.

"Our hometown was quite unsupportive of our new, healthy lifestyle," John told us later. "Everyone we knew was completely indifferent to health or fitness. We felt rather isolated, and we were looked on as freaks."

"But John was due to retire in a few months," Sally took up the story, "So we decided to look for a city that regards the health and fitness culture as the norm and the couch potato culture as abnormal. We wanted a community that nurtures every aspect of a health-enriching lifestyle."

Locating a health-conscious city wasn't easy.

The Reids wrote to dozens of cities and communities requesting information on health and fitness resources and activities, and asking about the existence of year-around lapswimming pools and natural foods supermarkets.

Many of the brochures they received boasted about how well each city's hospitals could treat disease. But, with a single exception, not one piece of Chamber of Commerce literature mentioned a word about opportunities for staying well.

The exception was Durango, Colorado.

## A City Committed to Health and Well-Being

In the literature John received from the Durango Chamber of Commerce was a publication entitled *Along the Animas—Tracking the Health of Durango, Colorado.* Written by the area's graduate student nurses class, it combined statistics and interviews with residents to present a very thorough profile of the holistic health of Durango and its people. On the premise that the health of a community is inter-related to its environmental, economic, social, educational, and cultural aspects, the nurses had reviewed every issue from climate to air and water purity, waste disposal, lifestyle, fitness resources, and health care. Their very complete assessment also included opportunities for intellectual activity and spiritual growth.

Interviewees described Durango's lifestyle as "active"; "the pace here is slower and good for health"; "it probably forces us Type-A personalities to slow down a bit"; and "Durango has fewer couch potatoes than Los Angeles." Interviewees from all walks of life indicated that they had moved to Durango for its recreational opportunities, climate, scenery, and the low level of urban stress. Very obviously, Durango's lifestyle emphasizes physical fitness while residents are more aware and supportive of physical activity, diet, and other health-promoting behaviors.

The Reids flew to Durango for their next vacation and their expectations were thoroughly fulfilled. Today, they raise their own organic fruits and vegetables beside the Animas River and their days are filled with exhilarating bicycle rides in summer, and exciting cross-country ski trips on deep powder snow in winter.

"Every decision to move is a trade-off," Sally pointed out. "Like every high altitude city, Durango has minor air pollution in winter, and we have tourist traffic in summer. But all in all, we can honestly say that Durango is thoroughly committed to the health and well-being of its residents. Health and fitness is a top priority for just about everyone here."

It may sound like pie in the sky—and you won't find it mentioned in most Chamber of Commerce literature—but a surprising number of other U.S. cities come equally close to qualifying as citadels of healthful living.

By way of example, here is our selection of the United States' fifty most healthful cities ranked from first to last in order of healthfulness. The gold, silver, and bronze medal categories are our own idea and are self-explanatory.

## *The Healthiest Places to Live and Retire*

| Rank | City/State | Healthfulness Score | Population |
|------|------------|---------------------|------------|
| **GOLD MEDAL CITIES** | | | |
| 1 | Boulder, CO | 63 | 90,000 |
| 2 | Eugene, OR | 61 | 110,000 |
| 3 | Ann Arbor, MI | 61 | 112,000 |
| 4 | Madison, WI | 60 | 187,000 |
| 5 | Chapel Hill, NC | 59 | 45,000 |
| 6 | Santa Fe, NM | 59 | 80,000 |
| 7 | Colorado Springs, CO | 59 | *300,000 |
| 8 | Davis, CA | 58 | 50,000 |
| 9 | Gainesville, FL | 57 | 90,000 |
| 10 | San Diego, CA | 57 | 1,100,000 |

## SILVER MEDAL CITIES

| 11 | Durango, CO | 56 | 16,000 |
|----|-------------|-----|--------|
| 12 | Bloomington, IN | 56 | 56,000 |
| 13 | Prescott, AZ | 55 | 30,000 |
| 14 | La Crosse, WI | 55 | 55,000 |
| 15 | Albuquerque, NM | 55 | 510,000 |
| 16 | Corvallis, OR | 54 | 50,000 |
| 17 | Bradenton-Sarasota, FL | 54 | *300,000 |
| 18 | Bozeman, MT | 53 | 30,000 |
| 19 | Huntsville, AL | 53 | 175,000 |
| 20 | Columbus, OH | 53 | 650,000 |

## BRONZE MEDAL CITIES

| 21 | Seattle, WA | 53 | *2,000,000 |
|----|-------------|-----|-----------|
| 22 | Los Alamos, NM | 52 | 22,000 |
| 23 | Alamogordo, NM | 52 | 32,000 |
| 24 | Sun Cities, AZ | 52 | 64,000 |
| 25 | St. Petersburg, FL | 52 | 260,000 |
| 26 | Minneapolis-St. Paul, MN | 52 | *2,300,000 |
| 27 | Silver City, NM | 51 | 12,000 |
| 28 | Missoula, MT | 51 | 80,000 |
| 29 | Green Valley, AZ | 50 | 16,000 |
| 30 | Eau Claire, WI | 50 | 60,000 |

## RUNNER-UP CITIES

| 31 | Pensacola, FL | 50 | 70,000 |
|----|---------------|-----|--------|
| 32 | Austin, TX | 50 | 500,000 |
| 33 | Portland, OR | 50 | *1,400,000 |
| 34 | Kerrville, TX | 49 | 26,000 |
| 35 | Fayetteville, AR | 49 | 45,000 |
| 36 | Tucson, AZ | 49 | *800,000 |
| 37 | San Antonio, TX | 49 | 1,100,000 |
| 38 | Redding, CA | 48 | 65,000 |
| 39 | Clearwater, FL | 48 | 100,000 |
| 40 | West Palm Beach, FL | 48 | *500,000 |
| 41 | Mount Dora, FL | 47 | 7,800 |
| 42 | Cedar City, UT | 47 | 14,000 |
| 43 | Las Cruces, NM | 46 | *85,000 |
| 44 | Tallahassee, FL | 46 | 135,000 |

| 45 | Birmingham, AL | 46 | * 1,000,000 |
|----|----------------|----|-------------|
| 46 | Paradise, CA | 45 | 35,000 |
| 47 | Providence, RI | 45 | 175,000 |
| 48 | Moab, UT | 43 | 4,700 |
| 49 | Melbourne, FL | 43 | 60,000 |
| 50 | Boulder City, NV | 41 | 14,000 |

The maximum possible score for total healthfulness is 70. Where more than one city has the same score for total healthfulness, the city with the smallest population is listed first and the city with the largest population last. A good general rule is that the smaller the city, the more healthful it is.

The population figures are estimates for 1991. In most cases, they include the population of any small adjoining towns. In terms of rating healthfulness, we felt that this was usually more meaningful than quoting the official census count for the core city alone. Hence our figures may not agree exactly with those of the 1990 census.

Population totals marked with an asterisk (*) are those for an entire metropolitan area.

Due to the often exorbitant cost of housing in much of urban southern California and the Northeast, as well as for reasons such as poor air quality, we have minimized selections in some of these areas.

How these rankings were arrived at is carefully explained in the remainder of this book. You will find a detailed profile and report on the health aspects of each city in the second half of this book.

## *A City for Everyone*

While the fifty cities were chosen primarily with healthfulness in mind, we also endeavored to provide the greatest possible variety. As a result, they range in size from some of the smallest to some of the largest cities in the United States … from tropical beach resorts to winter sports centers …

from places where retirement checks power the economy to others in which it is fueled by hi-tech research, education and medical care ... from relaxed small towns to high-energy university centers ... from places which seem tailored for retirement to others which offer younger workers a variety of well-paid career choices ... and from places surrounded by spectacular natural beauty to others not quite as inspiring.

Nonetheless, the majority are interesting *both* for retirement *and* as places to pursue a career and to raise a family. Even though some of the northern cities may not be well known as retirement locales, nearly all our cities can qualify as good places to retire.

For example, few people might consider retiring from New Jersey to the Colorado Rockies. But that is exactly what some couples are doing.

We met one such couple while cross-country skiing at over 11,000 feet in the mountains west of Boulder, Colorado. Two years previously, this couple had moved from Trenton to Boulder (our top gold medal award city). Rather than retire to a life of ease in the Florida sun, they preferred to hike and ski-tour in the Rockies by day, and to audit classes at the University of Colorado, or to square dance, in the evenings.

It may still be unusual, but people have retired from West Palm Beach, Florida to Colorado Springs, Colorado and literally thousands have moved from California to retire in Montana or Oregon. In many cases, they found the move more satisfying than did many of those who headed in the opposite direction and joined the retirement stampede to the Sunbelt.

# 2

# Ranking the Healthfulness of the States

## *Are Some States More Healthful to Live in Than Others?*

State health statistics can provide a useful indication of how closely the lifestyle in each state compares to our ideal low-risk lifestyle. But the lifestyle variations they reveal are almost invariably due to social, economic and environmental differences.

Why, for example, is the heart disease rate only 128 per 100,000 annually in North Dakota, while in West Virginia it's 78 per cent higher—a whopping 218 per 100,000 annually? Why does Utah have the lowest cancer rate in the nation? Why do Wyoming, Nevada and Colorado share the dubious distinction of having the highest rates of lung disease? And why is the Deep South called "The Stroke Belt?"

Even professional statisticians are tempted to read too much into figures. Yet it's fairly safe to assume that Utah's low cancer rate—it also has the nation's lowest rate of major illnesses and the highest ranking for exercise—is due to its large Mormon population who abstain from tobacco and alcohol for religious reasons. North Dakota's low rate of heart disease has been linked to the low-fat content of its traditional diet. Likewise, West Virginia s high heart disease rate can be traced to a mix of cardiovascular risk factors in its Appalachian lifestyle. Widespread cigarette smoking in

15

rural areas—possibly linked with the western cowboy image—seems to explain the high lung disease rate in Wyoming, Nevada and Colorado. And a higher incidence of hypertension among the black population appears to explain the high rate of stroke in the Deep South.

Interestingly, none of the variations is due to inherent differences like climate or elevation, or even to air or water pollution. The fact that the life expectancy of a baby born in Delaware is 2½ years less than that of a newborn in Utah is due entirely to lifestyle variations.

Measuring the healthfulness of each state was recently simplified when the Northwest National Life Insurance Company ranked all fifty states by the healthfulness of their inhabitants.

For starters, the study used World Health Organization standards to define a healthy population as, "one that is in a state of complete physical, mental and social well-being and not merely the absence of disease or infirmity." Defined this way, health has many dimensions including anatomical, physiological, mental, cultural and environmental factors. As the NWNL report states, "the rankings look at health in a wide, holistic sense."

## Measuring the Healthfulness of States

The survey ranked the healthfulness of each state by measuring the levels of seventeen common health statistics selectively grouped into five categories. The five categories consisted of:

**The Lifestyle Factor,** which measures behavioral effects such as smoking, motor vehicle deaths, violent crime, risk for heart disease, and the educational level—that impact the overall health of each state's population. The five best-scoring states were: 1.Utah; 2.North Dakota; 3.Montana; 4.Nebraska; 5.Hawaii.

**The Access-to-Medical Care Factor**, which measures the availability of health care services to each state's population. The five best-scoring states were: 1. Connecticut; 2. New Hampshire; 3. Massachusetts; 4. New Jersey; 5. Hawaii.

**The Disability Factor**, which measures the degree to which injury and sickness impact the daily activity of individuals and their ability to work and to enjoy life fully (considered by public health professionals as a very important indicator of the overall health of a population). The five best-scoring states were: 1. Hawaii; 2. Alaska; 3. New Mexico; 4. California; 5. Texas.

**The Disease Factor**, which measures the impact of illnesses such as heart disease, cancer, AIDS, tuberculosis and hepatitis on the population. The five best-scoring states were: 1. Wyoming; 2. North Dakota; 3. Minnesota; 4. Colorado; 5. Nebraska.

**The Mortality Factor**, which measures the healthfulness of a population by noting the differences in the total death rate and by measuring the years of useful life lost by deaths before age 65. The five best-scoring states were: 1. North Dakota; 2. Hawaii; 3. Minnesota; 4. Iowa; 5. Utah.

The five group rankings were then totaled to assign each state an overall ranking as follows.

## Overall State Health Rankings

| | |
|---|---|
| 1. Utah | 10. Colorado |
| 1. Minnesota | 12. Vermont |
| 3. New Hampshire | 12. North Dakota |
| 4. Hawaii | 12. Maine |
| 5. Nebraska | 15. Virginia |
| 5. Connecticut | 16. New Jersey |
| 7. Massachusetts | 17. Rhode Island |
| 7. Wisconsin | 18. Montana |
| 7. Iowa | 19. Ohio |
| 10. Kansas | 20. Pennsylvania |

| | |
|---|---|
| 20. Indiana | 34. New York |
| 22. California | 34. Illinois |
| 23. South Dakota | 38. Kentucky |
| 23. Maryland | 39. Alabama |
| 25. Oklahoma | 39. Arkansas |
| 25. Wyoming | 39. Arizona |
| 25. Delaware | 39. South Carolina |
| 25. Michigan | 43. Oregon |
| 25. Missouri | 44. Florida |
| 30. Washington | 45. New Mexico |
| 30. Texas | 45. Louisiana |
| 32. North Carolina | 47. Nevada |
| 33. Idaho | 47. Mississippi |
| 34. Georgia | 49. West Virginia |
| 34. Tennessee | 50. Alaska |

**Note:** states which carry duplicate ranking numbers received the same overall healthfulness score.

Worth noting is that many of the most healthful states are in the north. Such popular retirement states as Florida, Arizona, Nevada and South Carolina are close to the bottom, while northern tier states like North Dakota, New Hampshire, Minnesota and Wisconsin score near the top in healthfulness. These examples serve to remind us that a warm, sunny climate cannot always offset poor health habits and high rates of urban stress.

Surveys such as this also reveal apparent contradictions. Despite their high rates of cigarette smoking, Colorado and Wyoming end up as tenth and twenty-fifth healthiest states respectively. But again, at risk of reading too much into statistics, a fairly distinct pattern seems to emerge. The most affluent states with the fewest industrial cities seem to predominate among the higher ranking states, while many of the poorest southern states, along with several rust belt states, appear more numerous among the lowest-scoring states.

Seen in this light, the state rankings do seem to generally correlate with the rankings of our 50 healthiest cities.

Some years ago, a similar survey ranked the 48 continental states in order of attractiveness for retirement. Although the retirement rankings bore little resemblance to the order of rankings for healthfulness, Utah also took top place as the nation's best state for retirement.

Although Utah may not be the home of any of our gold medal cities, it has always impressed us as a thoroughly safe and wholesome state with an abundance of both inherent and lifestyle qualities that enhance its overall healthfulness.

# 3
# Rating the Cities I: Inherent Man-Made Health Factors

## *Urban Stress and Pollution*

Urban stress is a measure of the combined effect of environmental, economic and social stresses on a city's quality of life. The quality of life in many large American cities has already fallen below minimal standards on the most basic social measures.

Uncontrolled growth has already turned much of urban Southern California into a dehumanizing morass of choked freeways, filthy air, crime, drugs, gangs, and more trash and sewage than the aging and weakened infrastructure can handle. Urban sprawl and shrinking open space have virtually annihilated the once-envied California lifestyle.

According to recent public health reports, one of every two California children currently remain without immunizations against childhood diseases, and fewer than 33 percent of tenth graders will graduate with their senior class. Among those in the lower socio-economic levels, health standards, life expectancy, and infant mortality rates are little higher than in many Third World countries.

Urban stress is created almost entirely by rapid population growth. The same rapid growth that is destroying

California's quality of life is having equally deleterious effects on the health of middle class urban Americans throughout the nation.

Urban stress resulting from the pressures of population growth is one of the major underlying causes of stress-related disease in the United States. Among the principal stress-related diseases that kill or cripple Americans are hypertension, heart disease, stroke, cancer, pneumonia, ulcers, and rheumatoid arthritis.

To examine how cities are coping with the stress of uncontrolled population growth, Zero Population Growth organization designed its now famous Urban Stress Test. By rating a city on each of eleven interrelated criteria, the Urban Stress Test arrives at an overall index which ranks each city in the hierarchy of stress.

The eleven criteria include: population change, crowding, education, violent crime, births, community economics, individual economics, hazardous waste, sewage, water, and air quality. Each of these criteria is an inherent but man-made factor that, directly or indirectly, influences the healthfulness and quality of life of each urban center (and of every other community as well).

Scores of surveys have confirmed that the incidence of stress-related diseases and dysfunctions in a population correlates closely with the level of urban stress. This implies that the most healthful cities are those with the lowest levels of urban stress.

Already people are becoming skeptical of the traditional paradigm that more and bigger is better. The votes of millions of Americans are indicating that clean air and water are more important than larger paychecks. One hallmark of a healthful city is that it places the health, welfare, and well-being of its residents ahead of profits, prosperity and business growth. Another more visible indicator is that a healthful city remains a friendly and pleasant place in which to own and drive an automobile.

Although we are becoming increasingly aware of the high price in declining health and quality of life that we must pay to live in a fast-growing city, few of us realize that the prime cause of urban stress is the private automobile.

## *Our Dehumanizing Cities Are Stressing Our Health*

In most other countries, the majority of city workers commute to the job by public transportation. But when the United States traded its public transportation system for private automobiles it locked Americans into a lifestyle that made us increasingly dependent on cars, mechanization, and consumption of energy. As every form of physical exertion was eliminated from the American way of life, the nation lost its vitality to the automobile.

The result is a soft, flabby, health-sapping existence which requires most families to own at least two automobiles and so many appliances that we consume several times as much energy per capita as any other nation. As the American economy continues its struggle against world competition, the stress of surviving in most American cities is so great that many people have no time to be concerned with their health.

Half of all U.S. families are unable to afford even a modest facsimile of the American dream. The cost of housing, automobiles, and utilities is turning urban life into a nightmare. Meanwhile, the price of medical treatment has soared to such heights that, even with insurance, most Americans can no longer afford to be sick.

Today, the stress of urban living is taking an increasing toll on human health. Urban commuting has become a major source of chronic stress and the basic cause of millions of cases of stress-related disease.

## Gasoline Overkill

Scores of surveys have revealed that traffic congestion is the most important factor in determining the quality of urban life. In all too many cities today, driving in rush hour traffic has become sheer misery. Many large cities are so congested that the rush hour begins as early as 11 a.m. By mid-afternoon, it can take five minutes to creep a single block. Bumper-to-bumper driving, gridlock, and long tie-ups have become pandemic in dozens of U.S. cities.

In and around the hundred largest metropolitan areas, public discontent has already begun to dampen our longtime love affair with the automobile. According to the Federal Highway Department, if no improvements are made, freeway congestion will quadruple by the year 2010. The fastest-growing cities will have ten times as many cars as at present.

In Southern California, freeway speeds are already down to 33 mph and are expected to drop to 15 mph by the end of the century. As almost half of all urban space is occupied by cars, American cities are being carved up and disfigured by more and more freeways, roads and parking lots.

## The Tyranny of the Automobile

In large, fast-growing cities, owning and driving an automobile has become the single most stressful factor in the American way of life. Anyone who doubts this need only try driving to a shopping mall on a weekend afternoon. Once safely at home after the twice daily hassle on the freeways, many urban and suburban dwellers prefer to spend their evenings and weekends at home rather than brave the traffic to go out again.

The family car that once enhanced our prestige and standard of living is now destroying our quality of life. Instead of providing freedom and mobility, the auto has become a form of enslavement. Making it all even more stressful is the increasingly burdensome cost of automobile ownership, insurance, and operation. Most families are forced to spend one-fifth of their incomes for an obligatory form of transportation which is becoming less and less efficient and attractive. Indeed, financing automobile ownership keeps one-half of all Americans permanently in debt.

## *Toxic Air: Profile of Peril*

In sixty metropolitan areas of the United States, air quality reaches unsafe levels at least several times each year. And in several large metropolitan areas in Southern California, the air is unhealthy to breathe on an average of 232 days each year. Meanwhile, the Clean Air Act Coalition reports that over 100 million Americans live in cities with air so polluted that breathing is hazardous to health.

The main risks to health are breath-robbing levels of carbon monoxide and ozone. But all air pollutants can damage the lungs of a person who exercises outdoors. Since outdoor exercise plays an essential role in a low-risk lifestyle, it is fairly obvious that the majority of American cities do not qualify as healthful places to live.

Among the worst polluters are chemical, tire, and pesticide plants; petroleum refineries; and smelters, which spew cadmium and other heavy metals into the atmosphere. If the air is significantly polluted in the community in which you currently live, this fact might weight your decision to relocate to a more healthful area. You can check local levels of air pollution by calling the local office of the EPA.

## *How Smog Sabotages Health*

While we like to place the blame for air pollution on power plants and industry, emission from private automobile exhausts remains the largest source of air pollution. Automobiles are the major cause of the familiar yellow-brown clouds of stagnant, urban smog.

Smog causes some degree of harm to everyone who inhales it. People who consistently breathe air that fails to meet

EPA standards tire more easily, the cells in their lungs begin to thicken and die, and their lungs lose elasticity. A recent Harvard University study revealed that air pollution kills over 80,000 Americans annually, far more than are killed in traffic accidents.

Of the constituents of smog, automobiles are primarily responsible for carbon monoxide, nitrous oxides, hydrocarbons, and ozone.

When hydrocarbons and nitrous oxides are emitted from auto exhausts they are transformed by sunlight into ozone. A toxic form of oxygen, ozone is the most hazardous component of smog. Ozone build-up can occur in any area of heavy traffic during warm, sunny weather. Ozone's effects are worst during hot summer afternoons between May and September.

Federal standards consider the ozone level unhealthy when it builds up to .12 parts per million (ppm). Yet almost every U.S. city exceeds this standard at least once each year. In most areas, whenever ozone levels exceed .2 ppm for one hour or more, a health alert is given. People at risk are advised to remain indoors and not exercise. However, research has shown that levels as low as .08 ppm can affect lung tissues and cause chest pain and headaches.

Ozone is doubly dangerous because it cannot be screened out by nasal cilia and it is breathed directly into the alveoli, causing irritation, coughing, congestion, suppressed immunity and premature aging of the lungs. People exercising outdoors at .15 ppm frequently encounter breathing difficulties and chest discomfort, both of which can linger for hours. Inhaling ozone while exercising can also inflame the lungs and reduce their capacity while simultaneously irritating the throat. People with asthma are particularly susceptible to ozone. Animals exposed to ozone for long periods have shown symptoms of emphysema and have suffered from deterioration in lung capacity.

Yet as this was written, 94 U.S. cities were violating the Clean Air Act and ozone levels were the highest on record.

## *A Shapeless Destroyer of Vitality and Health*

Odorless and colorless, carbon monoxide abounds in the air of congested cities, especially in California. It results from incomplete combustion of gasoline. Carbon monoxide combines with hemoglobin in the bloodstream to prevent the red blood cells from transporting oxygen to tissues, heart, and other organs.

As a result, carbon monoxide causes pulmonary problems and is particularly hazardous to anyone with heart disease or angina. Carbon monoxide also impairs coordination and ability to concentrate.

Carbon dioxide is another colorless gas spewed in enormous quantities from auto exhausts, particularly during winter. Although not directly hazardous to health, carbon dioxide is largely responsible for the greenhouse effect and global warming. Many suspended particles of dust, soot, and dirt in smog also cause eye irritation.

## *Acid Rain Menaces Health*

Yet another health-damaging pollutant is acid rain, created when sulfur dioxides and nitrogen oxides are released into the atmosphere by the burning of fossil fuels. Upon exposure to sunlight, they are transformed into dilute forms of sulfuric and nitric acids. Clouds transport acid rain aerosols nationwide in such quantities that they overload the planet's ability to absorb them. Vast quantities of acid rain are steadily strangling all life in forests and lakes from California to New England. So destructive are these acids that they have already eaten away the outer surfaces of hundreds of marble and stone structures.

With equal potency, the acids inflame the lungs of all who inhale them, and over the long term may cause permanent scarring of lung tissue. Health damage to the lungs of Americans by acid rain is so widespread that the American Lung Association estimates it costs the nation $15 billion annually in medical treatment.

## *Our Gas Guzzling Lifestyle May Be Ending*

Continuing to live in a city with polluted air may have other far-reaching lifestyle effects. Already, No-Drive Days, which require 20 percent of all drivers to leave their cars at home on one day each week are being instituted in badly polluted areas. And much more stringent controls appear likely in the future.

The goal of the new Clean Air Bill is to cut emission of toxic chemicals and acid rain 75 percent and to give every U.S. city clean air to breathe. Terms of the bill call for cars nationwide to meet the rigorous California tailpipe emission standards. In heavily-polluted areas, gas stations may be restricted to selling a blend of oxygenated gasoline. And by 1997, ten percent of new cars may be powered by low-pollution methanol fuel designed to reduce atmospheric ozone. Among the worst-polluted U.S. cities are Los Angeles, Houston, New York, Chicago, Baltimore, Philadelphia, and Milwaukee. Many cities at high elevations, such as Denver, also suffer from heavy carbon monoxide pollution.

Under consideration, however, is a newly-proposed Los Angeles Air Quality Plan that goes far beyond proposed federal standards in reducing tailpipe emission. Under these standards, new autos may emit only .25 grams of hydrocarbons per mile (gpm) and .4 gpm of nitrogen oxide. Currently, federal standards permit .41 gpm of hydrocarbons. If adopted the new California standards will probably stimulate similar standards across the country.

To upgrade air quality, the federal government may, in the future, force cities to levy punitive tolls and parking surcharges to penalize commuting by cars with only one person. Another probable move is to withhold federal highway funds from major cities that fail to reduce tailpipe emission by a specified amount. And bans may be extended to prevent driving on certain days and in certain places.

Under the proposed Los Angeles Plan, gasoline may be banned altogether by 2007. Car pooling will become mandatory, free parking will be severely restricted, and limits will be placed on the number of cars per family. For Americans who continue to live in or near large, polluted cities, automobile ownership will become increasingly less attractive and personal mobility will certainly be reduced.

## Bicycle-Friendly Cities Score High on Healthfulness

In future years, the bicycle is likely to emerge as a far superior alternative to short-distance automobile travel, at least in fine weather. Today's multi-geared, high-performance bicycle is the most energy-efficient vehicle ever designed for land travel. Beneficial to health, and completely non-polluting, the bicycle requires only a minimum level of fitness to use. Unfortunately, millions of Americans are too unfit to pedal a bicycle—or for that matter, to walk—even one mile. However, today's hi-tech bicycles are so efficient and easy to pedal that a moderately fit person can readily cover distances of ten to twenty miles or more, often in less time than it takes to drive a car the same distance through congested city streets.

Already, most healthful cities in America have recognized the advantages of the bicycle by constructing bikeways and bicycle paths and by instituting other aids to urban bicycle travel.

It has been our experience that any city which is recognized as being *bicycle-friendly* or which advertises itself as *bike friendly*, especially if it has a full-time bicycle coordinator, is likely to offer an exceptionally high quality of life and livability. We have found that being *bicycle-friendly* is a more dependable indication of a city's healthfulness than almost any other guideline or statistic.

## *Lethal Landfills Threaten Our Drinking Water*

All over America, mountains of trash are leaching contamination into surface and underground water supplies, endangering the safety of drinking water. Attempts to dispose of garbage by incineration have proved equally hazardous to health, producing huge amounts of heavy metals, dioxins, and hydrochloric acid.

America's throwaway philosophy has created a major nationwide garbage crisis. Although Americans constitute only 5 percent of world population, we generate 25 percent of the world's waste. Currently totaling 160 million tons annually, U.S. refuse is expected to increase to 193 million tons by the year 2000.

Our mounting levels of garbage are creating an increasingly stressful situation because most landfills serving major cities are already choked. Meanwhile, public opposition and the NIMBY (not in my backyard) attitude is making it extremely difficult and expensive to create new landfills. By 1995, only half as many landfills will be in operation as now. At about the same time, half of all U.S. cities will have exhausted their present landfills.

Massachusetts has already used up all available landfill space, and several northeastern cities have been trucking garbage as far as 80 miles to dumps in Ohio and Pennsylvania. Recycling is the only workable solution to shrinking landfill space. To preserve their quality of life, most healthful cities are already immersed in active programs to recycle all aluminum and tin cans, glass bottles, plastic, cardboard, and newsprint.

Not surprisingly, then, another unfailing indication of a healthful city is the presence of a strong and vigorous recycling program. Any bicycle-friendly city that also has a strong recycling program is almost invariably a superbly livable city with an exceptionally high quality of life.

## The Pathology of Pesticides

Landfill contamination is not the only source of water pollution. Manmade pollution is leaching into soil and water all over the country. According to the EPA, underground water supplies in 38 states have been contaminated by agricultural pesticides. The situation is worsened because many of America's underground water supplies are steadily vanishing. Water in lakes, rivers, and aquifers is being used with profligate disregard for future replenishment. At Tucson, for example, the water table has dropped 170 feet since 1960. All over Florida, California, and Arizona, farmers are abandoning irrigation due to shrinking water supplies.

As supplies diminish while contaminants increase, the concentration of contaminants is also steadily rising. In the lower Mississippi Valley, increasing rates of certain types of cancer have already been linked to waterborne pesticide contamination.

## The Stress on Our Coasts

Man-made pollution doesn't stop at smog and landfills. Excessive amounts of agricultural pesticides flowing into the ocean periodically set off a flush of algae blooms, suffocating and poisoning millions of fish. Residents of beach resorts along the Gulf of Mexico and New England coast are all too familiar with *red tides* that leave their beaches littered with millions of dead and rotting fish. Meanwhile, a toxic bouillabaisse of sewage and chemicals has contaminated over one-third of the nation's shellfish beds. Many types of coastal fish are no longer safe to eat.

At the same time, our beaches and shores are being steadily eroded, and the culprit is largely the same carbon dioxide that we daily spew out in huge amounts from our automobile exhausts. Carbon dioxide is a major cause of the greenhouse effect. As global warming steadily melts the Arctic ice cap, seas all over the world are gradually rising. At many places on the Atlantic coast, the high water mark has moved 50 feet inland during the last half century. As the Arctic ice cap continues to melt, scientists predict that in future decades, storm waves will range thousands of feet inland, destroying hundreds of low-lying cities and beach resorts.

From California around the Gulf of Mexico to the Carolina Banks, Long Island and Cape Cod, the oceans are steadily stripping the nation of its sand dunes and beaches. In California, hundreds of beachfront homes and hotels have toppled into the Pacific. Not only have hundreds of miles of beach disappeared, but many of those sections left intact have been badly littered by a tidal wave of trash and garbage.

As landfill space runs out, the oceans are being increasingly used as a gigantic garbage dump. Particularly around the Gulf of Mexico and on the middle Atlantic coast, beaches have been littered with trash and filth that has included fecal matter, balls of grease and oil film, discarded video cassettes, plastic six-pack yokes, plastic jars and bottles of every size, and styrofoam cups and egg cartons plus an array of medical waste ranging from hypodermic needles to catheter bags, sutures, bandages, and even still-intact blood samples.

Most beach resorts use a fleet of trucks to clean up the debris. But undeveloped shores are often left uncleaned. Nor can trucks stop erosion. And efforts to restore beaches by pumping up fresh sand, notably at places like Miami Beach and Delray Beach, Florida, have been only partially successful. The reason is that dumping fresh sand on an already-eroded beach steepens the beach angle. Eventually, the sand will wash away once more.

Exacerbating the problem is that over half the U.S. population lives within 30 miles of the seacoast. Population density figures show that our coastal areas are saturated with an average 267 persons per square mile, compared to only 46 elsewhere.

While the onslaught of litter, red tides, and erosion may not directly affect health, taken together they could prove extremely stressful to anyone who has counted on enjoying long beach walks or ocean swimming for exercise and health.

## *Evaluating Urban Stress*

Evaluating the level of urban stress for cities with a population of 100,000 or more has been greatly simplified by publication of Zero Population Growth's Urban Stress Test. By applying the Stress Test to statistics measuring eleven different criteria that arise from rapid population growth, ZPG has come up with an Overall Rating of Urban Stress for each of 192 cities and metropolitan areas in the U.S.

After awarding a score of from 1 (best) to 5 (worst) for each of the eleven criteria, the average of these scores becomes a city's Overall Rating for urban stress. For the 192 cities reviewed in the 1988 Stress Test, Overall Ratings ranged from a low (best) of 1 .6 for Cedar Rapids, Iowa to a high (worst) of 4.2 for Gary, Indiana.

Due to the time required to assemble the various statistics used by ZPG, some of the data can be several years old at the time of review. Usually, however, data for inherent criteria of this type is fairly slow to change. And once established, a trend tends to continue. Thus a city's Overall Rating is unlikely to show sudden or dramatic change.

Hence the Overall Ratings of ZPG's Urban Stress Test appear to be the best indicator available of the quality of life, and therefore, of the healthfulness of a city, in terms of man-made and environmental stress.

For cities in this book too small to have been ranked by ZPG, we have evaluated their urban stress level ourselves, using data as close as possible to that used by ZPG and using a similar scoring system. Admittedly, statistics for smaller cities are not as readily available as for cities of 100,000 or more. While data such as that for violent crime is readily available for each county, statistics for other criteria may not exist for smaller communities. In such cases, we either omitted the factor, or obtained a local estimate.

In this book, Overall Ratings from the ZPG Urban Stress Test are preceded by the symbol ZPG (for example, Urban Stress: ZPG 2.6). Overall Ratings which we evaluated ourselves are preceded by the symbol EST (for example, Urban Stress: EST 2.6).

Stressfully high ratings for any of the eleven criteria are commented on in the description of each city in this book, as are below average levels.

Here is a review of each of the eleven criteria used in the ZPG Urban Stress Test.

### 1. POPULATION CHANGE
The U.S. population has doubled since 1945 and is growing at the rate of two million annually, with the greatest increase among those of lower socio-economic status in the largest cities. By increasing the use of energy and automobiles, a growing population acutely affects health on all levels.

Utilizing recent population change statistics, ZPG's Population Change rating presents a broad perspective in the dynamics of population change taking place. ZPG considers model communities as those having stable populations over time, with modest gains or losses. Stressed communities have large numerical population increases (or losses) and population growth rates exceeding 10 percent annually.

Thus any city with a population growth rate in excess of 10 percent annually is likely to suffer from growing pains that can stress the health of its residents.

### 2. CROWDING
This is ZPG's measurement of the percent of housing with more than one person per room. In model communities, only 1-2.1 percent of housing units are crowded, whereas in stressed communities 7 percent or more of housing units are crowded.

### 3. EDUCATION

ZPG measures educational attainment based on the percentage of the population 25 or older with a high school education (1980) and a community's educational expense per pupil for the 1984-85 school year. Model communities are defined as those in which 80 percent or more of residents are high school graduates. In stressed communities, fewer than 55 percent of adult citizens have a high school education.

### 4. VIOLENT CRIME

ZPG considers that violent crime statistics are far more reliable than those collected on other types of crime. Violent crimes may also be a better indicator of population-related stress.

ZPG's measurement is based on the rate of violent crime per 100,000 population for 1985 and 1986, as well as the change in crime rate from 1980 to 1986. Model communities are those which report violent crime rates of fewer than 350 per 100,000 inhabitants and an increase in crime rate of 3.5 percent or less.

### 5. COMMUNITY ECONOMICS

ZPG rates a community's economic standing based on its unemployment rate in 1987 and its 1987 Moody's Bond Rating. Model communities have unemployment rates below 4.6 percent and a *Best* quality rating from Moody's. Stressed communities have unemployment rates exceeding 9.4 percent and a *Speculative* rating from Moody's.

### 6. INDIVIDUAL ECONOMICS

ZPG combines data on the percentage of both families and individuals living in poverty in 1979 and the change in per capita income from 1979 to 1985. (The most recent poverty statistics were those for 1979.)

In model communities, fewer than 5 percent of families and 6 percent of individuals live in poverty, while per capita income topped $12,500 annually and had increased more than 56 percent from 1979 to 1985. In highly stressed communities, 17 percent or more of families and 21 percent or more of individuals live in poverty, while per capita income falls below $9,000 per year and had increased less than 35 percent between 1979 and 1985.

### 7. BIRTHS
ZPG's Births factor assesses the percentage of all births in 1985 to females under twenty, 1985 crude birth rates in each community, and 1985 infant mortality rates.

In model communities, the teenage birth rate is below 9 percent of all births, the crude birth rate falls between 14.5 and 16.5 and the infant mortality rate is less than 8.5 deaths per 1,000 live births. In stressed communities, the teenage birth rate soars to 19 percent and higher, the crude birth rate reaches 23 or more, and the infant mortality rate is greater than fifteen deaths per 1,000 live births.

### 8. AIR QUALITY
Using county and metro area data, ZPG assesses cities that did not, as of 1985, meet primary (long term) and secondary (24 hour) EPA air quality standards for six pollutants considered most dangerous (carbon monoxide, nitrogen dioxide, ozone, sulfur dioxide, lead, and total suspended particles). Secondary standards apply only to sulfur dioxide and total suspended particles.

Model areas meet long term and 24 hour standards while stressed communities do not meet EPA standards on four of the seven possible measures.

### 9. HAZARDOUS WASTES
ZPG's Hazardous Wastes rating is based on the number of Superfund sites listed by the EPA for the city and/or county, in addition to the number of potentially hazardous waste sites under EPA investigation.

Model cities have no hazardous waste sites reported by the EPA. Stressed communities have four or more sites within the city limits or seven or more sites in the county. ZPG added additional penalizing for any city with greater than twenty potentially hazardous waste sites.

### 10. WATER
Based on U.S. Geological surveys made in 1984-86, ZPG assesses the availability and quality of ground and surface water.

The top cities on this scale have water availability and quality in the *good* range, meaning that the water supply is of adequate quality and is sufficient to serve the city's present population. (Incidentally, no U.S. city qualifies for a *best* rating in which the area's water supply would be of high quality and in abundant supply.)

Stressed communities have water resources considered to be in danger, where resources are already drying up and contain pollutants.

### 11. SEWAGE
ZPG's Sewage assessment is based on data from the EPA that reports on the quality level and capacity of wastewater treatment for municipalities around the country in 1986.

Model communities have facilities that provide greater than secondary treatment of all wastewater. Stressed Communities either do not provide at least secondary treatment for any wastewater or discharge raw sewage.

(Secondary treatment removes at least 85 percent of the conventional pollutant found in domestic sewage. Advanced treatment removes a higher percentage of conventional pollutants and also removes *exotic* pollutants such as phosphorus.)

ZPG additionally penalizes any city whose treatment facilities had an existing sewage flow that exceeds the design flow.

## How ZPG Arrives at an Overall Rating

Here is an example of how ZPG rates these eleven criteria (on a scale of 1-to-5) and averages them to arrive at an Overall Rating. Data is for Eugene, Oregon, considered one of the most healthful cities in the nation.

Population change 3
Crowding 1
Education 1
Violent crime 1
Community economics 2
Individual economics 4
Births 3
Air quality 2
Hazardous wastes 1
Water 2
Sewage 3

Total 23
Overall Rating 23/11=2.1

ZPG's Overall Rating is given for each city in this book with a population of 100,000 or more and is preceded by the symbol ZPG. For Eugene, Oregon it is listed as:

**Urban Stress: ZPG 2.1.**

For states in which the largest city has a population below 100,000, ZPG has also awarded an Overall Rating to the largest city in that state. Thus, in some cases, a ZPG Overall Rating may exist for a city with a population below 100,000.

As explained earlier, for cities in this book for which no ZPG Overall Rating exists, we have attempted to estimate the Urban Stress Overall Rating ourselves, using the best data available. Such estimates are listed as:

**Urban Stress: EST 3.2.**

## How Population Size Affects Health

With a few notable exceptions, the size of a city's population relates on a straight line basis to its level of urban stress. As a general rule, the higher the level of urban stress, the lower is a city's overall healthfulness.

The exceptions occur when, despite a population count of 250,000 or more, a city has maintained a high quality of life and livability. Although relatively rare, this combination can lead to even a large metropolis being ranked as a relatively healthful place to live.

Nevertheless, most large metropolitan areas are definitely *not* the most healthful places in which to live. As a result, a nationwide exodus has swept the country as people move from huge, unmanageable cities to smaller towns and communities. For many people, economic considerations delay this move until retirement. Which explains why retirees are leading the way back to Main Street. Throughout the United States, former urbanites are relocating to smaller cities, ideally with a pace so relaxed that one can drive a car without stress—or ride a bicycle safely, if preferred—and where life is relatively free of congestion, pollution, pressure, and crime.

Many people are moving today to what urban planners call a Second Tier City. With a population between 50,000 and 250,000, these midsized cities are large enough to offer a vigorous economy plus all the facilities and services, and the intellectual and cultural life, of a much larger center. Most medium-sized cities also have reasonably-priced housing and first rate medical care.

Those who prefer still smaller communities are finding even lower levels of urban stress in cities with a population between 15,000 and 50,000. Certain cities in this range—such as college towns and resorts which cater to people of higher education and affluence—also tend to provide a range of services and facilities comparable to those of much larger cities.

According to ZPG's Urban Stress Index, the most livable cities have a population of 121,000 or less, while the worst have an average population size of 785,725 or more. To maximize health, a good rule is to aim for a city with the highest possible quality of life and livability.

## *Very Small Communities Can Be Health-Defeating*

Beware, however, of small communities that are so provincial that people gawk at strangers and so conformist that no adult dare ride a bicycle or exercise for fear of appearing different. The danger in selecting a very small town is that you will very probably discover that your level of education, income, and cultural interests are much higher than those of the majority of residents.

Although many Americans fondly dream of retiring to the friendly, small town in which they grew up, most exurbanites have become far too sophisticated to fit in. If you are a reasonably well-educated, cosmopolitan, health-conscious resident of a metropolitan area, you would probably be much more at home in such trend-setting cities as Boulder, Colorado; Madison, Wisconsin; or Seattle, Washington—high energy places full of pedestrian malls with sidewalk cafes, New Age bookstores, ethnic and vegetarian restaurants, bike paths, and universities.

By contrast, most very small communities lack a choice of fresh fruits, vegetables, and whole grain breads. There is usually no place to hike and few adults ever swim or ride a bicycle, let alone play tennis or practice yoga. Frequently, the focus of cultural life revolves around high school sports or gossip in the local cafe.

At the other extreme, most of us would be equally well advised to avoid such fashionable large cities as San Francisco, Boston, or Washington—or most places in Hawaii or Alaska—where housing is exorbitantly priced and living costs among the nation's highest.

## *Rating Urban Stress by Population Size*

Based on the 1-to-5 scale used for ZPG'S Overall Ratings, here is how population size relates to the level of urban stress. For the average city, the larger the population, the poorer its rating for urban stress.

Cities with a population of 100,000 or less have an average rating of 2.5 for urban stress. ZPG ranks this level as consistent with a *Warning* of possible urban stress.

Cities with a population of 100,000-149,999 have an average rating of 2.8 for urban stress. ZPG also ranks this level in the *Warning* zone for possible urban stress.

Cities with a population of 150,000-249,999 have an average rating of 2.9 for urban stress. Though still within the *Warning* zone, this is considered an above-average stress level.

Cities with a population of 250,000-499,999 have an average rating of 3.2 for urban stress. ZPG considers this level to be in the *Danger* zone.

Cities with a population of 500,000-999,999 have an average rating of 3.4 for urban stress. This level is well within the *Danger* zone.

Cities with a population of one million or more have an average rating of 3.8 for urban stress. This level reaches even higher into the *Danger* zone.

Based on these guidelines, the population figures quoted for each city in this book can be a useful indicator of the extent of urban stress which is likely to exist in the average city of that size.

Anyone seeking a complete report on ZPG's Urban Stress Test, or information about any subsequent Test reports, should contact Zero Population Growth, 1400 Sixteenth Street N.W., Suite 320, Washington D.C. 20036 (202-332-2200).

### Other Man-Made Influences That Can Be Stressful To Health

Whether you're retiring, or seeking a more healthful city in which to live and work, this book focuses primarily on aspects which are fairly slow to change. But when it comes to housing, or the cost of living, or finding a job, information on these topics is often a more perishable commodity. Both housing availability and costs, and the cost of living, can fluctuate with changes in the economy or with opening or closing of a major plant or military base. Likewise, the employment situation in any city can change almost overnight.

So rather than attempt to rate these less stable factors, we have confined ourselves to commenting on the housing, cost of living, and job scenes. Nonetheless, to ensure that your information is as current as possible, we recommend writing or calling the information sources (given at the end of each city profile in this book) and asking for the most recent information on housing costs and availability, the cost of living, and the employment outlook in your field. Naturally, no one dependent on full-time employment should consider moving to a new city without a firm commitment of employment there.

## *Housing*

A significant man-made stress factor can be the high cost of shelter accompanied by a shortage of homes, condominiums, rental apartments, or mobile homes. Actual shortages have been few in recent years, but in places like Southern California or New England newcomers often face a shortage of *reasonably-priced* places to live.

A brief appraisal of the recent housing situation is given for each city, together with an indication of the price range in relation to the regional or national average.

Naturally, fluctuations in population or the economy can cause information to change. So it should be regarded only as a guide which was based on conditions at the time this book was written.

## *Affordability*

A high cost of living can have a detrimental effect on health. As used in this book, *affordability* is the cost of living in any city with housing costs excepted. Affordability is, therefore, a measure of how far your income is likely to go in meeting the costs of food, utilities, transportation, maintenance and medical care.

For the 260 largest U.S. cities, the current cost of living is reported by the American Chamber of Commerce Researchers Association. But for smaller cities, we have had to rely on local estimates.

Due to lower distribution costs, food and automobile fuel costs tend to be lower in larger cities while lower wage scales bring down the cost of repairs and maintenance, and also health care, in smaller towns. Among other factors affecting affordability is an equable climate that reduces energy needs for heating and cooling. Proximity to a hydro-electric plant, or to plentiful coal or natural gas sources, may result in significantly lower utility costs. Municipally- owned utilities also often charge lower rates than those which are shareholder-owned. An efficient local bus service can help cut the cost of car operation, and proximity to agricultural areas can help lower the cost of fruits and vegetables.

## *Employment Opportunities*

Since they're comparatively free of the pollution created by heavy industry, oil refineries, or chemical plants, healthful cities have economies which tend to center more around hi-tech, computer, aerospace, and medical care research, and around office parks, health care, education, and tourism. It is in these fields that most jobs in healthful cities lie.

Meanwhile, as the supply of younger workers has begun to diminish, opportunities for part-time or seasonal jobs for retirees is starting to improve. It has already become common to see gray-haired bag boys and clerks in supermarkets, or elderly saladmakers in fast food eateries. Generally, part-time work is most plentiful in cities with a low proportion of other retirees, students, ethnic minorities and women aged 35-55. Nowadays, too, many large cities have placement agencies which are able to locate older workers in retail stores or the tourist trade.

# 4
# Rating the Cities II:
# Inherent Natural Health Factors

## *Environmental Health Benefits*

Climate, elevation, the inspiration of scenery and the mineral content of soil and water rank among nature's environmental influences on health. Unlike urban stress, which is entirely man-made, environmental influences all emanate from nature and are only moderately affected by man-made pollution.

## CLIMATE

The most healthful climate is that which is most supportive of living the low-risk lifestyle.

For most people, that translates into a pattern in which the temperature is as close as possible to 65°F in every season, and in which they can exercise outdoors every day in the year; weather changes are frequent but moderate; sunshine is abundant but varied by brief cloudiness; and which is as free as possible of extremes of heat and cold. Specifically, that calls for winter daytime temperatures of 60°-72° with a relative humidity of 35-40 percent, and summer daytime temperatures ranging between 70° and 80° with a relative humidity of 55-65 percent.

With the exception of a few places in Southern California, few cities have climates which can match these parameters.

Yet in practice, people are able to live long, healthful lives in just about every type of climate in the United States. So it's important to realize that, while the optimal climate just described is an ideal target to aim for, it is totally feasible and practical to lead an equally healthful lifestyle in a less-than-perfect climate.

## *The Most Healthful Place in America*

For example, if we use longevity as a measure of healthfulness we find that for many decades, the most healthful place in the United States, has been an area of Polish farms and small communities in west central Nebraska. The climate here is often frigid in winter and uncomfortably hot and humid in summer. Yet more people per capita lived to a ripe old age here than anywhere else in the United States. The explanation was not the healthfulness of the climate but the active, stress-free lifestyle enjoyed by the inhabitants.

When we separate racial, cultural, and economic differences from climate and geography, we find that people are able to live long and healthful lives in Vermont, Florida, Colorado, or North Dakota. Canada's cold climate doesn't prevent it from ranking fourth in overall life expectancy among all the countries in the world. By comparison, the warmer and sunnier United States ranks twelfth.

Nor is constant sunshine and eternal warmth a guarantee of good health. Tens of thousands of retirees have found that, after a few months, the long, hot summers of places like St. Petersburg, Palm Springs, or Phoenix can become enervating and monotonous. After testing out the Sunbelt for a year or two, thousands of other Americans have concluded that a mild, four-seasonal climate without too much snow, heat waves, or other extremes, is more stimulating and enjoyable.

## *Many Healthful Cities Are in the North*

Based on the ranking system used in this book, some of the healthiest cities and states are in the north. Understandably, too, those who enjoy cross-country skiing or snowshoeing for outdoor exercise will find a northern climate appreciably more healthful. We might mention that during fifteen years of living in northern Colorado, we cannot recall a single winter day when we were unable to exercise outdoors. Naturally, cross-country skiing was one of our favorite activities.

The various cities in this book are located in so many different climatic regions that to describe them all in detail would fill another book. Instead, we have scored the healthfulness of each city's climate based on how well it allows residents to follow a low-risk lifestyle. Naturally, if you dislike snow sports, you would not opt to live in Colorado, Vermont, Wisconsin, or Minnesota. Nor if mountain hiking and cross-country skiing were your favorite forms of exercise would you choose to live in Florida. Nonetheless, a city with a heavy winter snowfall can be just as healthful for a skiing buff as is a snow free city in South Texas to someone who prefers to bicycle every day of the year. Both cities can be equally conducive to living the low-risk lifestyle.

We have certainly given high scores to climates that closely approximate the ideal climatic pattern outlined earlier. But we have also given moderately high rankings to cities with other types of climates that are stimulating, free of extremes and conducive to any type of health-enhancing outdoor exercise. Thus our climate scores must be viewed in the light of your personal preference.

The cities in this book offer a wide choice of climates, ranging from tropical to alpine, and with a variety of settings from desert canyons to pine forests, and from seashore to high mountains. For a detailed description of any city's climate, send a postcard (or phone) to the information source given for each city in this book. Alternatively, you can write index of U.S. government publications and records on the climate of states and cities throughout the United States. The index is available free from the National Climatic Data Center, Federal Building, Asheville, NC 28801-2696 (704-259-0682).

## How Weather Affects Health

Researchers in the field of bio-meteorology—the study of the effects of weather on human health—have produced some interesting discoveries that may be helpful in evaluating the salubrity of a climate. Pioneers like the late Dr. Helmut E. Landsberg, and institutions such as the Health, Weight, and Stress Clinic at Johns Hopkins Hospital, in Baltimore, have discovered many of the body mechanisms through which weather may affect our mood and health.

They have found that changes in weather can cause corresponding changes in the body's thyroxine, serotonin, steroid, and amino acid metabolism, factors which directly affect our nerves and organs. For instance, falling barometric pressure allows the body to absorb more water from the intestines. This excess fluid can create edema (swollen ankles) or it may compress tissue in the brain, causing us to feel despondent, irritated, and depressed.

Undoubtedly, the most common influence of the weather on health is a type of mild winter depression and mood slump called Seasonal Affective Disorder (SAD). Bio-meteorologists have discovered that SAD is a light-sensitive dysfunction that results from continually staying indoors during periods of dark, sunless winter days and long nights. Most people call it "cabin fever." Regardless of the name, researchers have found that this mild seasonal depression can be swiftly cured, and completely prevented, by actively exercising outdoors for at least an hour each day.

During periods of cloudy, rainy winter weather or prolonged snowstorms, people who do not exercise daily outdoors—and who, therefore, are not following a low-risk lifestyle—may experience slowed reaction time and become lethargic, irritable, and unfriendly.

In almost every case, those who follow a low-risk lifestyle and exercise outdoors on at least four or five days each week, are minimally affected by weather changes or extremes. Nonetheless, for those who prefer calm weather to storms, it's worth knowing that southern California, southern Arizona, and southwestern New Mexico are comparatively storm-free, while winter storms and blizzards occur regularly in the high country of Colorado, northern New Mexico, Utah, and other northern tier states. Also prone to summer windstorms, thunderstorms, and hurricanes are the coasts of the Gulf of Mexico, Florida, and the Atlantic states.

## *The Effect of Weather Changes on Human Behavior*

Careful observations have also shown that rapid changes in temperature, humidity, and barometric pressure may worsen the pain of rheumatoid arthritis, while the incidence of perforated duodenal ulcer also increases under these conditions.

Health records show that in cities that experience frequent cold fronts and very cold temperatures, there is greater risk of heart attack, angina, stroke, asthma attacks, glaucoma, migraine headaches, colic, sinusitis, and middle ear infection in people who are already prone to these dysfunctions. But there is no increased risk to healthy people who follow a low-risk lifestyle.

In cities which experience extended periods of heat and high humidity, bio-meteorologists have found that riots and urban violence are more common, mortality rates increase, sexual activity declines, and there is an increase in migraine headaches, blood clots, ulcers, and skin rashes. Under these conditions, hospital patients tend to experience an increase in visual disturbances and dizziness, chest and digestive pains, and cramps. Hot, humid weather can also be energy-sapping and emotionally stressful to those who do not follow a low-risk lifestyle.

Almost everyone finds that occasional showers can be refreshing and stimulating, but for those who do not exercise regularly outdoors, continual rain can lead to frustration and depression. Similarly, a period of unbroken high winds heightens anxiety in many people.

High heat and low humidity—a common summer combination in low-lying desert regions—can stress both mind and body, and slow almost everyone down to some extent. Many people become irritated and disagreeable whenever the mercury remains above 80° for a prolonged period. Violent crimes increase and there are noticeable increases in heat-provoked heart attacks and stroke. Hot, dry winds can also trigger migraine, malaise, and depression, and they can slow reaction time and interfere with concentration.

Winter sunshine benefits almost everyone. It is most intense in southwestern Arizona and in bordering states such as New Mexico, Colorado, Utah, West Texas, Southern California, and the rest of Arizona. Among other states, only south Florida can match the winter sunshine record of the American Southwest. Compared to Tucson, which has over 260 clear days annually, the Florida Gold Coast has only 140 and the Pacific Northwest only 80.

All other things being equal, we'd certainly aim for a climate that has the highest possible amount of sunshine, particularly in winter, but also year 'round.

# ELEVATION

Among inherent geographic variables, elevation appears to make the great difference to health. Statistics have revealed that, throughout the world, the higher the elevation, the lower the incidence of heart disease and most cancers. Furthermore, should a person who lives at a higher elevation experience a heart attack, it is less likely to prove fatal than in a person who lives near sea level.

New information emerging from such sources as the American Heart Association, and the University of Colorado Health Services at Denver, is showing that high altitude alone does not reduce a healthy heart's performance. Two studies reported in 1986 at the fifty-ninth Scientific Session of the American Heart Association confirmed that going to a high altitude does not have an adverse effect on a healthy heart. In many cases, high altitude can actually improve cardiac performance.

These studies have led some cardiologists to send patients to elevations of 6,000-7,000 feet to speed recovery from recent heart attacks. The rationale behind this is that after a few weeks in the oxygen-thin air the body's red-blood cell count increases, enabling the blood to transport more oxygen. As a result, the quantity of blood pumped by the heart is reduced by up to 20 percent. Naturally, this eases the burden on the heart.

During these studies, researchers found that the heart's pumping capacity was well preserved in healthy persons at elevations as high as 29,000 feet, while two heart functions actually showed a suggestion of improved performance. Thus once a heart-healthy person becomes acclimatized, living at a moderate altitude of 5,000-7,500 feet may significantly reduce risk of heart disease. Supporting this conclusion is the fact that several societies of exceptionally long-lived peoples, namely the Vilcabambans, Hunzas, and Abkhasians, all lead active lives in the Andes, Himalayas, or the Caucasus at elevations of 5,000-8,000 feet.

## America's Longevity Belt

The same dry, sunny climate, and 5,000-8,000 feet elevations found in these citadels of longevity, also occur in such Rocky Mountain states as New Mexico, Utah, Colorado, Wyoming, northern Arizona, and parts of Nevada and Montana.

Here are such healthful and eminently-livable cities as Boulder, Colorado Springs, and Durango in Colorado; Cedar City, Utah; and Los Alamos and Santa Fe, New Mexico.

But living at higher elevations isn't all pluses. Winters are generally colder and snowfall heavier than at lower elevations on the same latitude. The oxygen-thin atmosphere is so fragile that in winter, some degree of smog hovers over almost every town and city. And risk of skin cancer increases with altitude.

Generally not due to elevation, however, are the above average rates of lung disease in most high-altitude western states. The culprit is widespread cigarette smoking, seemingly sparked by a desire to conform with such popular images as the Marlboro Man and the cigarette-puffing western cowboy.

A final caveat: we're talking here about elevations not exceeding 8,000 feet. No one with heart disease should move to an elevation higher than they are currently living at without the approval of a physician.

Despite the previously enumerated drawbacks to living at higher altitudes, as a general rule, the higher the elevation, the more healthful it is. Again, this applies only to elevations not exceeding 8,000 feet.

The health benefits for the elevation of each city in this book are scored as follows:

| Elevation | Score |
|---|---|
| sea level to 1,500 ft. | 1 |
| 1,500-3,000 ft. | 2 |
| 3,000-4,500 ft. | 3 |
| 4,500-6,000 ft. | 4 |
| above 6,000 ft. | 5 |

# TERRAIN THERAPY

Terrain therapy is the name for the visual healing that occurs whenever we look upon an inspiring scene of natural beauty. Whether a city is filled with trees and flower-bordered parks, or looks out over a nearby range of bold mountains, wild desert landscapes, sea and lake shores, forests or wetlands, natural beauty can be a powerful and ever present natural healing force.

For decades, physicians have observed the healing benefits of natural scenes on their patient's health. To help speed recovery, patients at many Adventist hospitals are routinely wheeled outdoors to experience the uplifting effects of sun, air, and verdure.

To live in a city sheathed in green trees, or in one that has a craggy mountain range soaring abruptly skyward from the city limits, is to constantly experience a visual medicine that can change your entire inner ecology. People who live in cities with aesthetic natural settings experience a constant uplifting of spirits. Others report an intoxication with nature that frequently inspires hope where only hopelessness existed before. By invoking strong feelings of peace and well-being, almost any refreshing scene of deep woods or far horizons has a perceptible healing power. As a familiar Sierra Club saying puts it: "A large granite mountain cannot be denied, it speaks in silence to the very core of our being."

While the health benefits of terrain therapy have been only partially explained by science, several studies indicate that a nurturing panorama, or the ability to spend time outdoors in a natural setting, definitely helps to mobilize the body's healing resources.

When Robert Ulrich Ph.D., of the University of Delaware, studied the recovery rates of patients in a hospital, he found that those occupying rooms in a wing that overlooked trees and verdure recovered 8 percent faster, and they also needed fewer painkillers, than those in another wing which looked out on a plain brick wall. The benefits are believed due to boosting of the immune system by the positive emotions invoked through the visual contact with nature.

Another experiment in the U.S.S.R. found that evergreen trees like spruce and fir give off a scent that stimulates the brain to lower blood pressure and heart rate and to smooth out irregularities in heart action. Two other authorities also confirm that living where you can exercise outdoors may add significant benefits to your health.

### Exercising Outdoors Is Healthier

Kenneth Cooper, M.D., exercise physiologist and author of *The Aerobics Program for Total Wellbeing* (New York, Bantam: 1988) believes you are more likely to improve your heart and lungs when you exercise outdoors than when exercising indoors, such as on a treadmill or stationary bicycle. His observations show that heart rates are higher when exercising in the open.

Well-known bio-optics expert John N. Ott also recommends exercising outdoors. His studies show that we need to spend more time outdoors to orient ourselves to nature and the sky. Exposing our eyes to the full spectrum of sunlight benefits both the eyes and the entire body. Indications have also shown that being indoors under artificial light for long periods can heighten risk of hypertension, eye disease, and some forms of cancer.

Other observations show that being surrounded by natural beauty helps to overcome depression and makes us feel good while simultaneously boosting the competence of our immunity and lowering our risk of cancer and infection. Moreover, this euphoria lasts for as long as we are able to continue looking out on, or being among, physically beautiful scenes. The uplift never fades.

In these days, as so many cities pave over and develop every last square mile of their land, denude their forests, and stripmine their hills, it is increasingly important to live in a place that provides the benefits of terrain therapy. A city endowed with trees, green parks, flower beds, woods, hills, shores, desert canyons, or nearby mountains—and where you can still walk safely beside a creek or river while you feel the crunch of dried leaves underfoot—remains one of those special places that continue to offer the rejuvenating effects of terrain therapy.

An assessment of the value of terrain therapy is given for each city in this book. Since terrain therapy has never been evaluated before, our rankings are based on the author's personal estimate supported, in many cases, by comments from local residents.

As is usual with our scoring system, number 5 indicates that a city has been ranked highest for its potential to provide terrain therapy, while a score of 1 indicates that a city has a very low level of inspiring natural scenes and settings.

# WATER AND SOIL

Hard water is rich in calcium and certain other minerals while soft water is mineral-free. Earlier studies showed that heart disease appeared to be lower in hard water areas. But more recent studies have revealed that it is the magnesium contents of drinking water, rather than calcium, which is responsible for the lower rates of heart disease. Incidence of both cholesterol blockage in arteries, and coronary artery spasm, are lower in areas where the water has a high content of magnesium.

Animal studies have confirmed that a high magnesium level in drinking water reduces serum cholesterol levels and significantly reduces the overall rate of heart disease. Strong indications also exist to show that a high level of magnesium in drinking water tends to reduce the magnitude of a heart attack should one occur. It also significantly lowers risk of coronary artery spasm, a type of angina caused by contraction of muscles in coronary artery walls.

Since magnesium is a muscle relaxant, it helps to dilate blood vessels throughout the body, not only reducing risk of artery spasm but lowering blood pressure at the same time. These facts were revealed recently during a large study of 58,218 women at Harvard Medical School and Brigham and Women's Hospital, in Boston. The study showed an inverse relationship between intake of magnesium and blood pressure readings. Newly emerging evidence is also beginning to show that diabetes is more common in areas with a low magnesium content in the drinking water.

Although statistics on the magnesium content of drinking water are not widely available, a good general rule is that the magnesium content of water is above average in these areas: North Dakota, South Dakota, Oklahoma, Nebraska, and Kansas, plus all of New Mexico but the northwest corner; eastern Montana and eastern Colorado; western Arkansas and western Missouri; all of Texas but the southeast corner; northwest Utah. Perhaps it is more than a coincidence that these same primarily mid-western states also hold the longevity record for the continental United States.

Selenium is another essential trace element that appears in foods grown in the soils of the Midwest, Southwest, and Central states, while it is frequently deficient in soil in the northwest, northeast, and Florida. By reducing free radical damage to body cells, dietary selenium is believed to lower the risk of breast and other cancers.

Today, however, produce from selenium-rich areas is shipped all over the nation, thus fairly guaranteeing a supply in the diet of everyone who eats whole grains and cereals. If you suspect your diet is low in selenium, supplements are available in every healthfood store.

Although neither magnesium nor selenium content is scored in this book, we have presented this information to help you evaluate these nutritional factors on your own.

# 5

# How a City's Lifestyle Influences Health

The basic premise of this book is that in the *healthful* cities we have chosen, a significantly greater proportion of people are living and practicing a low-risk lifestyle than in the average U.S. city.

Even in our most healthful city, there are obviously people who perceive their life expectancy as short, who have no desire for a long, healthy life, and who die twenty years before their time from diseases they could easily have prevented.

What we do claim is that in our healthful cities, more people regard exercise, eating a low-fat diet, and other health-promoting lifestyle steps as the norm rather than the exception. Thus both the community and one's peers are likely to provide appreciably more in the way of facilities, support and approval for anyone attempting to live healthfully. This makes it much easier to practice and to stay with a pro-health lifestyle.

And we may well *have* to depend on a low-risk lifestyle to preserve our health in future years.

Anyone counting on bionic body parts, high-powered drugs or other futuristic medical treatments to bale out their ailing health as they become older is likely to be disappointed. While mainstream medicine is supremely successful in repairing mechanical defects from cataracts to torn cartilage, and from every type of burn, injury, trauma, and emergency, when it comes to chronic disease many Americans have un-realistic expectations of what medical science is actually ca-pable of achieving.

## *Profits From Sickness*

Most of us forget there are two sides to medical science. One part, mainstream medicine, is fueled by for-profit hospi-tals and pharmaceutical manufacturers. At best, any kind of mainstream medical treatment is likely to be unpleasant and expensive. Most treatments for chronic disease, such as coro-nary artery disease, stroke, cancer, Type II diabetes, osteopo-rosis, emphysema, and renal disease amounts to little more than a quick fix and a patch-up.

A by-pass operation cannot possibly reverse all the dam-age caused by years of high-fat food, sedentary living, stress, and smoking. Unless the patient adopts and stays with a low-risk lifestyle permanently, there is a 60 percent chance that the by-pass will close again within ten years. In patients who continue their destructive health habits, the by-pass often closes within two years.

Balloon angioplasty sounds like a cheaper and safer al-ternative to by-pass surgery, but in 30 percent of cases the artery narrows again within six months. Powerful drugs to prevent angina, hypertension, or transplant rejection have unpleasant and adverse side effects ranging from male impo-tence to gallstones, dry mouth, nausea, and fatigue. Trans-plant recipients are often sick on one day in five for the rest of their lives.

New developments may bring improvements in the fu-ture. But in a high proportion of cases, the benefits of drugs and medical treatment do not always outweigh the risk and unpleasantness. Despite billions spent on cancer research, two of every three cancer patients still die of the disease, or from the side effects of treatment, within five years.

## *The Hazards of Hi-Tech Medicine*

Millions of Americans have learned the hard way that hi-tech treatment doesn't guarantee a successful outcome. Literally millions of people have failed to get well through medical treatment, or have been turned into invalids by chemotherapy and other aggressive treatments. According to *U. S. News* (March 12, 1990, page 25), experts estimate that up to one-third of all medical services performed in America are of dubious value and may even be harmful. And, according to the magazine, during 1989 some 50,000 Americans may have died from procedures they didn't need.

Further confirmation comes from a recent Rand Corporation study of several common surgical procedures frequently performed in the United States. The Rand Corporation concluded that:

Thirty percent of heart by-pass surgeries were of debatable value and 14 percent were unjustified. (Cost: $37,000 each.)

Thirty-two percent of carotid endarterectomies (removing plaque from neck arteries to prevent stroke) were of debatable value and 32 percent were unjustified. (Cost: $9,000 each.)

Thirty-six percent of pacemaker implants were of debatable value and 20 percent were unjustified. (Cost: $9,000 each.)

The literature carries frequent reports of unnecessary operations, pacemaker installations that weren't needed, and the high risk of becoming infected while in a U.S. hospital. For instance, a study by Harvard Medical School researchers for the New York State Health Department, and announced in *Public Citizen Health Letter* (April 1990, page 4), estimated that 354,000 hospitalized patients are injured and 89,000 die each year in U.S. hospitals as a result of medical negligence. These figures closely resemble those of a similar review of California hospital records made in the 1970s.

As modern medicine increasingly turns away from traditional humanistic healing practices towards sterile biochemical, hi-tech and harsh pharmaceutical treatments, an alienation is growing between the public and the medical profession. The family physician has been replaced by a physician-businessman who must use production line methods to compete. Often lacking sufficient time to make a careful examination and take a medical history, he must depend on quantifying lab tests for diagnosis, many of which are notoriously undependable. Errors in diagnosis are so common that many doctors routinely order additional tests merely to cover themselves against possible litigation suits.

As a result, costs are often exorbitant for medical care of mediocre quality. Anyone who is counting on this kind of medical treatment to help keep them alive and well in their later years is not being realistic.

### The Disease-Free Lifestyle

The other side of medical science has been far more successful. Preventative medicine, as it's called, is concerned with learning how to live a healthy, active life while staying free of the same chronic diseases that mainstream medicine is trying to cure.

Preventative medicine has made such spectacular progress in recent years that we already know how to stay healthy and avoid becoming sick. By adopting a low-risk lifestyle, science has proved that we can reduce the risk of getting a chronic disease by at least 66 percent, and in many cases by 90 percent or more—at least until very late in life. Instead of risking the loss of our life savings to pay for medical treatment that may not succeed, preventative medicine costs absolutely nothing. In fact, following a low-risk lifestyle may well save us money.

Obviously, nothing we're saying here is intended to discourage anyone from consulting a physician for a diagnosis, nor to avoid taking medical treatment when mainstream medicine offers the best solution. Yet every day, thousands of Americans consult doctors for problems they could easily prevent, and in many cases solve, by following a low-risk lifestyle. In fact, the low-risk lifestyle has made a mockery of many forms of mainstream medical treatment for chronic disease.

## Drugless Therapy—the Medicine of Tomorrow

For example, the Pritikin Program has achieved thousands of cases of dramatic improvement and recovery from heart disease, hypertension, Type II diabetes, obesity, and other chronic diseases without using surgery or drugs. The Pritikin longevity centers are located in California and Florida. Under medical supervision, these centers teach a new stress-free way of living, and a new way of exercising and eating, to be followed and maintained for the rest of one's life. Almost invariably, those who stay with this low-risk lifestyle regain their health and enjoy optimal health and fitness for the rest of their lives.

The Pritikin centers were achieving these results as far back as 1976. Out of 893 patients attending the first 26-day Pritikin Program, 85 percent of hypertensive patients who were taking medication lowered their blood pressure and left drug free. Over half of those taking insulin for Type II diabetes were able to cease taking it. Sixty-two percent of those taking drugs for angina were able to stop taking the medication, and many others reduced their dosage. The overall rate of reduction of cholesterol and triglycerides was 25 percent. And overweight patients lost an average of thirteen pounds. But the crowning achievement concerned 64 patients who had been recommended for by-pass surgery by their physicians. After five years on the Pritikin low-risk lifestyle, 51 still did not require surgery.

Thousands of similar cases of dramatically improved health have been documented at the numerous cardiac rehabilitation centers which have since appeared all over the country. In some cases, patients who were unable to walk across the room without chest pain found themselves able to walk four to five miles after a month or so on a fat-free diet plus a gradually-increasing exercise program.

It wasn't until 1989, however, that Dean Ornish, M.D., and Larry Scherwitz, Ph. D., were able to prove, at the 1989 American Heart Association Conference in New Orleans, that coronary artery blockage already in place could be reversed through a low-risk lifestyle. Using sophisticated medical tests, the researchers demonstrated that for the 28 people in their study group coronary artery blockage had decreased from 40 percent to 37.8 percent after a year or more on a low-risk lifestyle. Meanwhile, in a control group of twenty persons who merely followed the American Heart Association's recommendations (cut fat intake to not more than 30 percent of calories, exercise moderately, and stop smoking), average artery blockage increased from 42.7 percent to 46.1 percent. Put another way, 82 percent of those in the low-risk lifestyle group improved while 53 percent of the control group became worse.

While a reduction in blockage of 2.1 percent may not sound like very much, it often results in a tremendous increase in blood flow to the heart. For example, a 5 percent regression in atherosclerosis can easily double blood flow to the heart. And half the people in Ornish's study had a blockage reduction of more than 2.1 percent. In fact, several had a reduction of 5 percent, indicating a doubling of blood flow in the coronary arteries.

## *The Anti-Cancer Lifestyle*

In the same vein, the National Cancer Institute recently announced that by A.D. 2000, we could cut cancer incidence in half by simply upgrading our lifestyle. Institute experts believe that 75 percent of all cancer deaths are preventible by lifestyle changes. Study after study is now implicating animal fat and protein, overeating, excess body weight, lack of exercise, and substance abuse (alcohol, tobacco etc.) plus unresolved emotional stress as major factors in causing cancer. Between 35 and 60 percent of all cancer cases are related to diet.

According to World Health Organization statistics, Japan has the world's lowest death rates from cancers of the breast, prostate, and colon, and the lowest overall death rate from cancer of any modern country. Compared to an average intake of 3,500 calories daily with 40 percent from fat as in the United States, the average Japanese eats only 2,500 calories of which only 25 percent are from fat. Again, this is lower than the maximum 30 percent of calories from fat recommended in the United States. And the difference is clearly reflected in Japanese mortality from heart disease, which is only one-third of U.S. levels.

## Secrets of Wellness

Eat more fruits, vegetables, and whole grains, and less fat and foods of animal origin is the clarion call of virtually every major health advisory agency. Among hundreds of studies to demonstrate that vegetables help prevent cancer is a recent discovery by the Cancer Research Center of Hawaii. After studying 1,200 men and women, the Center found that women who routinely ate a variety of vegetables were seven times less likely to get lung cancer than those who ate fewer vegetables. In men, the risk was three times greater.

Another six year study of 6,500 Chinese in China by researchers from Cornell University, Oxford University, and the Chinese Academies of Preventative Medicine found that, in China, the mortality rate from heart disease is barely one-sixteenth what it is in the United States. Most Chinese are still eating the diet of their ancestors, which is high in fruits, vegetables, and whole grains. Only 15 percent of their calories are derived from fat. Not surprisingly, the average cholesterol level in China is only 127 mg/dl (milligrams per deciliter) compared to 212 in the United States. Their low-fat diet also gives the Chinese an exceptionally low rate of colon cancer.

Part of the study, based on animal research, strongly suggested that animal protein promotes tumor growth. In the United States, 75 percent of all protein is from animal sources, compared to only 10 percent in China. The study also found strong indications that the higher the intake of protein the greater the excretion of calcium by the kidneys. One result is that Chinese women have very low rates of osteoporosis despite having a calcium intake only half that of American women.

Osteoporosis, or bone loss, afflicts 24 million Americans, mostly women, and is responsible for 1.2 million bone fractures annually, usually in the hip or spine. The result is that one American woman in three, aged over 65, has at least one fractured vertebra. Millions of others have bones so fragile they hesitate to move for fear of skeletal injury.

Yet it is well documented that osteoporosis is caused by sedentary living, a diet high in protein and low in vegetables, lack of Vitamin D from staying indoors, and cigarette smoking. The disease can be almost entirely prevented by doing exactly the opposite, namely by walking briskly in the outdoors for several miles each day, by avoiding smoking, and by eating a diet high in fruits, vegetables and whole grains, and low in animal protein.

Name almost any other chronic disease, from cataracts to Alzheimers, and you will find strong evidence that it can be postponed, or prevented entirely, by living a low-risk lifestyle. For instance, hypertension is the major cause of stroke and almost half of all American women over 55 have hypertension. In more than half of these cases, normal blood pressure could be restored by permanently following a low-risk lifestyle. Additionally, much of the kidney disease so prevalent in the United States has been linked to a diet high in animal protein.

## Healthy Cities Support a Low-Risk Lifestyle

The greatest triumph of medical science has not been heroic operations, PET or CAT scanners, or blockbuster drugs, but the discovery that by adopting a pro-health lifestyle we can eliminate most of the risk of dying from any of the killer diseases mentioned so far. There is one catch, however. To reap the benefits of a low-risk lifestyle means that we must live that lifestyle every day for the rest of our lives. We can obviously do that much more easily by living in a city where a low-risk lifestyle is the norm rather than the exception.

Most literate Americans are aware of the need to live a low-risk lifestyle. But in most cities, people are bombarded by fast food ads and by friends and relatives who tempt them with high-risk foods and sedentary activities. As a result, in the average city, people tend to grow old quickly and slide into chronic disease by age 50.

Certainly, not everyone in our healthful cities eats sanely or exercises regularly. But overall, there is less temptation. More restaurants feature salad bars. Talking and thinking about health and life extension is not a cultural no-no as it is in most traditional cities.

In healthful cities, the first question many couples are likely to ask each morning is, "What exercise shall we do today?" In healthful cities, people know that failing to exercise compromises their aliveness and their ability to function each day.

Most Americans are aware that they could enjoy better health and a richer life by upgrading their lifestyle. But most of us are too complacent to change. Unfortunately, the alternative to change may be a by-pass operation, angioplasty, a hip replacement, or a lifetime on unpleasant maintenance drugs.

## *Health Insurance That Doesn't Pay*

Even those options may not be available in the future. Already, a crisis is facing the health insurance industry. Behind it is the fact that millions of Americans neglect their health for decades, then expect the insurance company or the government to bale them out with sophisticated medical treatment. Some insurance companies are flatly refusing to pay thousands of dollars for these expensive operations.

The truth is that medicine has become technologically able to deliver more care than any government, employer, or individual can afford. Premiums for health insurance are so high that 10 percent of the cost of a new American car goes to insuring the health of the workers who built it. The result is that most workers retiring in the future will receive fewer health insurance benefits.

Many experts believe that the U.S. health insurance industry is on the verge of collapse. It seems inevitable that within a few years health insurance in the United States will have to be nationalized. Almost all other industrialized nations already have a national health insurance plan. These plans provide primary health care for everyone. But expensive hi-tech treatment is usually rationed. In England, for example, kidney dialysis and by-pass operations are usually not available to those over 65.

## *Health Care May Be Rationed*

In the United States, we still assume that everyone is equally eligible to receive medical care. But in the future, expensive operations may be reserved for younger workers who have more productive years ahead.

Furthermore, demographic changes are threatening to imperil future health care for all mature Americans. As aging baby boomers begin to swell the ranks of the retired, by early in the next century those over 65 will constitute one-fifth of the population. Meanwhile, the number of younger employed people will continue to shrink. Eventually, there will be only two workers to support each retired beneficiary. Instead of contributing fourteen percent of their paycheck to supporting older generations as at present, workers will have to give up 40 percent in payroll taxes. The burden of paying for social security and medicare will become so great that many experts predict both will be abolished in favor of a national welfare program based on need.

Nor will there be sufficient younger people to fill the huge demand for health care workers. Experts already foresee a colossal dependency problem developing, with too few workers available to care for the soaring numbers of older people who are chronically ill.

Something many of us overlook is that health insurance does not protect us from ill health, it merely cushions us from most of the exorbitant costs of medical treatment. Even then, many policies require us to meet a sizeable deduction after which they pay only 80 percent of costs.

Medicare pays far less. Yet for all too many people, having health insurance merely destroys any incentive to live a healthful lifestyle.

## Nature's Own Health Insurance

To ensure our survival in the aging society of the future, a low-risk lifestyle—nature's own health insurance—is far more dependable, and far more affordable than any form of medical insurance.

Naturally, we are not suggesting that anyone stop paying their health insurance premiums. But most of us forget that even the best policy, and even the best of hi-tech care, can't always save a person from dying in agony. Yet we can substantially reduce the risk of a painful death by adopting a pro-health lifestyle—an achievement far easier to accomplish in a health-oriented community.

That nature's own health insurance has the support of many top health authorities is evident by the incentive programs offered by many corporations to employees who stop smoking, eat a low-fat diet, and begin an exercise program.

Former HEW Secretary Joseph Califano has said that the best way to lower health care costs is to avoid the need for medical services. And Dr. Joseph L. Kelly, M.D., in the *Journal of the American Medical Writers Association* (December 1989) wrote: "We can eliminate the need for sophisticated health technology if we simply stay well. Now that we know so much about what causes disease, it's up to all of us to take more responsibility for our own health."

## The Low-Risk Lifestyle Is Our Biological Heritage

For many people, an even more pressing reason to adopt a low-risk lifestyle came with the discovery in 1988 that between 98 and 99.5 percent of man's genes are virtually identical with those of a baboon or chimpanzee. Anthropologists have theorized that the human lineage arose in Africa about 8 million years ago and that man shared the same ancestors as most higher primates.

Most people think of early man as a big game hunter. But observations of modern hunter-gatherer tribes have revealed that, even with spears, snares, and bows and arrows far superior to those available to early man, today's primitive hunter is still a very inefficient procurer of game for the table. The conclusion today is that, until modern man appeared some 35,000 years ago, our ancestors lived primarily on coarse plant foods gathered by women. Even though early man did occasionally scavenge meat killed by predators, it consisted entirely of wild game and was relatively low in saturated fat.

The most authoritative opinion is that our organs haven't changed appreciably in the past 100,000 years. Our digestive system remains almost as it was in our paleolithic ancestors. Today we carry the same DNA as the higher primates—genes that prepared us for a physically-active lifestyle and a diet largely composed of fruits, vegetables, tubers, and wild grains. When our cells are deprived of this lifestyle and diet, they wane and weaken, our arteries become clogged, our bones waste away, our immune system fades, and we eventually become a victim of chronic disease.

In simpler societies and in Third World countries, people continue to follow a lifestyle and eat a diet far closer to that for which our genes evolved. Nutritionally, physically, and psychologically, life in these societies remains close to that of our primate ancestors.

When we exclude infectious diseases and complications due to childbirth, people in many simpler societies are actually fitter and healthier than people in any western nation. Instead of increasing with age, as in western societies, body fat and cholesterol remain at the same low level throughout life. Serum cholesterol is typically 125 mg/dl while both adults and the elderly enjoy a level of fitness and stamina far superior to that of most Americans.

Regardless of age, their daily lives revolve around hill walking, lifting and other equally vigorous activities. Even among the elderly, fitness is the norm. Compared to the increasing number of younger Americans who are overweight and out of shape, younger people in primitive societies are invariably fit and lean. By contrast, hardening of the arteries begins in most American males by age two and is well established by the early twenties.

Researchers believe that the physical deterioration seen in most Americans by age 40 is entirely due to the inappropriate way in which we eat, exercise, and cope with stress.

## Safeguard Your Health the Natural Way

What, then, *is* the ideal lifestyle?

Essentially, it mixes the ancestral peasant diet of fruits, vegetables, and whole grains common in undeveloped countries with the modern sanitation, refrigeration, medical care, and freedom from infections and childbirth complications that prevail in modern, affluent nations. When these are combined with a physically-active lifestyle similar to that found in many Third World countries, then we have a close facsimile of the lifestyle for which our genes were selected during evolution.

Seen in this light, it becomes evident that the chronic diseases that kill 75 percent of Americans arise out of a conflict between mind and body. Our hi-tech minds have trapped our animal bodies in a mechanized world designed to eliminate all physical exertion and most forms of traditional foods. We weren't designed to sit all day watching a video screen, or to fight freeway traffic, or to deal with angry customers, or to eat high-risk foods in a fast food eaterie.

The modern mechanized world and hi-tech lifestyle our minds have created is alien to our primate bodies. Our genes continue to program us for the lifestyle and diet that our ancestors lived some 35,000 or more years ago. Our bodies still thrive on vigorous exercise and on a diet of coarse plant foods, exactly the opposite of what we encounter in modern life.

By changing our lifestyle habits to more closely resemble those of our ancestors, the low-risk lifestyle enables our primate bodies to function more compatibly with our hi-tech minds.

The message of this book is that all the measures we need to improve and maintain our health are much more likely to exist in the nation's healthiest cities than in the traditional American community.

## *Whole Person Health Is Revolutionizing Medical Thinking*

To achieve optimal wellness calls for an integrated approach to enhancing health on the physical, psychological, nutritional, and emotional levels simultaneously. That means not only eating appropriately but also exercising both body and mind, minimizing the effects of stress, and maximizing opportunities for volunteer work, spiritual growth, and social contacts.

Thus a low-risk lifestyle doesn't consist merely of exercise and diet. It means cultivating a variety of personal aspects, each of which can contribute more humor, fun, and enjoyment to life. Most people who take up a pro-health lifestyle soon feel so good that they want to go on and feel even better.

We also need a Whole Person approach to health because good health habits are synergistic. Each healthful habit boosts the benefits of all other health-enriching habits.

For example, Dr. James Fries, associate professor of medicine at Stanford University, believes that when walking is combined with other health-promoting habits such as staying trim, eating a low-fat, high-fiber diet, and eliminating substance abuse, many chronic diseases can be postponed or avoided entirely. Dr. Fries is author of the Addison Wesley book *Aging Well*.

### Where to Live the Low-Risk Lifestyle

Each city in this book is scored on the resources it offers for each of the nine principal factors that contribute most to a low-risk lifestyle.

These are:

▶Health awareness of the population—based on education, affluence, and attitude toward health

▶Nutritional awareness—the overall attitude toward healthful eating

▶Fitness resources and activities—including the overall attitude toward exercise and staying trim

▶Stress management resources

▶Opportunities to exercise the mind in later life—through intellectual, cultural, and creative activities

▶Opportunities for social contacts

▶Opportunities for volunteer work

▶Opportunities for spiritual growth

►Quality of health care—including the extent, where known, of professional and licensed alternative and holistic health care practitioners and facilities

The next chapter reviews the ways in which each of these lifestyle factors influences health and enhances a city's healthfulness.

# 6

# Rating the Cities III: Lifestyle Factors That Influence Health

What actual health benefits could you reasonably expect from living in a healthful city rather than in a traditional city?

Although you're likely to benefit from lower levels of urban stress by moving to one of our healthful cities, and possibly from other inherent factors such as higher elevation and terrain therapy, the major influence affecting your health is the extent to which living in a healthful city enables you to more closely follow a low-risk lifestyle.

Naturally, the earlier in life that you adopt a low-risk lifestyle, the better your quality of life and the more years of healthful living you can anticipate. But several studies have recently shown that, even late in life, significant health benefits accrue to anyone adopting a low-risk lifestyle.

For example, a recent computer study by Kenneth G. Manton, Ph.D., professor and director of Duke University's Center for Demographic Studies, indicates that by adopting an optimally healthful lifestyle, a 30-year-old man or woman could reasonably expect to add fifteen years to his or her statistical life expectancy. And these would be healthy, active, productive years, not years of old age and senility.

Another study of 7,000 residents of Alameda County, California, (described later under Opportunities for Social Contacts) revealed that by practicing seven simple good

73

health habits—each similar to those in the low-risk lifestyle—a 45-year-old male could extend his life expectancy by eleven years. Specifically, he could increase his life expectancy from approximately 73.2 years to 84.7 years, while a 50-year-old man could increase his from 74.3 to 85.6 years.

With increasing age, the increase in life expectancy diminished. Yet even at age 75, the pro-health habits could add five years to a man's average life expectancy. Thus this study clearly demonstrates that it is never too late to adopt a low-risk lifestyle. Incidentally, the study also showed a proportionate but somewhat lower life expectancy increase for women.

When you consider that life expectancy tables are based on the mortality rates of people who live in both healthful and traditional cities—and that barely 15 percent of Americans can be truly described as health-conscious—adding eleven-and-a-half or fifteen years to your life expectancy is not really an exceptional achievement. For millions of Americans, and particularly for those who follow the often inappropriate way of life of a traditional city, adopting a low-risk lifestyle might extend their lives by as much as 35 years.

## *Thirty-Five Years of Extra Life*

That may sound exaggerated. But it is the actual statistical difference between the life expectancy of a 37-year-old, overweight, divorced male who lives in New York City, smokes two packs of cigarettes and takes several alcoholic drinks daily, performs no exercise, and is employed at a dull, routine office job ... and a slender, happily married Norwegian male, also aged 37, who abstains from all forms of substance abuse, and who leads an active outdoor life working on his own farm.

(When you break it down to basics, the Norwegian farmer's lifestyle quite closely parallels the low-risk lifestyle commonly practiced in America's more healthful cities.)

Obviously, the Norwegian has not extended his life expectancy by 35 years. The dramatic 35 year difference is due to the American's counter-productive habits that are destroying his health and shortening his life.

Were the American to adopt the low-risk lifestyle, it is highly probable that he could soon increase his life expectancy by 35 years, or possibly more.

Does eleven-and-a-half or fifteen or even thirty-five extra years of health-filled living sound worth having? If you are currently living in a traditional city, and are not following a low-risk lifestyle, you may be able to extend your life significantly by moving to a more health-oriented community.

For a deeper understanding of the factors involved, here is an analysis of each of the nine criteria by which we evaluate the lifestyle-enhancing benefits of each city.

# HEALTH AWARENESS OF THE POPULATION

Awareness of the need to follow a low-risk lifestyle is greatest among well-educated people in the 35-65 year age bracket. This trend has been confirmed by at least a dozen different surveys and studies. Moreover, since educated people tend to earn higher incomes, health awareness and moderate affluence go together. For instance, natural foods supermarkets exist only in upscale neighborhoods. And a study by the Centers For Disease Control showed that as income rose, so did the number of people who exercised. For people with incomes exceeding $40,000 annually, 10.5 percent exercised sufficiently to benefit health compared to only 6.3 percent of people with incomes of $15,000 or less.

That many people from lower socio-economic levels tend to ignore health advisories isn't surprising when you consider that one-fourth of the U.S. population reads below the high school graduation level. Since most health advice is printed, many less educated people are unsure or confused about what health steps to take. Over half of all people who die of heart attacks never graduated from high school, and the majority of obese women have lower levels of education and income.

Studies show that life expectancy is highest in the more affluent suburbs of resorts and of cities with a population of 125,000 or less. This trend is especially clear in not-too-large cities in which a principal campus of the state university is located. Not only is a state university a source of culture and education for residents of all ages, but it also draws several hundred highly-educated faculty members. Additionally, hi-tech industries and computer firms cluster around many state universities, adding more hundreds, or thousands, of well-educated, well-paid and health-conscious residents. Moderate affluence also brings more leisure and greater autonomy, two important pluses in reducing stress and extending life.

## *Baby Boomers Are the Most Health-Conscious Generation*

Studies are also showing that baby boomers—those born between 1946 and 1964—are the most health-conscious of any age group. Most baby boomers with higher education grew up on a diet of jogging, recreational bicycling, yoga, vegetarian eating, and herb teas. As they enter middle age, these better-educated baby boomers are still obsessed with youth. Millions ride bicycles for exercise and cross-country ski. Other millions have turned back the clock and refused to conform with traditional stereotypes of aging. Next to teen-agers, people 40 and over have the highest divorce rate. Many middle aged women are too busy pursuing exciting careers to have time to experience the empty nest syndrome.

Close behind on the health scale is today's younger generation of retirees. More than half of American men are retiring between ages 55 and 62. The majority are healthier, younger, more affluent, better educated and more independent than any previous generation. Instead of growing stiff and old, millions of today's grandparents are embarking on adventurous new paths to personal growth. Both they and the baby boomers are high-energy people who prefer an active lifestyle. Instead of crafts, hobbies, and gardening, they are demanding year around lapswimming, tennis, mountain bicycling, and more walking and heart exercise trails.

Martha Moyer, on the staff of the Del Webb Corporation, confirmed this trend when she recently wrote us from Sun City West. "We are seeing the interests of retirees shift from sedentary activities, such as arts and crafts and bowling, to higher energy activities such as exercise classes and lapswimming," she wrote.

Based on these and similar indications, our Health Awareness rating is a measure of how receptive and supportive a community is to the need to live a low-risk lifestyle.

## NUTRITIONAL AWARENESS

The Nutritional Awareness of any city is an estimate of how closely people in that city follow the dietary guidelines of the major health advisory agencies.

Among these agencies and associated sources are such prestigious researchers as the National Research Council, the National Cancer Institute, the American Heart Association, the Surgeon General, the Framingham Study, and the Pritikin Institutes for Longevity. The National Research Council's Health and Diet study involved a three-year review of 5,500 other studies, each made by a prominent scientist, and consisted of the most comprehensive report on diet and health ever undertaken. Included in the review were such landmark studies as the Seven Countries Study, which first incriminated saturated fat rather than cholesterol as the major villain in causing cardiovascular disease.

Acting separately, each agency has released a set of dietary guidelines designed to prevent such chronic diseases as heart disease, cancer, stroke, and hypertension.

When the cancer prevention guidelines issued by the National Cancer Institute turned out to be almost identical with those issued for preventing coronary artery disease by the American Heart Association, the National Heart, Lung and Blood Institute, and other top advisory agencies, it swiftly became apparent that the same animal-derived foods had been causally-linked to more than 75 percent of all chronic disease.

The result was that, in 1990, nine large voluntary and government health agencies published a special report entitled *The Healthy American Diet* in which they pooled their dietary concepts to create a single recommended diet designed to prevent all, or most, chronic diseases.

When we analyzed this diet (or better still, the original dietary recommendations of each individual agency), it came as no surprise to learn that this diet is almost identical to that on which our ancestors thrived until recent times and which our genes lead us to accept as man's natural diet.

## *Dietary Blueprint for Healthful Living*

When we analyzed the dietary recommendations and findings of each of the top advisory services, we found that they presented this overall picture of the most healthful diet for man.

►Americans are urged to lose no time in cutting by half or more their daily intake of calories from fats and proteins from animal sources, and at least doubling their intake of calories from fruits, vegetables, and whole grains.

►Saturated fat, it has been found, is two to five times more capable of blocking the arteries with cholesterol than is dietary cholesterol itself. This doesn't mean that cholesterol is any safer than before. It simply implies that saturated fat is several times more dangerous. Among the principal sources of both are whole milk, cream, butter, cheese, ice cream, egg yolks, animal fats of all kinds, hydrogenated vegetable oils, all fatty meats—especially organ meats, palm or coconut oil, and many commercially fried foods.

▸Polyunsaturated oils, like corn and safflower oils, once considered a safe substitute for animal fats, have now been linked with lowering of good cholesterol and immuno-suppression. Today, monounsaturated oils like olive and canola oils, plus Omega-3 oils found in fatty fish, are considered the safest oils to eat.

▸A high-fat diet has been directly linked to cardiovascular disease, hypertension, stroke, diabetes, cancer of the breast, colon, and prostate, plus obesity and blood clots. Several sources consider the American Heart Association's top limit of 30 percent of calories from fat to be far too high and recommend cutting fat intake so that only 10 to 20 percent of calories are derived from fat, the majority of which should come from vegetable sources.

Recent research has revealed that renal disease is becoming increasingly common as we burden the kidneys with two to three times as much protein as we actually need, and most of that is from animal sources. Evidence is also emerging linking tumor growth, osteoporosis, and cardiovascular disease with an excess of animal protein. As the diet advisories tell us, most Americans should cut intake of meat, eggs, and whole milk dairy products in half. Other foods to avoid are smoked, pickled, fermented and salt-cured foods, and foods charred by grilling or boiling.

## Eating for Health and Long Life

In place of foods of animal origin, a number of agencies recommend that we at least double our intake of coarse plant food. This is sound advice since there is a significantly lower incidence of almost every chronic disease in societies which consume large amounts of fresh fruits, vegetables, and whole grains. In fact, we should eat twice as many fresh vegetables as fruits and they should include beans, dark green and yellow-orange vegetables, cruciferous family vegetables like broccoli and brussels sprouts, and green peppers, onions, and garlic.

Virtually every type of vegetable has been found to help prevent cancer. A recent study at the University of Nebraska Medical Center (reported in *Nutrition and Cancer*, vol 12, no 2, 1989) showed that in animals, cruciferous vegetables may even slow the spread of cancer once it has developed.

We should also eat generously of whole grain breads and cereals. And, of course, we should eat fruits of all types.

Our digestive systems also demand a high intake of the same kinds of fiber that our ancestors consumed. No food of animal origin contains any fiber. Nor does adding bran to a low-fiber diet supply the complete mix of soluble and insoluble fiber our intestines require. To obtain these, we must eat a variety of fresh vegetables, fruits, and whole grains. Studies show that risk of colon cancer is lowest in people who consume 20-30 grams of fiber or more each day. The National Cancer Institute has recommended that Americans double or triple their average fiber intake of only ten grams each day.

At the same time, we must avoid overeating. After saturated fat, the highest dietary health risk factor is an excess of calories. Numerous lab animal studies have shown that moderately cutting back on calories (especially from fat) while maintaining a full supply of essential nutrients, boosts the animals' immunity, lowers their blood pressure, reduces risk of most chronic diseases, keeps them more active and youthful, and extends their lives by as much as 50 percent.

Coupled with regular exercise, a low fat, high-fiber diet also creates exceptional levels of energy, stamina, and endurance.

### Sizing Up a City's Nutritional Awareness

How can we tell how well these guidelines are being followed in any city? The best clues are the prevalence of natural foods supermarkets; of unusually well-stocked produce departments in regular supermarkets, especially if they carry a varied selection of tropical fruits and a section devoted to organically-grown produce; of farmers' markets, produce stores, and other good sources of fresh fruits and vegetables; of the availability of whole grain breads that are totally free of fats, oils, sweeteners, preservatives, and refined flours (which is not true of most commercial supermarket breads); of the number of vegetarian restaurants and ethnic restaurants, such as Indian, Italian, and Chinese, which frequently offer a tasty cuisine low in fat and animal protein; and of well-stocked salad bars in regular restaurants. Another good indication is the proportion of residents who are macrobiotic, vegetarian, Seventh Day Adventist or Mormon, all of whom consume less fat and animal protein and enjoy far better health than the general public.

Based on these and similar indications, our Nutritional Awareness rating is a measure of how closely a community is following the dietary recommendations of the major health advisory agencies.

# FITNESS RESOURCES AND ACTIVITIES

This factor estimates the awareness of the need for regular exercise in a particular city, and measures the extent to which exercise facilities and fitness programs are available.

In recent years, an avalanche of new research discoveries have demonstrated that regular exercise can benefit every part of the body, right down to our cells. And, of course, being as fit as possible and maintaining one's ideal weight play an essential role in the low-risk lifestyle.

After following over 13,000 men and women for eight years, the Institute for Aerobics Research, in Dallas, reported (in the *Journal of the American Medical Association*, November 3, 1989) that the more physically fit you are, the longer you will live. Specifically, the most physically-fit people in the study were three times less likely to die in any given period than the least fit. Furthermore, the most fit people were eight times less likely to die of cardiovascular disease than the least fit.

Another well-designed study by Ralph Paffenbarger, Ph.D., of Stanford University School of Medicine, followed 17,000 Harvard graduates for sixteen years. This study, too, found that, within limits, increased amounts of physical exercise can reduce mortality by 40 percent while simultaneously adding several years to a person's life expectancy. Based on the number of calories used while exercising, the study found that men who expended 2,000 calories per week on exercise showed a significant reduction in life-shortening diseases of the heart and arteries. The most sedentary among the men in the study showed a mortality rate almost double that of those who expended 2,000 or more calories per week.

Yet another major study, the Lipid Research Clinic's Mortality Follow-Up Study, followed 3,106 healthy men aged 30-69 for eight-and-a-half years. Results showed that the least fit men in the study—those with the highest levels of blood pressure, cholesterol and triglycerides—were 3.2 times more likely to die of heart disease than the most fit men.

The conclusion of these, and scores of other recent studies, is that a high aerobic fitness level alone can lower the risk of dying from any chronic disease, regardless of diet, stress, genetics, or family history. Furthermore, exercise bestows a wide range of additional benefits, all proving that taking care of yourself physically is one of the best health investments you can make.

### Regular Exercise Benefits the Whole Person

Regardless of age, exercising regularly builds a lean, firm, strong body; it retards, or even reverses, the aging process; it improves cardiac efficiency and oxygen uptake; and it lowers both blood pressure and resting heart rate. Exercise boosts sexual vigor, significantly lowers risk of cardiovascular disease and of several types of cancer, and cuts the risk of osteoporosis. It reduces symptoms of anxiety, stress, tension, and moderate depression. It mobilizes more energy and stamina, and reduces fatigue. Exercise also helps lower the proportion of body fat and plays a key role in maintaining one's weight at the ideal level.

Exercise helps retain the muscle mass of youth intact and improves definition of every muscle. By helping you to look and feel good, it boosts self-esteem and increases immunocompetence. As we grow older, exercise greatly enhances the quality of life. By exercising regularly, men and women of any age can stay vigorous, vital, alive, and youthful, and in the process minimize any risk of senility or a crippling fall. Through regular exercise, we can help beat most types of chronic disease and get to spend an extra ten to twenty years with our mate and our grandchildren.

Put another way, the risk of not exercising can be 1,000 times greater than any risk involved by starting a gradually-increasing exercise program. (Naturally, this assumes you have your doctor's permission to exercise.) Yet surveys show that over 92 percent of all American adults fail to exercise sufficiently to benefit their health. One woman in five is completely sedentary. And one of the principal reasons why people fail to exercise is that they live in a city with a pre-dominantly couch potato lifestyle.

### Health Hazards of Sedentary Living

In people who fail to exercise regularly, a progressive decline in cardiovascular efficiency occurs, leading to a serious decrease in maximum oxygen uptake; muscles atrophy, leading to a loss of strength and flexibility; and an overall physical deterioration sets in and becomes steadily worse.

Nor do many of America's most popular recreations involve worthwhile exercise. The Centers for Disease Control consider it unlikely that the following activities provide any significant benefit to health: pleasure boating, bowling, fishing, golf, horseback riding, softball, surfing, or water skiing. None involve rhythmic contraction of large muscle groups, considered a necessity by the CDC for improving fitness and health.

As sedentary people grow older, their joints and ligaments stiffen and they lose height and bone mass. An inactive lifestyle increases risk of heart disease, cancer, diabetes, and osteoporosis. Most people who require joint replacements have been sedentary for decades.

Obesity is pandemic in America, a condition growing out of our high-fat diet and sedentary lifestyle. Of 30 recent cancer and diet studies, 26 found more cancer among people who were significantly overweight, and who consumed a high calorie diet. The cancers included tumor of the breast, colon, rectum, prostate, thyroid, endometrium, kidney, cervix, ovary, and gallbladder. By reducing body weight through exercise and a low-fat, low calorie diet, the NCI estimates that risk of cancer at all ten of these sites could be dramatically reduced.

## Prescription for Restoring Youthful Vitality

Among recent discoveries by exercise physiologists is that exercising for an extended period of time burns off fat more effectively than a short, intense workout. Thus one measure of a healthful city is that it offers resources for taking long walks, long swims, or long bicycle rides.

Another effective way to lose weight is to combine the three main types of exercise, namely aerobic, stretching, and strength-building exercises. Combining all three in your exercise program ensures that you use the maximum number of muscles.

While aerobics is the core of a well-balanced exercise and fitness program, most authorities consider strength-building and flexibility training as equally essential. The American College of Sports Medicine recommends that adults perform a strength-building workout at least twice each week. To prevent back pain and to improve flexibility, a stretching routine such as yoga postures should also be done at least twice each week.

Another measure of a healthful city is the availability of facilities and programs for combining all three exercise forms into a well-rounded exercise program.

## Strength-Building Exercises

Strength-building exercises employ calisthenics or free weights or Nautilus-type progressive-resistance exercise machines. By working pairs of opposing muscles, these exercises have helped thousands of men and women of all ages to overcome back pain and to avoid surgery. Various studies have also found that strength-building exercises help maintain bone density, especially in women.

Tens of thousands of older men and women regularly perform strength-building exercises, including many in their 70s, 80s, and even 90s. Instead of steadily losing strength, as sedentary people do, those who perform strength-building exercises find that, regardless of age, they can work tirelessly all day. The majority have far more stamina than most younger people.

After studying several thousand older people who took up a strength-building exercise program, several surveys have confirmed that, within 90 days, the majority of men and women can double the strength of their arms, legs, and other muscles, even if they have been sedentary for years.

Thus yet another important measure of a healthful city is that it offers programs and instruction in all types of strength-building exercises for men and women of all ages. It should also have an abundance of weight rooms and progressive resistance exercise machines. Availability of Nautilus-type knee exercise machines is especially important for building up the quadricep muscles, and preventing or rehabilitating knee dysfunctions.

## Stretching and Flexibility Exercises

Failing to stretch and maintain flexibility causes the body to become stiff and to age rapidly. Stretching exercises, or yoga, for a minimum of 25 minutes at least twice each week, is considered the minimum for maintaining flexibility.

Most physiologists agree that maintaining a supple body is the best way to prevent arthritis. Inflexible muscles are more easily injured, while aerobic exercise without flexibility training can lead to cartilage wear in joints.

Regardless of age, stretching and flexibility exercises, regularly performed, can restore natural resilience and suppleness and can maintain flexibility for life.

Ideally, a healthful city should offer classes in *hatha yoga,* for people of all ages, several times each week. Alternatively, other forms of flexibility training are equally acceptable.

## Aerobic Exercise

Aerobic exercise involves the large muscle groups in rhythmic, dynamic movement to promote cardiovascular fitness. Exercising at a brisk pace benefits the heart, lungs, and circulation as well as every other body part and organ. For example, one bonus is that, after exercising for 30 minutes or more, clouds of endorphin are released in the brain, creating an exuberant feeling of relaxation and well-being that lasts for hours.

Among the most beneficial types of aerobic exercises for adults are brisk walking, race walking, brisk bicycling, rowing, continuous swimming, square dancing, and cross-country skiing.

To provide an alternative form of exercise when it's too cold or wet to exercise outdoors, a healthful city should provide swimming, dancing, or some alternative form of indoor exercise (which could also be stretching or calisthenics).

## *Bicycling*

Bicycling involves zero impact and minimal damage to joints or cartilage. However, to derive cardiovascular benefit from bicycling, you must spin the pedals briskly at a cadence of 60-95 rpm or more. To do this you must ride a high-performance bicycle with a wide range of gears. Thus one requirement of a healthful city is a choice of nearby low-traffic country roads where you can ride safely for 10 to 35 miles or more without having to stop. By contrast, merely dawdling on a bicycle path, or around the neighborhood on a department store bicycle provides little or no fitness benefit.

Don't worry about hills. Today's 18 and 21-speed bicycles can soar up hills. The more hills, the better your workout. Alternatively, if traffic-free dirt roads are available, you can ride on those using a mountain bicycle. Most, though not all healthful cities, are also bike-friendly communities with a network of quiet roads and bicycle paths that can take you swiftly all over town. Hundreds, if not thousands, of adults in these cities ride bicycles, and there is usually at least one bicycle club with organized rides of varying distances.

Generally, the West, Northwest, Southwest, Midwest, and Northeastern states provide the best bicycling, while the Southern states, and especially South Florida, offer the fewest opportunities to bicycle.

## *Cross-Country Skiing*

Considered the most aerobic of all exercises, cross-country or Nordic skiing involves both arm and leg muscles simultaneously. Studies show that trail skiers develop greater lung capacity, deliver more oxygen to vital body organs and tissue, and burn more calories than in any other exercise. The smooth gliding motion of ski-touring is relatively low-impact and easy on the joints.

Cross-country skiing is at its best in the high, dry powder snow of the Rockies in Colorado and Utah. But you can also enjoy it in National Forests all across the northern tier of states. And cities like Minneapolis have lighted trail networks for night-time skiing.

Almost any place with four feet of snow cover during winter offers good Nordic skiing. The technique is easier to learn than downhill and no lift tickets are required. But it often takes a drive of 30-40 miles under wintry conditions to reach the ski trails from such Colorado cities as Boulder or Durango. By comparison, Alpine or downhill skiing, in which you are hauled uphill on a lift, provides few fitness benefits.

Among healthful cities providing cross-country skiing are: Boulder, CO; Bozeman, MT; Cedar City, UT; Colorado Springs, CO; Durango, CO; Eau Claire, WI; La Crosse, WI; Los Alamos, NM; Madison, WI; Minneapolis-St. Paul, MN; Missoula, MT; and Santa Fe, NM.

## *Rowing, Canoeing*

Rowing an expensive racing shell with a sliding seat exercises the entire body. But rowing a skiff, or even paddling a canoe continuously—especially against a wind—provides efficient aerobic conditioning for the upper body.

To row or paddle successfully, you need a sheltered area on a calm river, lake, or salt water lagoon. The area must be relatively free of fast motor boats and water skiers. Its vast waterways give Florida top place for still-water rowing or canoeing. We've personally found the intracoastal waterway especially good, since shoals and mudbanks discourage water skiers, jet skis, and speedboats while rowboats or canoes can glide over them with impunity. Those who enjoy exercising on the water will find a variety of opportunities in our healthful cities.

## *Square Dancing*

Three million Americans aged 50 or over enjoy square dancing. In fact, active dancing of all types provides such a good fitness workout that it is often recommended for recovering heart disease patients. Square, folk, round, and aerobic dancing all combine rhythmic exercise with joy, fun, and social contact. Dancing also helps to create a strongly positive self-image. Across the nation, more than 500 ballrooms are open on any one night, while adult dances are often held at church, recreation, and senior centers to taped music. Steps can be swiftly learned and partners are easy to find. However, aerobic dancing or jazzercise may stress the joints of some older people.

To check on availability of square dance classes and activities in any city, consult the National Square Dance Directory, available in most public libraries. Also, look in the yellow pages under *Exercise and Physical Fitness Programs* or *Dancing Instruction.* Most healthful cities offer a variety of opportunities for active dancing.

### Swimming

Year around heated pools for adult lapswimming are in woefully short supply in the United States. Many cities have built Olympic-size pools, only to turn them over to frolicking children and divers. No provision is made for lapswimming, and as far as fitness is concerned the millions of dollars spent on these pools has been totally wasted.

Fortunately, year around lapswimming is available in most of our healthful cities. The best pools are 50-meter Olympic-sized pools operated by private swim clubs, or by the city parks and recreation department, with definite hours reserved for adult and senior lapswimming. Lapswimming opportunities are also often available at Ys, health clubs, and at some country clubs. Other pools are usually too small and too crowded. Twenty meters is the minimum acceptable length for lapswimming. Where water is not too contaminated for human contact, dams, lakes, and rivers can provide good seasonal opportunities for distance swimming.

For the privilege of having a full 50-meter lane all to yourself at a private club or natatorium, you should be prepared to pay somewhat more than the usual fee at a municipal pool. Regardless of the fee, however, wherever a city offers an opportunity to swim 10, 20, or 50 laps two or three times a week throughout the year, this fact is usually noted in this book.

A low-impact exercise, swimming builds strong arm, shoulder, neck, and back muscles, while helping keep the whole body flexible. For those with joint problems, many pools also offer water exercise classes.

## Tennis

Thousands of superbly healthful older men and women—many in their 80s—owe their fitness to a lifetime of playing fast singles tennis. Many of our healthful cities have outstanding municipally-owned tennis facilities, including instruction by pros. In other cities, you must play at private clubs. But wherever a city is considered a good tennis town, and has the courts, complexes and clubs to prove it, this fact is noted in our city profiles.

## Walking and Hiking

The most popular and least expensive of all aerobic exercises, brisk walking promotes flexibility and strengthens major muscle groups in the arms, legs, and back. In fact, walking briskly for four or five miles a day tones the entire body, while creating a wonderfully relaxed feeling of total well-being.

Thousands of older men and women also practice race walking, a faster and more demanding variety of competitive walking that offers benefits equal to running but with far less risk of injury. Thousands of other adults prefer to work out on *pars cours* (heart exercise) trails. The idea here is to walk approximately 100 yards from one exercise station to the next.

At each station, you stop and perform a calisthenics-type exercise, such as doing fifteen sit-ups. You then walk (or jog) to the next station. Most *pars cours* trails have fifteen to twenty exercise stations.

In all too many American cities and communities, residents have no place to walk. By contrast, almost all our healthful cities offer a choice of walking trails, many with hills, and the majority also have pars cours trails and race-walking clubs. In these same cities, walking and hiking clubs are also popular.

Actually, hill and mountain hiking provide the greatest fitness-walking benefits. Wherever outstanding walking opportunities exist, they are noted in our city profile reports.

## *Healthful Cities Support Maximum Fitness*

Several recent studies have suggested that a mere twenty minutes of brisk walking three times a week can significantly reduce risk of heart disease. However, those content with a minimum amount of exercise are missing many other major benefits.

According to the Institute for Aerobics Research, a woman who exercises only to the point of being moderately fit has a mortality rate more than twice that of a woman who is optimally fit. In other words, a woman willing to exercise for a longer period five to six times a week, and to become *really* fit, has less than half the risk of dying in any given period than does a woman who is only moderately fit. For males, moderately fit men have a mortality rate 23 percent higher than optimally fit men.

As you learn to enjoy exercise, you'll find it well worthwhile to make an extra effort to achieve optimal fitness rather than to be satisfied with merely a moderate level of fitness. Thousands of people in our healthful cities are already exercising every day rather than a mere three times a week. Thus you're likely to find plenty of support from adult fitness buffs in our healthful cities.

Also confined almost exclusively to America's most healthful cities are Masters Training Programs through which adults and seniors can compete with others in their age group. Some of our cities also hold an annual Senior Games. And the Senior Olympics are often held at or near one of our healthful cities.

### *Few Cities Provide Information on Their Fitness Resources*

Incidentally, trying to extract information about fitness resources and exercise programs from Chambers of Commerce, or other sources, is often harder than pulling teeth. In many cities, fitness facilities and activities are separately operated by as many as twenty different entities. It is, therefore, quite difficult to tally the fitness resources of any community without having lived there for an extended period.

With three exceptions (Durango, CO; Prescott, AZ; and Seattle, WA), not a single city we visited had catalogued its fitness resources, nor did any literature list the resources for staying fit and healthy. Many employees in information offices smoked and were overweight, and few, we found, ever exercised themselves. One tip-off, we discovered, is that any city that advertises itself as a "golf capital," or has a slogan like "where golf is king," is unlikely to be very fitness-oriented.

The best source of information about exercise and fitness opportunities is a city's parks and recreation department. Addresses for both the Chamber of Commerce (or the Convention and Visitors Bureau) and the parks and recreation department are given in our city profiles.

# STRESS MANAGEMENT RESOURCES

This guideline evaluates the extent of facilities and programs offered by each city to minimize the harmful effects of unresolved emotional stress.

Almost every disease or dysfunction has been linked to stress. Stress arises when we are faced with a life event that appears to threaten our security, comfort, pleasure, or prestige. Whenever we perceive an event as threatening or hostile, negative feelings such as anxiety, cynicism, or fear are aroused. With hair trigger speed, the brain transforms these negative feelings into the biochemical and physiological reactions of the *fight or flight response*, a primitive survival mechanism that in earlier times prepared us to meet immediate physical danger.

Adrenalin squirts into the bloodstream, placing the entire body in an emergency state. Platelets in the bloodstream prepare to clot to prevent blood loss from possible wounds, thereby increasing risk of a stroke or heart attack. Arteries constrict, sending blood pressure soaring and increasing risk of coronary artery spasm or stroke. Glycogen pours out of the liver to power the muscles for action. When this energy remains unused—as it frequently must in modern society— we feel tense and uncomfortable and we experience increased anxiety, depression, and inability to relax. Among stress hormones released into the bloodstream is cortisol, which suppresses the immune system, significantly increasing risk of cancer, infectious disease, or rheumatoid arthritis.

Millions of Americans who perceive the world as threatening or hostile, or who feel cynical, anxious, or depressed, live in a permanent state of emergency with the *fight or flight response* constantly simmering. Soon, their hypertension becomes chronic, their blood platelets remain clumped, their immunity stays suppressed, and they live at a heightened risk of heart disease, stroke, cancer, and a whole series of potentially-lethal infectious diseases. Usually, the higher a city's level of Urban Stress, the higher the proportion of residents living stress-filled lives.

But life doesn't *have* to go on being stressful. Stress management programs exist to help us cope with stress, and also to transform the personality so that what we once perceived as hostile now appears as harmless and neutral. In the process, stress disappears, and with it most stress-related risks to health.

Stress management programs fall into two categories:

1. Systems for coping with stress, such as deep muscle relaxation and biofeedback, in which students are taught to prevent the destructive effects of stress by learning to deliberately relax the body.

2. Systems that transform the personality so that instead of perceiving a life event as hostile and unfriendly, we see it as non-threatening and harmless. In this category are yoga, the teachings of Unity and other New Thought churches, A Course in Miracles, the Master Mind Technique, and a variety of therapies based on the highly successful twelve-step system used in Alcoholics Anonymous and similar self-help programs.

## *Stress Management Programs Are Most Common in Health-Conscious Cities*

Both forms of stress-management have gained wide acceptance in the more cosmopolitan and sophisticated cities of America. They have also been widely adopted by corporations and institutions. Frequently, classes are offered at minimum cost by hospitals, churches, parks and recreation departments, community colleges, adult education departments, medical schools, and even by senior citizen centers. Through stress management classes offered by these and similar institutions, stress can be dissipated or buffered from harming the body.

To a great extent, however, stress management programs are available only in health-conscious cities. This guideline measures the availability of stress management programs and resources for each city in this book and ranks them accordingly.

# OPPORTUNITIES TO EXERCISE THE MIND IN LATER LIFE

This guideline measures the extent of opportunities for personal growth through intellectual, cultural, and creative activities for adults.

At least a dozen studies, each authored by a prominent psychologist, have confirmed that to remain physically healthy and active, we must exercise our minds as well as our bodies. The brain is like a muscle. It atrophies when not used. To enjoy perfect health throughout life, we must keep our minds as elastic and youthful as we did in our twenties. This translates into using our minds to the greatest possible extent throughout life.

For instance, a study of 58 people aged 65 and over, made in Omaha by the International Institute of San Diego during the 1980s, proved that the more people use their minds, the more they are likely to live a long, healthy life.

The 58 subjects were split into two equal-sized groups. Group 1, the painters, actively studied art and painted. Group 2, the non-painters, did nothing. After eleven years of studying and painting, 67 percent of the painters remained alive compared to only 12 percent of the non-painters. Each of the painters was mentally alert and none were confined to bed. By contrast, only 62 percent of the surviving non-painters were mentally alert and 38 percent were confined to bed.

This, along with several similar studies, has clearly demonstrated that with regular mental activity and learning the mind ages more slowly than any other organ. In almost every healthy person, intelligence gradually increases to age 50 and remains constant into the 80s and 90s, and even beyond. But this is true only when we regularly use mental gymnastics to keep our minds flexible and resourceful so that we continue to sharpen our ability to keep on learning.

## The Most Mind-Dulling Activities

Sadly, millions of older Americans give up on learning and mental activity and slide into a steady diet of watching TV and spectator sports and playing bingo. Unfortunately, these passive, mind-dulling activities neither exercise the mind nor place any demand on our intelligence or creativity. As a result, our western society considers it normal for older persons to become feeble-minded and to suffer from senility and neurological disorders like Alzheimer's. For decades, it had been assumed that senility was inevitable with increasing age. But studies at the National Institute on Aging, and elsewhere, have shown that decline in intellectual function is much less common than was earlier believed, while senility is almost always due to a disease state, or to over-medication, and not to aging. In reality, much of what has been attributed to senility is now believed due to progressive inactivity of the mental process.

To keep the mind active, and to stay healthy, we must seek out learning and intellectual challenge. Provided we keep learning, intellectual growth continues throughout life. When we stop learning, much of the zest and excitement of living is lost. The annals are filled with examples of men and women who became intellectual giants in their 80s and 90s, and who experienced radiant health in the process. Bernard Shaw and Bertrand Russell were still actively writing in their 90s, while the paintings of Pablo Picasso reveal that he underwent an explosion of growth between ages 82 and 92.

## The Mind—Use It or Lose It!

It is much easier to keep on learning and challenging the mind in a community that prizes such traits as intellectualism, liberal thinking, and mental creativity. Academic qualities such as these are valued most highly in college towns, especially in those where the main campus of the state university is located. For personal and intellectual growth, we'd look for a city in which the state university is the major industry, and in which the college faculty, plus scientists from clustering hi-tech research parks, comprise at least 25 percent of the population, with the student body adding another 25 percent or so. This doesn't leave much room for couch potatoes.

The result is that a university town like Gainesville, Florida, has more in common with other university towns such as Boulder, Colorado or Chapel Hill, North Carolina than it does with neighboring Florida towns only a few miles away. Their academic quality, their stable economy, and their neighborhoods that rarely deteriorate have long made college towns popular for retirement. With a highly-educated populace monitoring the city fathers, college towns tend to have far superior schools, infrastructures, parks, libraries, museums, and other amenities, while resources for health and fitness are usually outstanding. The quality of hospitals, and of medical and dental care, is also often exceptional.

Most larger colleges or universities sponsor a series of plays, concerts, classic films, ballet, chamber music recitals, and lectures by visiting celebrities. And provided the institution is *state-funded,* most of these inspiring cultural activities are open to local residents, usually free or at nominal cost.

Furthermore, 36 states waive tuition for retired residents at state-supported community colleges and universities. From Princeton University to a dozen top-ranking state universities, gray-haired retirees are auditing classes without charge, satisfying their thirst for knowledge as they listen to top professors and lecturers. More than one-third of all students in college today are over 30 years of age, and they include many retirees who are enrolled in credit courses and are training for a second career.

At almost all state-funded institutions of higher learning, local residents are able to use the library and the university swimming pool, gym, running tracks, tennis courts, and other fitness facilities. To ensure that all these facilities *are* open to local residents, call or write the University's Public Information Officer. This source can supply a calendar of events, tell you exactly when classes and facilities are open to local residents, and even recommend college courses or programs which seniors may audit.

## Bookstores: Indicators of a City's Intellectual Support

Another important indicator to a city's potential for intellectual growth is its number of bookstores. For example, Austin, Texas has four times as many bookstores as nearby San Antonio, which is more than twice as large. In part, this reflects the presence in Austin of the main campus of the University of Texas. But San Antonio's literacy record is dragged down by its huge population of 217,000 functionally-illiterate residents.

While state university centers obviously rank high among America 's healthiest cities, they are not the only places where one can keep the mind honed and active. Other cities and resorts, many with populations as low as 25,000, offer stimulating classes in continuing education for adults of all ages. Others have free universities at which anyone with something useful to teach may offer a class.

Even in smaller communities, an individual can sharpen the mind with such interests as astronomy and cosmology. Learning a new language, or learning to play an instrument, builds new neural pathways between brain cells, making the mind more active and alive. Books of puzzles and brain bogglers can challenge the mind for weeks at a time. Even quite small towns often have great book groups and classes in computer sciences that stimulate the mind. Some retirees buy a microscope and take up botany and biology. The world today is filled with exciting new knowledge and ideas. It's important, however, to follow a discipline that employs constructive thinking based on reason, rationalism, and logic. Venturing into speculative metaphysics, such as theorizing about Unidentified Flying Objects, or other non-provable subjects, does little to sharpen or hone the mind.

98

The extent of a city's cultural activities is another good indicator of opportunities for staying intellectually active. The availability of good libraries, museums, art galleries, theater, opera, ballet, concerts, lectures, music and drama festivals, and good FM music stations provides a direct clue to a city's overall healthfulness.

# OPPORTUNITIES FOR SOCIAL CONTACTS

This guideline measures the opportunities offered by each city to avoid loneliness and isolation by joining and participating in a wide variety of social, civic, and church groups and organizations.

Several important studies have each confirmed the health risks that arise from social isolation and loneliness. For example, a study of 7,000 residents of Alameda County, California, by Lisa F. Berkman, Ph.D. and S. Leonard Syme, Ph.D., showed that the more social contacts a person has, the longer they live and the healthier they are. This conclusion held up even when subjects had other poor health habits.

The study revealed that people with close, intimate relationships, especially marriage, underwent less stress and depression. Unresolved emotional stress arising out of loneliness-caused depression appears to suppress immunity and to open the way for cancer and pneumonia as well as other life-shortening health risks like heart disease. The study showed that unmarried people with few friends and relatives, and who spurned opportunities for social contacts, had a death rate twice that of people who enjoyed an abundance of social relationships.

Another study by Dr. William Ruberman (published in the *New England Journal of Medicine* in 1984) followed 2,320 men for several months after they had suffered a heart attack.

Results showed that those who led isolated and stressful lives were four times more likely to die than were those who enjoyed lower stress levels and more social contacts.

Still another study by Dr. Richard Hessler, professor of Sociology at the University of Missouri, followed 1,700 men and women aged 75 and older for twenty years. By the study's end, only 129 remained alive, of whom 90 percent were women. The study concluded that loneliness was a key factor in the high mortality rate of older men. Apparently, retirement disrupts many relationships men develop through work, and older men tend to make few new contacts. Women, by contrast, eagerly join social, civil, and church groups and meet many more people through whom they can maintain relationships as they grow older.

## Health-Oriented Cities Offer More Social Contacts

For optimal health, everyone—whether male or female, single or married—needs a strong social network of relatives and friends. For health-conscious people, making new associations is usually much easier in a health-oriented city. Most sophisticated, cosmopolitan cities with a population of 80,000 or more offer a distinct singles lifestyle, with a variety of singles groups, each appealing to people of different ages. University towns that are also home to several hi-tech industries, frequently have a large population of mature and well-educated single people. In larger centers, it is not uncommon to find such highly-specialized groups as singles associations for men and women over 50 who are at least five feet, ten inches tall. Invariably, there are adult sports and activities clubs and endless classes plus dance, social, and civic groups to join. In larger centers, churches also have singles groups with weekly gatherings for members of all ages. The health-oriented cities describes in this book generally have a far superior array of opportunities for social contacts than does the average traditional town.

To swiftly build a network of friends and relationships we'd recommend that single men and women choose to live in a city with a population of between 80,000 and 125,000. By contrast, social contacts are more difficult to make in smaller towns and remote suburbs where single people are seldom invited to a bridge game or a dinner party.

Cities that cater predominantly to retired people aged 60 and over are also likely to have a disproportionately large population of single women. In many retirement cities, among the over-60 population, there are frequently four women to every man.

Among the best ways to meet new friends is to enroll in classes or study groups, or to volunteer—two other health-building lifestyle steps for which each of our cities has been rated. Reaching out and investing yourself in service and philanthropic institutions can also help you to reap the benefits of altruism.

Playing tennis is another great way to meet new friends. Single women might also consider taking up sports bicycling—an activity often found only in healthful cities and which tends to be dominated by single men.

The laughter and good feelings that are part of social intimacy provide another health bonus. Tests have shown that laughter increases antibodies in saliva that defend the body against infections and colds. Laughter also significantly lowers risk of heart disease and cancer; it lowers blood pressure; it also raises the pain threshold and reduces the impact of stress.

No statistics exist to measure a city's opportunities for social contacts. Instead, we have attempted to evaluate the chances for making new associations based on the factors described in this section.

# OPPORTUNITIES FOR VOLUNTEER WORK

Helping and caring for others has long been confirmed as a powerful health therapy. Hence this guideline measures the extent of opportunities that exist in any city for meaningful volunteer work of the type that is likely to benefit health.

When Linda Nelson, Ph.D., a sociologist at UCLA, examined reports of 100 natural disasters, she discovered that rescuers almost invariably experienced an exhilarating feeling of power, energy, and well-being. Several studies, in fact, have shown that those who help others experience increased energy, lower blood pressure, reduced stress, and a greater level of self-esteem and immunocompetence. This translates into a significantly reduced risk of cancer and infections. Almost everyone who expresses altruism also experiences a state of calm and well-being equivalent to that of a runner's high.

Confirming these discoveries is a recent study by the University of Michigan Survey Research Center which followed 10,000 people for ten years in Tecumseh, Michigan. Results showed that people who did volunteer work had a significantly higher life-expectancy than non-volunteers. For instance, men who did no altruistic work had a death rate two-and-a-half times as great as those who performed volunteer tasks.

Similar results were reported by a still ongoing study by the Institute for the Advancement of Health, in New York City, which revealed that people who help others feel better and have fewer diseases and stress-related problems.

## Healthful Cities Are Caring Cities

Few cities are unable to satisfy a person's need for volunteer work. But a health-oriented city—that is, a caring city—is often better organized in that it usually has one or more clearing houses for volunteer assignments. Often entitled

Caring Callers, Helping Hands, or Sunshine Services, these organizations match volunteers with the most suitable job and time slots, which frequently results in a more healthful and satisfying volunteer experience. In larger cities, the United Way and the Retired Senior Volunteer Program (for people over 60) frequently recruit volunteers for public service work.

For maximum health benefits, volunteer work must bring you into close contact with those being helped. Donating money, or raising funds by selling in a thrift store, provides fewer health benefits than directly helping the needy on a person-to-person level. You must also have a genuine desire to help, and you must not be coerced into helping by others. For maximum health benefits, you must work at something you are good at and it must satisfy a real need to do something that is meaningful to you. It should be work that makes you feel good. If possible, also, it should challenge the upper limits of your capabilities.

Locating a volunteer job that meets these requirements is obviously much easier if you can apply through one of the more than 400 volunteer clearing houses that exist in U.S. cities. Among smaller and medium-sized cities, these clearing houses tend to be more numerous in communities that are dedicated to answering pressing social needs and to promoting responsive and responsible caring. Through their volunteer clearing houses, many of the cities in this book offer literally thousands of opportunities to express altruism, generosity and unselfishness that can indirectly benefit health. Meanwhile, surveys are showing that in traditional cities, and especially in larger metropolitan areas, residents are gradually reducing their involvement with others.

A well-organized volunteer clearing house can direct you to any of the major government-sponsored volunteer programs, ranging from VISTA (Volunteers in Service to America) to SCORE (Service Corps of Retired Executives) to the Senior Companion Program, the Retired Senior Volunteer

Program, the National Volunteer Agency, and the National School Volunteer Program. Other openings range from serving food in soup kitchens to teaching, counseling, fund raising, helping house the homeless, coaching Little League players, helping battered spouses, or organizing recycling groups. Virtually every kind of support group welcomes volunteers and you can work in hospitals, libraries, or museums; or you can teach the illiterate to read; or you can deliver meals on wheels.

To locate sources of volunteer work in any city, look in the yellow pages under such headings as: *Volunteer Action Center; Volunteer Information and Referral; Social Services; or Community Organizations.*

Through a volunteer job you may also acquire new skills and expertise that can lead to a second career that offers both financial and emotional rewards. Another built-in benefit of volunteer work is the opportunity it provides to meet new people and to make new friends.

# OPPORTUNITIES FOR SPIRITUAL GROWTH

Investigations are revealing that all forms of spiritual belief and faith exert a powerfully beneficial effect on health and long life. In a study of 1,000 long-lived Americans, the Committee for an Extended Lifespan found that virtually every long-lived person has strong spiritual beliefs. The same study also found that over 50 percent of healthy, long-lived people defuse stress by turning their problems over to a higher power for solution while they continued to relax and enjoy life.

Evidence is growing that those who practice the Golden Rule—who treat others as we'd like them to treat us—enjoy better health and live longer than those who spurn spiritual beliefs. Several studies have found that people with strong spiritual beliefs have stronger immunity, lower blood pressure, and cleaner arteries than the general public.

Specifically, all forms of prayer, meditation, and spiritual belief appear to minimize the effects of stress and to mobilize our defenses against disease. When the benefits of prayer were analyzed by Dr. Harold Bloomfield, director of psychiatry at the Holistic Health Center in Del Mar, California, and by other investigators, it was found that spiritual faith fosters a strongly positive attitude. In turn, these positive emotions boost such health-enhancing physical mechanisms as the immune system.

Additionally, most of the world's major religions urge their followers to shun stimulants, substance abuse, and promiscuous sex, while both the Mormon and Seventh Day Adventist churches, as well as an increasing number of New Age churches, are leading members towards vegetarianism and simpler living.

Adventists, in fact, follow a series of health-improving guidelines that require regular exercise, getting adequate sleep, and eating a vegetarian diet. These guidelines foster a positive attitude that boosts self-esteem and empowers the immune system. The guidelines also very closely resemble those described in this book for living a low-risk lifestyle.

## Spiritual Faith Lowers Risk of Disease

By way of proof, a study of 50,000 Utah Mormons found their cancer risk was only 50 percent that of the U.S. general public, while the Mormon heart disease risk was only 25 percent, giving Mormons a life expectancy seven years longer than that of the average American. A similar study of California Adventists revealed that the cancer risk for Adventists was 47 percent lower than for the California general public. In fact, non-smoking Adventist males have a lung cancer risk only half that of non-smoking males in general.

However, top researchers believe that spiritual faith alone bestows health benefits that are even more powerful than the lifestyle steps endorsed by most churches. According to Meyer Friedman, one of the leading discoverers of Type-A behavior, spiritual faith may be the basic need of people with Type-A personalities. Meyer believes that spiritual faith can relieve and reverse the deep-seated anxiety that leads to cynicism and hostility, the two most destructive traits in men prone to heart disease.

Reflecting the same views, Kenneth Pelletier, Ph.D., of the University of California, San Francisco recognizes that people with Type-B personalities—that is, hardy, healthy, relaxed people—are least affected by stress. He reports that people with Type-B personalities frequently have a strong spiritual dimension in their personality.

Several studies of churchgoers have shown that people with strong spiritual faith experience 30-40 percent less heart disease than the general public. A study of churchgoers in Washington County, Maryland showed that churchgoers had a heart disease rate 40 percent lower than that of the overall county population, while among male churchgoers aged 45-64, the heart disease rate was 50 percent below that of the general county population.

Dr. Herbert Bensen, nationally acclaimed author of several books on the health benefits of relaxation and meditation, originally identified the healing benefits of these practices by taking them out of their traditional spiritual framework. But when he combined them once again within a context of spiritual faith, he found their healing powers greatly multiplied.

As many as half of all healthy, long-lived people have not formally belonged to a church. They have believed, instead, that a powerful force in the universe was working through them and they saw themselves as a media for the spread of love and service. Whatever one's personal views—whether agnostic, traditional, New Age, or following an eastern philosophy—seems to make little difference. With or without religion, health benefits accrue to those with strong spiritual beliefs and faith. What counts most is that spiritual people view the world as a friendly, loving, hospitable, and non-threatening place.

## *Healthful Cities May Offer More Choices for Spiritual Growth*

Based on these and similar factors, this guideline estimates the extent of opportunities for spiritual growth in each city in this book. While the influence of Adventist and Mormon churches is undeniable, many mainline Jewish, Protestant and Catholic churches are now beginning to recognize that preserving the ecology and staying well are no longer secular problems. Unity and other New Age churches have long recognized the importance of a Holistic approach to health. And movements such as yoga and zen, that are based on oriental philosophies, also support a simpler lifestyle with greater emphasis on natural foods, exercise, and positive perception.

Through their cosmopolitan and sophisticated population, many of the healthful cities in this book offer a markedly wider choice of opportunities for spiritual growth and healing than does the typical traditional city. State universities seem to act like magnets to attract a wide variety of sources for spiritual growth and for developing human potential. Not only are the conventional churches here, but so are most New Age churches, plus a variety of yoga, macro-biotic, and other forms of spiritual and human potential organizations.

# QUALITY OF HEALTH CARE

This guideline measures the availability and quality of comprehensive medical care available in each of our cities. Medical care is described as comprehensive when it embraces not only conventional physicians, drugs, and hospitals but also holistically-oriented M.D.'s and licensed health professionals in such alternate fields as naturopathy, chiropractic, nutrition, and acupuncture. The existence of holistic physicians and alternative health-care practitioners in any city implies that that city is open and receptive to preventative medicine and to a low-risk lifestyle.

Holistically-oriented M.D.'s are medical doctors who prescribe mainline medical treatment when it is obviously the best solution, but who also recommend alternative, non-medical treatment, or lifestyle change, when medical treatment can be harmful or of dubious value.

Holistic healing and alternative therapies have become increasingly popular, particularly in college and university towns and in other sophisticated and cosmopolitan cities, especially in California. One reason is that many mainline medical treatments have become economic or political issues. Instead of being given the most beneficial treatment for your illness or dysfunction, the medical treatment you actually receive is more often determined by the extent of your insurance coverage, and what it will pay for, coupled with a desire to minimize risks of a litigation suit.

We should not forget that the purpose of a low-risk lifestyle is that, through accepting responsibility for the care and feeding of our own bodies, we can minimize dependence on mainstream medical treatment. Doctors, drugs, and hospitals are always there if we need them. And for periodically-recommended check-ups such as pap smears, mammographies, and prostate or rectal examinations, mainline medical treatment provides a useful service. Nowadays, however, these tests, as well as most routine types of medical care are available in almost any U.S. city with a population of 20,000 or more.

### Are Big University-Affiliated Hospitals Really Better?

Until recently, it was thought that the high-powered medical center hospitals affiliated with major universities invariably provided the best medical care available. As far as hi-tech and heroic operations go, this is probably still true. But when *Medical World News* published a survey of 20,000 patients who had recently used the services of 89 hospitals (March 13, 1989, page 74) it turned out that those with the best patient satisfaction were almost all rural and small town hospitals with fewer than 200 beds. Based on personal care factors such as swift nurse response to patient calls, special dietary needs, and speedy reports on tests, small hospitals easily outranked the big university-affiliated medical centers on every score but technical skill.

Some of the nation's largest university-affiliated medical center hospitals are located at or near some of the healthful cities described in this book. That's because many of our cities also happen to be the location of a major university. It should also be borne in mind that most hospitals today are operated by aggressive, profit-making corporations. Most score high on the kind of technical skill needed to handle a by-pass or implant operation, but many tend to rate low in patient care.

While they cannot handle hi-tech operations, most smaller hospitals today are as well equipped to deal with routine illnesses or injuries as are the largest hospitals. Nowadays, most hospitals in smaller towns are completely modern, scaled-down versions of big city hospitals. Virtually all have operating and recovery rooms, delivery, and nursing facilities, a blood bank, a 24-hour emergency room, and an outpatient clinic.

Most smaller hospitals have coronary units with the most modern medical and surgical equipment required to handle heart attacks. Even communities with a population of 20,000 usually have a 24-hour emergency cardiac care system able to respond quickly to any emergency.

Undoubtedly, a major university-affiliated medical center draws scores of top specialists who can be consulted in nearby medical complexes. Thus we have awarded an extra point to any city with a major medical center and hospital. By the same token, we have also awarded an additional point to any city in which a choice of skilled holistic M.D.'s and other licensed alternative health care professionals are available. Additionally, this guideline appraises the reputation and availability of all types of medical care, including existence of Veterans Administration and military hospitals, health maintenance organizations, health education units, and all other community health services.

# 7
# How the Healthfulness of Cities Is Scored and Ranked

Each city in this book has been awarded a Total Healthfulness Score. By comparing scores, you can swiftly see how the healthfulness of one city stacks up against that of another.

To understand the scoring system, let's begin with Urban Stress.

### Ranking Urban Stress

The Urban Stress Overall Rating is given at the commencement of each city review together with the population count and elevation. It appears either as:

**Urban Stress: ZPG 2.9**
**or**
**Urban Stress: EST 2.9**

The initials ZPG indicate that the rating was compiled by Zero Population Growth (ZPG) while EST indicates that the rating was estimated by the author using a similar formula to that employed by ZPG. The significance of the Urban Stress Overall Rating is fully explained in Chapter 3.

Because the Urban Stress Overall Rating is itself a composite of eleven other stress-related factors, it has a greater impact on health than any of the other criteria we use. For this reason, we have doubled the number of points used in its scoring, from one-to-ten instead of from one-to-five.

In compiling the Urban Stress Overall Rating, ZPG's actual ratings range only from a high of 1.6 to a low of 4.2. Thus, the scoring system used in this book is as follows:

| Range of ZPG and EST Urban Stress Overall Ratings | Points Awarded in This Book | Comments |
|---|---|---|
| 1.60 to 1.85 | 10 | Excellent |
| 1.86 to 2.12 | 9 | Excellent |
| 2.13 to 2.38 | 8 | Very Good |
| 2.39 to 2.64 | 7 | Very Good |
| 2.65 to 2.90 | 6 | Average |
| 2.95 to 3.16 | 5 | Average |
| 3.17 to 3.42 | 4 | Fair |
| 3.43 to 3.68 | 3 | Fair |
| 3.69 to 3.94 | 2 | Poor |
| 3.95 to 4.20 | 1 | Poor |

For example, the Urban Stress Overall Rating for Boulder, CO is 2.1. Translated into the scoring system used in this book, this earns it a score of 9 and places it in the "Excellent" range. This score appears at the end of each city review after the identifying word "Urban." It is then tallied into each city's Total Healthfulness Score.

### All Other Health Criteria

The twelve other criteria used in arriving at each city's Total Healthfulness are scored by the following standards:

| | |
|---|---|
| 5 | Excellent |
| 4 | Very Good |
| 3 | Average |
| 2 | Fair |
| 1 | Poor |

These eleven other factors consist of the Natural Inherent Factors (Climate, Elevation, Terrain Therapy) analyzed in Chapter 4, and the Low-Risk Lifestyle Factors analyzed in

Chapter 6. In the city profiles, each is identified by a single key word as follows:

## *Abbreviations Used In Total Healthfulness Scores*

| | |
|---|---|
| Urban | scores the Urban Stress Overall Rating as just described |
| Climate | scores the healthfulness of each city's climate based on how well it allows residents to follow a low-risk lifestyle |
| Elevation | scores the benefits of higher elevation thus: |

| Elevation | Score |
|---|---|
| sea level to 1,500' | 1 |
| 1,500'—3.000' | 2 |
| 3,001'—4,500' | 3 |
| 4,501'—6,000' | 4 |
| 6,001' and above | 5 |

| | |
|---|---|
| Terrain | scores the estimated healing value of Terrain Therapy |
| Awareness | scores the Health Awareness of the population |
| Nutrition | scores Nutritional Awareness |
| Fitness | scores Fitness Resources and Activities |
| Stress | scores Stress Management Resources |
| Mind | scores Opportunities to Exercise the Mind in Later Life |
| Social | scores Opportunities for Social Contacts |
| Volunteer | scores Opportunities for Volunteer Work |
| Spiritual | scores Opportunities for Spiritual Growth |
| Care | scores the Quality of Health Care |

The scores for each of these thirteen factors appears at the end of each city profile, as in this example:

Scores: Urban 7. Climate 3. Elevation 3. Terrain 2. Awareness 4. Nutrition 4. Fitness 4. Stress 3. Mind 5. Social 3. Volunteer 3. Spiritual 2. Care 5. Total Healthfulness: 48.

The maximum number of points attainable is 70. In this case, the total number of points adds up to 48. Note that the higher the score, the better the rating. Note also that the maximum score for Urban is 10, while for all other criteria it is 5.

## *What Pleases Peter May Not Always Please Paul*

It's important to bear in mind that the cities reviewed here were handpicked by the author as potentially the healthiest communities in America. They were not obtained from a computer scan. Thus it's very possible that more than one potentially-healthful city does not appear in these pages.

Secondly, no place is perfect. From a healthfulness viewpoint, selection of every city has been a trade-off. One city may have outstanding resources for fitness, intellectual activity, and social and volunteer opportunities yet it may also be afflicted by some degree of air pollution and by moderately congested traffic. Nonetheless, we believe that we definitely have managed to select the majority of America's healthiest cities in this book.

Third, our Total Healthfulness Scores are not intended to rank these cities from best to worst. The scores are merely intended as a useful guide to the availability and quality of factors that most influence health. For example, a city with a total score of 25 has only half as many health-enhancing factors as a city with a score of 50. In the final analysis, it's still largely a question of choosing a city that most closely approaches your own personal preferences.

## *How to Check on Facts and Obtain More Information*

While all facts and information in this book were carefully checked prior to publication, all are naturally subject to change with the passage of time. Although more than 90 percent of this information will probably remain accurate through the life of this edition, we strongly recommend that you independently verify all the facts and information for yourself. You can do so by calling or writing to the information sources given for each city, and by visiting the city in person.

For information, write to the Chamber of Commerce or the Convention and Visitor's Bureau, and to the Parks and Recreation Department addresses given at the end of each city review. Ask specifically for information on living or retiring in that city (or for fitness activities if you write to the parks department). Some sources haven't much to offer. Others may charge for a newcomer's or retiree's kit. However, the majority will list your name with their bank and realtor members. Through them, you can obtain additional information and sample listings of rentals and houses for sale. Another way to quickly feel the pulse of any city is to take out a short term subscription to its local newspaper.

Once you've decided on a likely city, scout it out on your next vacation. Spend some time there during both summer and winter. Check out everything on the spot for yourself. Whatever you do, never give anything away, sell your home, or decide to move until you have *thoroughly checked out everything first.* And if you're dependent on a job, never move to another city without a firm commitment of employment there. Most authorities then recommend that, upon retiring or moving, you rent for a few months before purchasing a home in any unfamiliar community.

Significant information about jobs and housing or living costs may be mentioned in our city profiles. But for reasons given earlier, these factors are not ranked under any of our guidelines.

*Abbreviations used in this book:*

CoC — Chamber of Commerce
C&VB — Convention and Visitors Bureau
P&R — Parks and Recreation Department
EST — Author's estimate of Urban Stress
ZPG — Zero Population Growth

# AMERICA'S MOST HEALTHFUL CITIES: FROM A TO Z

**ALAMOGORDO, NM.** Population: 32,000. Urban Stress: EST 1.9. Elevation: 4,350'. Anyone seeking a livable, worry-free place in which to lead a low-stress, low-risk lifestyle might well consider this friendly, small town in southern New Mexico. Nestled on a sunny high-desert plain at the foot of the massive Sacramento Mountains, this sparkling, modern city reaches west to the high dunes of White Sands National Monument. Often described as a "hi-tech town on the federal payroll," Alamogordo is home to hundreds of well-educated affluent baby boomers who work at nearby defense-oriented federal installations. Add in approximately 1,700 military retirees and their families, and an almost equal number of retired civilians, and you have an exceptionally health-conscious and high-energy population whose preference for physically-active recreations helps explain why Alamogordo recently still lacked an 18-hole golf course.

The city's dry, sunny, moderate climate—with 300 clear days annually and a mere eleven inches of annual precipitation—makes outdoor activities enjoyable all year. From White Sands twenty minutes southwest to mountainous Lincoln National Forest in the mountains 30 minutes east, the area abounds in safe trails for hiking and bicycling; and, in winter, cross-country skiing. For those who prefer smoother indoor walking, the Older Americans Center hosts a one hour mall walk each weekday morning. Area Volksmarch clubs also hold monthly 10K group hikes. Adult lapswimming is available any weekday all year: at a heated pool in winter and outdoors in summer. A private spa also offers a pool and weights room. The mild climate is responsible for the long tennis season; twelve municipal courts (eight lighted) and three racquetball courts are available. Among a choice of community exercise classes, the city gym teaches a combined strength-building and flexibility class three times a week (for just 50¢ a session). Two square dance groups provide lessons and hold four dances a month. And canoe paddling can be enjoyed on nearby mountain lakes.

Local cultural groups plan to stage a series of symphony and band concerts, plays, ballet, and classic film presentations in the recently-renovated Flickinger Performing Arts Center. For science and physics buffs, this hi-tech city's Tombaugh Space Center displays the most recent space science developments and shows them off in a theater with a wrap-around screen 40 feet in height. Retirees can also audit the mostly vocational courses at the local community college, or enroll in a choice of free classes in the community program for lifelong learning.

Local fruit and nut orchards help boost the supply of natural foods while two healthfood stores supply most nutrition basics. Yoga is taught at community education classes, as is stress-relieving Swedish and foot massage. But there is no public transportation for those who prefer not to drive.

Another active series of classes, workshops, and social get-togethers emanates from the Older Americans Center. In cooperation with the Retired Senior Volunteer Program, the Center recruits the several hundred volunteers needed to help staff 86 different local agencies.

Another good source of fellowship are the city's predominantly mainline Protestant churches. Although relatively small, Alamogordo's 92-bed Memorial Hospital is a full-service facility and the cadre of 40 or so physicians represent almost every specialty. Also available nearby is a small military hospital and commissary.

The solar heating panels and evaporative coolers sprouting from rooftops help explain the low average level of utility bills and living costs. Recently, Alamogordo had several hundred homes for sale, from delightful older-style pueblo residences to modern ranch style homes, plus condominiums, rental apartments, and mobile homes, all at very reasonable cost. Property taxes were also considered low. Most job opportunities occur in hi-tech research, but openings can be affected by defense cutbacks.

Since all firefighters are also police officers, and vice versa, the high ratio of police to population helps explain Alamogordo's persistently low crime rate. The only drawback we found was that the infrastructure—water supplies, street drainage, sewers, and sewage facilities—appeared fully loaded. Any new population growth could boost property taxes.

Scores: Urban 9. Climate 4. Elevation 3. Terrain 5. Awareness 4. Nutrition 3. Fitness 5. Stress 2. Mind 3. Social 3. Volunteer 4. Spiritual 3. Care 4. Total Healthfulness: 52.

Information: CoC, Box 518, Alamogordo, NM 88310 (800-545-4021 outside NM; 800-826-0294 in NM; retirement video available at nominal cost). P&R, 511 Tenth Street, Alamogordo, NM 88310 (505-434-2867).


**ALBUQUERQUE, NM.** Population: 510,000. Urban Stress: ZPG 3.2 Elevation: 5,311'. Though it's never been called a citadel of health and fitness, Albuquerque has an abundance of resources for living the low-risk lifestyle—with strong peer support from the more affluent and highly-educated sectors of the city's population. Albuquerque's dynamic defense-related economy has transformed the city into a burgeoning metropolis sprawled across a flat desert plain. Yet a sheath of green trees cloaks the entire city. And sweeping abruptly skyward from the city's eastern limits, the towering Sandia Mountains provide a breathtaking backdrop visible from every suburb.

This combination provides such visual relief from the urban setting that it earns Albuquerque the highest rating for terrain therapy. Add in a high, dry, sunny climate ... the city's top-ranking hospitals and its active volunteer center ... a citizenry dedicated to preserving the environment and quality of life ... and the fact that Albuquerque has become an internationally recognized Mecca for the arts ... and that, in 1989, Albuquerque was rated by *Newsweek* magazine reporters as one of the best cities in which to live and work ... and it is obvious that this city has a bounty of healthful assets in its favor.

But as with any city this size, there are trade-offs to consider. On still winter days, a hideous layer of brown smog hovers above the city, the result of high-altitude temperature inversion caused by galloping population growth and congested rush hour traffic. The air has, at times, been so acrid with carbon monoxide that wood burning fires are banned in homes.

These caveats aside, you'll find the population young, affable, and vigorous, with a median age of 30 and an affinity for a lifestyle that is casual and elegant. Among the diversity of cultures are 24,000 university students and as many retired military couples.

Although brisk, winter days are dry and mild enough to be outside at all times. Over 20,000 acres of city open space, plus adjoining Sandia Mountain Wilderness and Cibola National Forest, offer at least 80 miles of hiking and cross-country ski trails that wind all over the Sandia Mountains. You can hike up to almost 11,000' and, spring through fall, the trails are bordered with masses of wildflowers. Within the city, sixteen miles of flatter trails provide easier walking.

In addition, several organizations arrange a series of race walks, fun runs, and walk or run meets, some for people 50 and over.

While we weren't too impressed by bicycling opportunities, a system of bicycle paths network part of the city. Daily lapswimming for adults and seniors is available at four heated parks department indoor pools, and at eight other outdoor pools in summer. Three pools also feature Masters swim workouts. For those over 62, a month of daily swimming recently cost only $5. Tennis is also popular here, with two large parks department complexes equipped with laykold and Omni courts. Other public and private courts abound.

To keep the mind active, the University of New Mexico hosts a brilliant series of lectures, concerts, plays, ballet, and opera featuring such top regional talent as the New Mexico Symphony, the Southwest Ballet, and the City Chamber Orchestra. Along with six theater companies, each with its own theater, an experimental theater on campus presents innovative dances and plays. Also here are mind-stimulating museums of anthropology, art, science, and natural history. In the works is a huge new performing arts center. And you'll find a mind boggling choice of adult education classes.

Nutritionally, corn tortillas are one of the best whole grain foods and scores of restaurants serve low-fat chile and other traditional New Mexican foods. During summer, roadside stands are piled with apricots, peaches, apples, and other local fruit. Nine thriving senior centers arrange a constant round of social activities for those 55 and over. And the Volunteer Agency of Albuquerque, a United Way program, matches the skills and talents of thousands of volunteers with the needs of more than 300 agencies.

Two major medical centers, 1,200 doctors, eight other hospitals, a V.A. hospital and a flourishing H.M.O. with over 100,000 members explains Albuquerque's reputation for providing exceptional health care.

Although the economy seems overly dependent on federal spending, Albuquerque generally offers a wide variety of career choices for those with technical skills. In the bone dry atmosphere, less expensive evaporative cooling is often used in place of refrigerated air. Even so, housing and living costs hover a bit above the national average. A wide selection of new and resale homes are normally available, together with condominiums and townhouses and large complexes of rental apartments.

Scores: Urban 4. Climate 4. Elevation 4. Terrain 5. Awareness 4. Nutrition 4. Fitness 5. Stress 3. Mind 5. Social 4. Volunteer 5. Spiritual 3. Care 5. Total Healthfulness: 55.

Information: C&VB, 625 Silver Avenue S.W., Suite 210, Albuquerque, NM 87125 (800-284-2282). P&R, One Civic Plaza, 6th Floor, Albuquerque, NM 87110 (505-768-3490).

**ANN ARBOR, MI.** Population: 112,000. Urban Stress: ZPG 1.8. Elevation: 766'. Often called the last of the real university towns, the special atmosphere of the University of Michigan—one of America's top ten state universities—permeates every corner of Ann Arbor. Hi-tech research and development parks mingle with historic districts of brick-paved streets lined by Greek Revival homes. And Ann Arbor's high quality of life has repeatedly won it awards as a safe, clean and family-oriented place to live.

All this has drawn a sophisticated, younger-than-average population of highly-educated, moderately-affluent baby boomers and younger retirees, almost all of whom are exceptionally health-conscious and into physical fitness and other health-enhancing activities. As always, the extent of interest in bicycling is a direct indication of a city's enthusiasm for living a low-risk lifestyle.

A major bicycling town, Ann Arbor has its own city bicycle coordinator and a splendid bikeway system on which thousands daily speed swiftly and silently throughout the city without creating pollution or congestion. The city's 700-member Bicycle Touring Society organizes frequent rides, while Ann Arbor also hosts a variety of bicycle events and races throughout summer. Supplementing bicycle transport is a dependable city bus service with quite frequent schedules.

Virtually every other fitness activity is well represented, from miles of groomed cross-country ski trails and ice-skating areas in city parks in winter, to canoeing on the Huron River in summer. Jogging and walking trails wind through the Arboretum and the Botanic Gardens. There are 22 public tennis courts and a Masters swim program, plus daily lapswimming at a variety of heated indoor pools and outdoor beach areas. From weight exercises to aerobics, yoga, martial arts, stretch-ercises, Feldenkrais flexibility training, Conditioning-for-Life and Trim-and-Slim Classes, the flourishing YMCA and parks department provide dozens of classes daily plus clinics to upgrade your form.

While its location 30 minutes west of Detroit precludes dramatic scenery, Ann Arbor's Huron River, wooded hillsides, and extensive parks and gardens provide terrain therapy year around. Despite the brisk, invigorating winters with 35" of annual snowfall, and the rather hot, humid Midwestern summers, there's hardly a day when a healthy person can't exercise outdoors.

Education and culture are a way of life in this university city and Ann Arbor provides a continuous bill of concerts, plays, lectures, festivals, and special events, many presented in the university's Power Center for Performing Arts. Bookstores abound, at least 50 major concerts are presented annually, and Ann Arbor has its own symphony, chamber orchestra, comic opera guild, civic ballet, and several theater groups. There are festivals galore. The university library is open to everyone and you can choose from hundreds of continuing education classes in everything from computer science to languages and astronomy.

Testifying to the high level of nutritional awareness are the numerous restaurants that have elevated vegetarian cooking to an art form; and each Saturday, the farmers' market is crammed with fresh produce. As is usual in a major university city, stress management classes abound. And like most other fitness activities, the Washtenow Walkers group provide as many opportunities for socializing as for exercise. A huge choice of volunteer opportunities exist through such organizations as the Retired Senior Volunteer Program and various social services and teaching-learning communities. All the world's major faiths are represented, as well as New Age churches, ashrams, temples, mosques, and Quaker meeting halls.

Ann Arbor's university teaching hospital gives the city world class stature for medical care. Also here is a V.A. teaching hospital and several general hospitals. Its dynamic university and thriving business climate customarily give Ann Arbor Michigan's lowest unemployment rate, and for those with skills, job opportunities are often good in hi-tech, automation, and robotic development firms, and for clerical and support staffs. Homes range from small starter houses to restored historic homes and luxurious subdivisions, plus condominiums for all tastes. Modern rental apartment complexes are also numerous and shelter costs seem only slightly above average. Rather unsightly are the thousands of parking meters, but we were told it is typical of Ann Arbor's casual attitude that most residents ignore tickets unless they accumulate half a dozen.

Scores: Urban 10. Climate 3. Elevation 1. Terrain 3. Awareness 5. Nutrition 5. Fitness 5. Stress 5. Mind 5. Social 4. Volunteer 5. Spiritual 5. Care 5. Total Healthfulness: 61.

Information: CoC, 211 E. Huron Street, Suite 1, Ann Arbor, MI 48104 (313-665-4433). P&R, 100 N. Fifth Avenue, Ann Arbor, MI 48104 (313-994-2780).

**AUSTIN, TX.** Population: 500,000. Urban Stress: ZPG 2.9. Elevation: 500'. The capital of Texas, and home of the University of Texas (UT)—largest university in the South—Austin lives in the shadow of politics and bears the unmistakable stamp of a center of learning. When you consider that Austin is ringed by a hi-tech research park, and that affluent baby boomers comprise the largest sector of the population, the city's enthusiasm for healthful living is understandable. Twenty-eight miles of walking and running trails meander along the quiet shores of Town Lake, and wind on through 10,000 acres of greenbelt that penetrates almost every corner of the city. Opportunities for intellectual and cultural enrichment abound. The high level of nutritional awareness is evident in the large, well-stocked natural foods supermarket. And the warm, sunny climate permits outdoor exercise throughout the year.

Motorboat-free Town Lake, bordered by green parks, is the first in a 150-mile stair-step chain called the Highland Lakes, which lead out into the lush Hill Country that surrounds the city. Despite Austin's freeways and busy four-lane avenues, with the many parks and extensive greenbelt areas, nature is never far away.

Half the population have lived here ten years or more, and together with over 60,000 students, they support strong recycling and anti-growth movements. Unfortunately, Austin isn't yet a great bicycling town. For enjoyable cycling, you must drive out 30 miles or more into the Hill Country. But in many other ways, Austin's residents display a high level of health and nutritional awareness.

During the long, hot summers, of course, most Austin residents exercise early in the day. Among fitness resources are 28 public swimming pools, mostly open air, plus attractive lake swimming in summer from beaches on several of the closed-in Highland Lakes. Private clubs provide heated pools for winter swimming. Instruction and tournaments are available at four tennis centers and at 24 parks with tennis courts.

124

Canoeing and rowing are encouraged at Town Lake, as well as on several other Highland Lakes. For ice skating, there's the Icecapades Chalet. An extensive series of fitness, body toning, and power walking classes are held at various community schools and recreation centers. Thousands of walkers, race walkers, and runners train daily on the city's 28 miles of greenbelt trails. And over 20,000 entrants compete in the Capitol 10K race each spring.

Many retirees keep their minds active by auditing classes at UT. Thousands of others sign up for language, creative arts, and vocational classes in the city's huge adult education program. Throughout the year, but especially in winter, UT imports a steady flow of top-caliber ballet, opera, drama, concerts, and lectures, most staged in the handsome Performing Arts Center. Among frequent performers are the Austin Symphony, plus other major symphony orchestras, and the Ballet Austin, one of only three professional companies in Texas. Ten other theaters stage scores of musicals, comedies, and both classic and innovative plays. A growing arts center, with many resident painters of note, Austin has three art museums and some 35 galleries.

Supplementing Austin's large natural foods supermarket is a thriving farmers' market where fresh fruits and produce are sold year around, and a series of low-fat and vegetarian cooking classes that are part of the Community Schools Program. The same Community Schools Program is the source of dozens of classes in almost every branch of stress management, from yoga to stretching and toning, foot massage, t'ai chi, and meditation.

As Texas' undisputed center for modern day churches and New Age thought, Austin caters to every type of metaphysical interest from holotropic breathwork to zen and kundalini yoga. Opportunities for social contacts range from dozens of singles groups to adult friendship centers. An annual fair is held to recruit men and women for the thousands of unfilled volunteer openings. A major regional medical center, with nine top-rated hospitals and 1,200 physicians, Austin also has its share of licensed professionals in such fields as chiropractics, foot massage, and nutrition. A military hospital is located at a nearby air force base, while the nearest V.A. hospital is in San Antonio, 75 miles south.

Away from the center, suburban homes are fairly reasonably priced while you'll find hundreds of elegant condominiums and well-located rental apartments, none of which are exorbitant. For decades, Austin has been popular with retirees seeking a large, cosmopolitan city. Growth in recent years has somewhat reduced the city's former high quality of life. But for a city this size, Austin still has many pluses—not the least of which is its affordable cost of living. In Austin's research and development-oriented economy, good career choices often exist for those with credentials.

Scores: Urban 6. Climate 3. Elevation 1. Terrain 4. Awareness 4. Nutrition 4. Fitness 5. Stress 4. Mind 5. Social 3. Volunteer 3. Spiritual 4. Care 4. Total Healthfulness: 50.

Information: CoC, Box 1967, Austin, TX 78767 (512-478-9383). C&VB, Box 2990, Austin, TX 78769 (512-478-0098). P&R, Box 1088, Austin, TX 78767 (512-499-2000).

**BIRMINGHAM, AL.** Population: (area) 1,000,000. Urban Stress: ZPG 3.5. Elevation: 650'. Once a grimy steel city known as the South's Johannesburg for its racial intolerance, Birmingham has made an amazingly swift transition from heavy industry to become the South's leading medical center. Its smokestacks replaced by glass-walled office towers, Birmingham has achieved such a superior quality of life that in 1989 it was rated the most livable city in America by the U.S. Conference of Mayors, and as one of the best cities in which to live and work by a critical group of *Newsweek* reporters.

Powering its economy is the huge University of Alabama (UAB) Medical Center, one of the nation's top medical schools. Despite all the impressive hi-tech research and equipment, however, some of the Center's greatest successes have been achieved by its Department of Preventative Medicine. Basing its Health Advancement Program on endorsing a low-risk lifestyle, the department offers a full lifestyle evaluation together with a health status assessment, a recommended fitness and exercise program, advice for a low-fat, hi-fiber diet, and careful medical supervision for the first few weeks of lifestyle change. To launch into a pro-health lifestyle with the full support of this prestigious medical school is certainly a valid reason for choosing to move to Birmingham.

The city scores fairly well on most other health counts. Its quiet, tree-shaded neighborhoods lie on gently-rolling hills that blaze with camellias, azaleas, and dogwood in spring and with golden colors in fall. Although summer days are rather hot and humid, it's tennis weather the rest of the year. Fall is brisk, winters short, snowfall negligible and the rainfall 55" annually. Counting more engineers per capita than any other southern city, Birmingham is a town of friendly, prosperous, and hospitable research and blue collar workers.

In response to a high citizen demand for exercise and fitness classes, several parks department recreation centers offer almost daily adult and senior organized walks, adult and ladies gym classes, jazzercise and aerobics classes, adult strength-training, and yoga, martial arts, and stretching courses. Fitness walking trails are available in parks throughout the city, while a nature center on the south side offers seven miles of wooded trails, and Oak Mountain State Park, fifteen miles out, has thirty miles of wooded trails. Drawing many world class runners here is the annual Pepsi Vulcan Marathon and a 10K run plus a major triathlon.

Well-kept tennis courts exist in many of the city's 70 parks. The best outdoor summer swimming is from the lake beach in the aforementioned park. Outdoor pools also exist in a variety of parks. But for winter swimming, you must go to the Y pool or to a private club. Private health and athletic clubs are numerous: some have Nautilus strength-building equipment, including knee machines for knee rehabilitation. Canoe paddling for exercise is available at Oak Mountain State Park.

From great literature to the cultural arts to esoteric research, opportunities for intellectual activity are legion. Birmingham's superbly well-stocked, ultra-modern library is the hub of the South's largest library system. The city's planetarium and hands-on Natural Science Museum provide displays of science and astronomy for kids of all ages. For nine months of the year, the stages of the Civic Center, the Clark, and the Town and Gown Theaters resound to a bustling schedule of chamber music and symphony concerts, ballet and grand opera, and Broadway plays and musicals. Adding zest to learning are frequent lectures by world class celebrities at the city's ten institutions of higher learning, almost all open to the public.

With a low-fat, high-fiber diet openly endorsed by UAB and other area health advisory agencies, it's a welcome sight to see open bins of stone ground whole grains crowding natural foods stores. To meet the demand, the Golden Temple store—and its healthfood cafe—is open seven days a week.

In this important medical center, yoga, massage, stretching, biofeedback, and every type of stress management technique is readily available. Many people go to work by city bus to avoid the stress of driving. Alternatively, you can laugh away stress at the local Comedy Club.

Singles groups, square dance lessons and sessions, and an active friendship club for seniors are just a few of the many opportunities for meeting others. Among a wide choice of volunteer openings is that of being an usher at one of the city's theaters offering cultural fare. Birmingham rates about average on opportunities for spiritual growth. But its vast 64-block medical center, specializing in everything from preventative medicine to transplants, rates it a 5 for health care. Also handy in case of a sports injury is the nationally-famous Alabama Sports Medicine Institute. A V.A. hospital, and eighteen other hospitals, complete the medical care scene.

Rapid growth has recently driven up housing prices to where a typical three-bedroom home costs around $90,000. Priced in proportion were rows of stylish condominiums, townhouses, and rental apartments. Living costs were slightly below the national average. Unaffected by federal spending, Birmingham offers qualified younger people superior economic opportunities, particularly in the health care field.

Drawbacks? Birmingham's dynamic, vibrant growth has created a rather high level of urban stress. The city could also use more natatoriums, tennis centers, exercise trails, and other fitness resources.

Scores: Urban 3. Climate 3. Elevation 1. Terrain 4. Awareness 4. Nutrition 4. Fitness 4. Stress 3. Mind 5. Social 3. Volunteer 4. Spiritual 3. Care 5. Total Healthfulness: 46.

Information: C&VB, 2027 First Avenue North, Birmingham, AL 35203 (205-252-9825). P&R, 400 Graymont Avenue West, Birmingham, AL 35203 (205-254-2391).

**BLOOMINGTON, IN.** Population: 56,000. Urban Stress: EST 2. Elevation: 750'. Set among the picturesque rolling hills of southern Indiana, Bloomington is a relaxed town that springs to life whenever Indiana University (IU) is in session. Known as a major music center, this All-American city blends small town warmth with the culture of a major metropolis. As a highly desirable residential city, Bloomington has also become popular for retirement. Among its highly articulate population are some 6,500 university faculty and employees, while the 32,000 student enrollment gives the city a perennially youthful air.

Its reputation as a bike-friendly city reveals that Bloomington is yet another stronghold of the health and fitness culture. Bicycling receives strong support from the city and the media. Quiet roads lead to six state and federal recreation areas nearby, and hundreds of riders take part in the annual Hoosier Hills weekend bicycle tour.

Together, the large Y, the university, the Older Americans Center, and the parks department offer an abundance of adult lap and Masters swimming, tennis (with free clinics for seniors), soft aerobics, and organized fitness walks and jogging. Six state and federal recreation areas close to Bloomington provide canoeing, lifeguard-patrolled lake swimming, and scores of miles of hiking trails. One park has a 50-acre mountain bicycle area. Most of the fitness resources of the university and Winslow Sports Complex are open to residents. Many adults take part in ice and roller skating. And the parks department features a daily health enhancement class for those over 50.

IU is America's tenth largest campus and the university's world renowned School of Music presents an almost daily series of concerts and recitals, plus top rung opera and ballet, at its Musical Arts Center. A steady flow of touring Broadway plays is staged at the splendid auditorium along with classic and contemporary drama, and a series of guest speakers and celebrities. With its Windfall Dancers, Bloomington Symphony, dozens of bookstores, and a strong continuing education program, Bloomington is guaranteed to keep the mind constantly inspired and active.

The Older Americans Center, and a dozen similar adult organizations, sponsor continual social dances and get-togethers. Men will find unlimited volunteer opportunities through the usual recruiting organizations. But Bloomington has also made a special effort to help women discover meaningful roles through volunteering. Through such active organizations as the American Association of

University Women, the Network of Career Women, the Commission on the Status of Women, and the Office for Women's Affairs, Bloomington provides outstanding opportunities for women volunteers. The city's 60 churches are augmented by a wide assortment of New Age faiths, plus others such as Baha'i. Bloomington also has a fairly adequate bus service.

Focusing on natural foods is Bloomingfield's Market and Deli, a complete natural foods store, while a huge assortment of fresh fruits and vegetables are sold each Saturday morning at the Community Farmers' Market. Among its many activities, Bloomington's flourishing Y provides stress management instruction, employing yoga, self-hypnosis, and other successful holistic healing techniques.

Providing state-of-the-art medical care is the 350-bed Bloomington Hospital, supported by 165 physicians and augmented by health education classes such as the monthly community lecture series, "Speaking of Health."

Bloomington's cost of living and housing hover slightly below the national average. Both old and new homes, condominiums, and rental apartments are usually plentiful, and there are several self-contained communities for independent active retirees. The only drawback we encountered concerned past problems with extensive deposits of toxic PCBs spread from a capacitor plant.

Scores: Urban 9. Climate 3. Elevation 1. Terrain 3. Awareness 5. Nutrition 4. Fitness 5. Stress 4. Mind 5. Social 4. Volunteer 5. Spiritual 4. Care 4. Total Healthfulness: 56.

Information: CoC, Box 1302, Bloomington, IN 47402 (812-336-6381). C&VB, 2855 North Walnut Street, Bloomington, IN 47404 (800-678-9828).

**BOULDER, CO.** Population: 90,000. Urban Stress: EST 2.1. Elevation: 5,500'. The ultimate health and fitness town, Boulder is a thoroughly civilized, cultured, caring, bicycle-friendly state university center that does its best to discourage growth and to promote the highest possible quality of life. Built snug against the craggy Flatiron range, and with dramatic vistas of the snow-capped Rockies reaching west, much of Boulder lies beneath a sheath of green trees. Together with its 56 flower-adorned parks, this combination earns it the highest score for terrain therapy.

Once a haven for anti-war activists, this youthful, high-energy city has matured into a trendy haven for affluent, highly-educated, physically-fit young professionals. Over 40 percent of the population are baby boomers and some 50 percent hold college degrees. Scores of world record holding athletes live here. As a result, Boulder has become the undisputed running, bicycling, Nordic skiing, and mountain hiking capital of the Rockies.

Endless miles of spectacular hiking trails begin at the city limits and wind through the foothills to mountain summits. There are two bicycles to every household and Boulder has 30 miles of city bike paths and its own bicycle coordinator. For miles around, the roads are filled with bicyclists while hundreds of miles of unpaved roads and old railroad beds provide splendid mountain bicycling. From the city, it's an hours drive to superb cross-country skiing on deep powder snow. You'll also find unlimited opportunities to hike and trail-ski through the mountains in nearby Indian Peaks Wilderness and Rocky Mountain National Park.

For daily exercise, Boulder has six 25-meter heated swimming pools, all devoted to lapswimming. Thirty miles of jogging and walking trails wind through the city. There are 52 public tennis courts, a heart exercise trail, and dozens of exercise studios, gyms, and athletic and racquet clubs. On Memorial Day, over 20,000 residents join in the Bolder-Boulder 10K run. And between them, the Y and the parks department offer a wealth of opportunities to lead an active life in the Colorado outdoors.

Home of Celestial Seasonings herb teas and the gigantic Alfalfa natural foods supermarket, Boulder has always been a nutrition-conscious town. Its several thousand followers of eastern philosophies include hundreds of vegetarians.

With a series of world class cultural events that include the Colorado Music Festival, a Shakespeare festival, a Gilbert and Sullivan festival, a Bach festival, and a summer arts festival, keeping the mind active is no problem in Boulder. Anyone 55 or over may audit unlimited courses at the University of Colorado (CU). As 84-year old CU student Irving Krakusin recently put it, "The mind must be fed with knowledge or it will die of starvation."

Both on and off campus, and throughout the year, there's a rich array of concerts, art films, plays, and lectures, many by leading celebrities. Also here is an outstanding public library and a free school where anyone may teach anything.

Singles clubs flourish for men and women of all ages, the Senior Center offers numerous social activities, and the city is dotted with ethnic restaurants and colorful cafes. Boulder has a volunteer services coordinator, while the library alone welcomes volunteers in sixteen different program areas. Spiritual worship opportunities range from mainline churches to a large Unity church plus flourishing Buddhist and yoga organizations. Besides two hospitals there are a military and a university teaching hospital in Denver 27 miles away. Boulder is also well supplied with holistic M.D.'s, naturopaths, chiropractors, and other alternative healing professionals. The city is also home to major institutes of Rolfing, transpersonal psychology and massage therapy.

Obviously, liberal thinking and intellectualism outweigh middle class conformity here, while hundreds of affluent residents deliberately drive older but well-kept cars to denigrate the automobile as a status symbol.

A wide choice of stress management classes is available, including yoga and biofeedback training. Also helping to beat the stress of driving is the extensive Boulder-Denver bus system which provides relatively good service throughout the area, with discounts for retirees. During summer, hundreds of people use the city bicycle paths to avoid driving.

Its wealth of resources for healthful living, plus the support of its predominantly health-conscious population, obviously makes Boulder a top choice for anyone seeking to adopt a low-risk lifestyle. The climate is dry, crisp, and sunny, with relatively little snow persisting on the ground in winter, and with few extremes of summer heat. But traffic is busy, parking is often tight, and on winter days Denver's brown smog drifts in to join Boulder's own high altitude air pollution.

Though growth in Boulder is restricted, the dynamic hi-tech economy is creating rapid growth in adjoining towns. Boulder's popularity has also driven up home prices and rents to about 20 percent more than in neighboring cities.

Scores: Urban 9. Climate 4. Elevation 4. Terrain 5. Awareness 5. Nutrition 4. Fitness 5. Stress 4. Mind 5. Social 4. Volunteer 4. Spiritual 5. Care 5. Total Healthfulness: 63.

Information: CoC, Box 73, Boulder, CO 80306 (303-442-1044). P&R, Box 791, Boulder, CO 80306 (303-444-3421 ).


**BOULDER CITY, NV.** Population: 14,000. Urban Stress: EST 1.9. Elevation: 2,500'. If your idea of healthy living is sunshine and relaxation, consider this sunny, laid-back small town close to Lake Mead in southern Nevada. Boulder City was originally founded to house workers building Hoover Dam in the 1930s. In 1960, Congress declared it an independent community and turned over the city, along with a substantial chunk of adjacent land, to the residents.

Determined to prevent Boulder City from becoming another Las Vegas, the city passed a growth control ordinance in 1979 limiting new dwelling units to 137 annually. This wise precaution has limited growth to a rate of 4 percent annually. Safe and virtually free of violent crime, Boulder City today is an uncongested oasis of cool green lawns and tree-shaded streets surrounded by spectacular desert. Shaded walkways line the few downtown blocks and most residential streets are curved. With all gaming banned inside the city, Boulder City has long been Nevada's most popular retirement town. The air is uncontaminated and the altitude breezy. And though health and fitness aren't a paramount community issue, Boulder City nonetheless has very adequate resources for anyone dedicated to following the low-risk lifestyle on his or her own.

Seen across the dry, brown desert hills, sunrise is glorious and sunsets are equally breathtaking. These same hills insulate Boulder City from the smog and frenzy of Las Vegas and its industrial suburb of Henderon, respectively located 24 and 12 miles distant. The city's median age of 51 years confirms that at least one person in four is retired. Many chose Boulder City for its freedom from sleet, hail, and snow. No one denies that summer days are hot, so hot that almost all outdoor exercise is done before 9 a.m. Yet 217 days each year are absolutely cloudless, and rain falls on only twelve days annually.

Swimming is available year around: at Lake Mead Beach in summer where you can swim parallel to the beach for at last half a mile; and during winter, adult lapswimming hours are reserved daily at the 25-meter municipal pool. Eleven tennis courts, plus racquetball courts, provide tennis buffs with a workout. And during calm, early morning hours you can canoe for miles on Lake Mead. A hiking trail starts in the city and, by now, should connect with another 3-mile trail built by the Civilian Conservation Corps in the 1930s. A variety of other desert and canyon hikes is available. And the parks department offers a choice of aerobics, jazzercise, and stretch-and-flex classes for both men and women.

Boulder City's adult education classes emphasize creative writing, great books groups, and computer operation, while the city's Cultural Center periodically presents the Nevada

Opera and regional orchestras and dance groups. For sophisticated cultural entertainment, most residents drive to Las Vegas, famed for its Master Series concerts featuring the Las Vegas Symphony, and for ballet performances by the Nevada Dance Theater. Some Boulder City retirees also commute to Las Vegas to audit tuition-free classes at the University of Nevada.

For fresh produce, most residents rely on local supermarkets. Anyone who can dance or play cards can find an abundance of social life. Volunteer assignments are handled by the local Retired Service Volunteer Program. And Boulder City's 38-bed hospital and team of sixteen doctors supplement the major medical facilities of nearby Las Vegas. Military retirees use the hospital at Nellis Air Force Base in Las Vegas. Two chiropractors provide an alternative to medical treatment.

Boulder City's controlled growth program has raised home prices slightly above the national average. Nonetheless, some 50 homes are usually on the market with rental apartments available at medium rates. Also usually for sale is a choice of mobile and manufactured homes, both popular in the mild year around climate. Municipally owned hydro-electric power and low property taxes keep living costs close to the national average. For career opportunities, younger workers must look to the industries of Henderson, a twenty minute commute. Some retirees have also found part-time work there.

Drawback? A gaming casino exists outside the city limits.

Scores: Urban 9. Climate 4. Elevation 2. Terrain 3. Awareness 3. Nutrition 2. Fitness 4. Stress 1. Mind 2. Social 3. Volunteer 3. Spiritual 2. Care 3. Total Healthfulness: 41.

Information: CoC, 1497 Nevada Highway, Boulder City, NV 89005 (702-293-2034). P&R, Box 367, Boulder City, NV 89005 (702-293-9255).

**BOZEMAN, MT.** Population: 30,000. Urban Stress: EST 1.8. Elevation: 4,755'. "No amusement parks, no water slides. No lines or crowds or traffic jams … a small city of cosmopolitan opportunities, a sophisticated town of uncommon amenities," is how Bozeman's publicity brochure describes this university town in southwest Montana. Forested mountains alive with elk, antelope, and eagles soar skyward from the city limits, and eye-pleasing panoramas reach in every direction. Within twenty miles are some of America's most spectacular peaks where the snowfall reaches 400 inches annually. World class Nordic ski trails start just beyond the city's edge, and on skinny skis you can glide over frozen rivers through a back country inhabited by deer, geese, and trumpeter swans.

An outdoor fitness Mecca with legendary cross-country skiing, Bozeman is home for the main campus of Montana State University (MSU). The air is clean, the skies are blue, the water is pure, and the crime rate is exceptionally low. These health-enhancing amenities are already helping to draw advanced hi-tech firms to MSU's budding research park. With a younger-than-average baby boomer population and 10,000 students, Bozeman fairly swarms with energy. The city is gateway to a vast mountain and forest recreational area that reaches south into the backcountry of Yellowstone Park.

Starting with a heart fitness trail in the city, walking and hiking opportunities extend out to 1,800 miles of National Forest trail where even a novice can reach high alpine meadows blanketed with wildflowers and then hike on to the summits of many of the easier peaks. The Big Sky Wind Drinkers running club sponsors dozens of fun runs, plus marathons and triathlons with a class for men and women over 40. There are Masters Thirty-Plus track and field meets, and an active women's hiking club with weekly all-day treks.

Internationally-famous Nordic skiers live in Bozeman, and the Bridger Ski Club offers USSA Masters training and citizen races for adults of all ages. Along the Gallatin Valley—where Bozeman lies—and in side canyons, on resort ranches, and at a dozen cross-country ski centers, is one of the greatest concentrations of groomed, lighted, and undeveloped ski trails in America. In summer, many trails are open to mountain bicyclists. The Gallatin Valley Bicycle Club arranges an active schedule of summer rides, with road races every other week. You can lapswim year around in Bozeman's 50-meter indoor pool (or at three other pools) and join in synchronized swimming or water aerobics. Tennis is played on 27 public courts. And in winter you can ice skate at three open air rinks, each with a warming hut. Lastly, the numerous spas and fitness centers all have Nautilus equipment, weights, and exercise classes.

Bozeman's thrilling scenery has drawn a dozen well-known western painters and their work is displayed in the city's ten art galleries. Opportunities for exercising the mind in Bozeman don't quite equal those for exercising the body. But the university does present occasional plays, concerts, lectures, and regional ballet and opera companies. A community summer theater, the university's highly-educational Museum of the Rockies (with planetarium), and a Shakespeare in the Park series round out opportunities to enjoy culture in Bozeman.

Nutritionally, Bozeman scores well with three natural foods stores, the Hearthstone Whole Grain Bake Shop and Natural Foods Cafe, and the New Asia Kitchen which features eight vegetarian Chinese entrees guaranteed free of MSG. Many people associated with the university are into zen and macrobiotics.

Anyone who participates in Bozeman's wealth of fitness recreations can make social contacts galore. Yoga, rolfing, biofeedback, and similar deep relaxation and stress-management techniques are all taught in and around the campus area. Volunteer work is easily found. And eastern philosophies flourish among the university population. Bozeman's Deaconess Hospital is well equipped to handle any emergency, while four chiropractors offer most non-invasive types of natural healing therapy.

The more desirable homes lie just outside the city limits, and a comfortable resale home recently averaged $80,000 with condominiums running around $62,000. MSU is Bozeman's major employer, with a small but growing group of hi-tech firms adding to the job market.

Drawbacks? Annually, 80 inches of snow falls in Bozeman. But summers are warm, dry, and sunny.

Scores: Urban 10. Climate 3. Elevation 4. Terrain 5. Awareness 5. Nutrition 5. Fitness 5. Stress 3. Mind 2. Social 3. Volunteer 2. Spiritual 3. Care 3. Total Healthfulness: 53.

Information: CoC, Box B, Bozeman, MT 59715 (800-228-4224). P&R, Box 640, Bozeman, MT 59715 (406-587-4724).


**BRADENTON-SARASOTA, FL.** Population: (area) 300,000. Urban Stress: EST 2.6. Elevation: 15'. Almost everyone knows of Sarasota's rich culture, its elegant country clubs, and candlelight and wine restaurants. But few realize that this wealthy Gulf Coast resort supports some of Florida's best fitness facilities. Back of the blue bays, the powdery white beaches and the fecund island resorts, legendary Sarasota has one of the best family Ys in the South.

With two swimming pools, four tennis courts, a one-quarter-mile lighted running track, and a fitness center with Neptune and stair machines, the Y offers a wealth of adult fitness programs. From a Masters triathlon training program (race-walk 5 kilometers, swim 1 kilometer and bicycle 25 kilometers) to a cardiac wellness and walking program ... and from slimnastics classes to choreographed music ... the Y's activities range all the way to its "Y-way to stress management" based on learning to identify tension and reducing it with exercise and by boosting self-worth.

But that's just a start. Adults and seniors can lapswim for several hours a day at Arlington Park Aquatic Center where hundreds participate in the 50-Mile Swim Program and others enjoy synchronized swimming to a musical beat. Sarasota has its share of jogging trails and both public and private fitness clubs. There are scores of public and private tennis courts, many with pro shops. Numerous launching ramps provide canoe access to miles of back bays and shallow rivers where you can enjoy a paddling workout far from the roar of motorboat cowboys, water skiers, and jet skis. Just a few miles out are three subtropical state parks with more superb canoeing, miles of walking trails, and open water swimming.

Bradenton—an unpretentious and less expensive beach resort next door to Sarasota—has several miles of beach accessible at low tide for running or walking. Here also is another fine Aquatic Center with its own active Masters swim program, many more tennis courts, a schedule of low-impact senior exercise classes, and a Nautilus Center with knee-rehabilitation machines.

Sarasota scores equally high for opportunities to exercise and stimulate the mind. Retirees can audit or take degree courses at both the University of South Florida and its associated New College. During winter, the eighteenth century Asolo Theater and the bayfront Van Wezal Performing Arts Hall host a hectic assortment of top-caliber drama, ballet, concerts, opera, and art films. Meanwhile, the Florida West Coast Symphony is based at the Music Center, and the Sarasota Opera, with its own orchestra, performs at the Theater of the Arts. Rounding out the picture is the New College String Quartet and a host of community and dinner theaters with commendable performances, plus an event-packed Florida Music Festival each June. For more scientific fare, Bradenton's Bishop Planetarium features a unique laser light presentation and an introduction to astronomy.

Home of more than 200 millionaires, Sarasota has long been a popular haven for affluent retirees. But an ever growing number of young professionals, lured by the fitness and cultural programs, are breathing new life into this traditional retirement town. For instance, to soften the impact of growth and busy traffic, Sarasota has a constantly ongoing program of beautification. Despite the concrete, the city's glorious sunsets, the rakish coconut palms, and the feathery Australian pines all make a significant contribution to terrain therapy. Naturally, the climate is deeply subtropical with long, hot, rather humid summers, short sunny winters and a liberal 54 inches of annual rain, most of which arrives during summer afternoon thundershowers.

Long known for eliminating loneliness, Sarasota's seven Friendship Centers provide a steady round of social events, dances, and educational programs. Bradenton's volunteer clearing house places over 300 adults in jobs with non-profit agencies annually. And area hospitals are so in need of volunteer help that most have their own director of volunteers. Retired physicians even staff Sarasota's Senior Friendship Center which treats only senior residents. Three large hospitals with a total 1,700 beds, and over 500 area physicians, provide some of Florida's best medical care. The area is also known for the excellence of its chiropractic physicians.

At present, a virtual moratorium exists on further homebuilding in Sarasota. However, since housing costs in Bradenton are some 30 percent lower than in Sarasota, several thousand canny retirees enjoy the glamorous life of Sarasota but live in less expensive, plain Jane Bradenton. However, several miles east of both cities are huge adult mobile home and manufactured housing parks, rental apartment complexes, and condominium communities, many with their own swimming pools, tennis courts, and social and fitness programs. But even in Bradenton, housing costs are still somewhat above average.

While home prices in Sarasota are still within reach of the more affluent retiree, they are all but out of reach of lower echelon workers. Since these workers can no longer afford to live in Sarasota, part-time employment opportunities for retired residents have improved in recent years. For qualified working adults, both Bradenton and Sarasota have enjoyed a strong economy in recent years, with a high employment rate and a wide range of career choices for health care workers and other trained personnel.

Drawbacks? The area's dense population creates fast traffic and considerable congestion while theft rates have been disturbingly high. Some overdeveloped beaches are being eroded and on weekends, public beaches are often crowded and parking is almost impossible.

Scores: Urban 7. Climate 4. Elevation 1. Terrain 4. Awareness 4. Nutrition 3. Fitness 5. Stress 4. Mind 5. Social 4. Volunteer 5. Spiritual 3. Care 5. Total Healthfulness: 54.

Information. Bradenton: C&VB, Box 788, Bradenton, FL 34206 (813-746-5989). P&R, 5502 33rd Drive West, Bradenton, FL 34209 (813-748-4501, Ext. 3251). Sarasota: C&VB, 655 North Tamiami Trail, Sarasota, FL 34236 (813-957-1877). P&R, 801 North Tamiami Trail, Sarasota, FL 34236 (813-365-4388).

**CEDAR CITY, UT.** Population: 14,000. Urban Stress: EST 1.8. Elevation: 5,800'. High on the side of a red sandstone plateau that sweeps up from Zion National Park, this prosperous Mormon college town offers an active outdoors lifestyle in a recreational paradise of spectacular evergreen forests and surrealistic rock formations. Cedar City is high and cool, and the town's well-kept homes surround the parklike campus of Southern Utah State College (SUSC), a four-year liberal arts and sciences institution complete with ivy-covered halls and solar-heated buildings. All around, on the forested slopes of Dixie National Forest, deer and elk graze among the juniper and aspen that creep down to the city's edge. Its academic flavor, freedom from crime, and high quality of life are drawing both Mormons and non-Mormons to retire in Cedar City.

In the brisk, invigorating climate, tennis can be played for nine months of the year. True, you must shovel snow several times each winter. But precipitation totals only ten inches annually, and 266 sunny days are recorded each year. This dry, crisp weather is ideal for hiking in nearby Zion or Bryce Canyon National Parks, or at Cedar Breaks National Monument or Brianhead Ski Resort, and a score of other uncrowded backcountry areas.

Winter sees vast areas of untracked, deep-powder snow and you can tour-ski through narrow canyons or on immense mountain slopes. During summer, the same trails are open for hiking and mountain bicycling. In fact, opportunities are phenomenal for fat-tired bicycling over old wagon roads or through the amazing geological wonders of such breathtaking routes as Spruce Mountain Trail and Hendrickson's Lake Trail. Hikers, too, talk in hushed tones when describing the Zion Narrows Trail, and the seven-mile trail to Kolob Arch, highest rock arch in the world. In fact, many of America's most exciting hikes and mountain bike rides begin a few miles from Cedar City. Equally dramatic are such road bike rides as the 23-mile run from Cedar City to Cedar Breaks National Monument, or the roads in Bryce Canyon National Park and others that go on to Escalante Canyon and Capitol Reef National Park. Meanwhile, several municipal swimming pools and tennis courts provide fitness exercise within the city.

At Cedar City's nationally-famous Shakespearian Festival, three plays are performed in nightly rotation, with three other contemporary plays staged at SUSC's Randall C. Jones Theater. Simultaneously, twelve ballet performances are given each August by the city-based American Folk Ballet, and by the Ballet West. Built around this festival are a score of other workshops and seminars in various fine arts, many attended by retirees. Again, during winter, six more plays are performed at the Randall C. Jones Theater. In this cultural milieu, opportunities flourish to participate in mentally stimulating extension and university classes.

As in other Mormon towns, we found fewer opportunities for volunteer work, while we also found little evidence of unusual interest in nutrition, stress management, social activities, or opportunities for spiritual growth. Basic health care is supplied by the 48-bed Valley View Medical Center and by twenty physicians.

Attractive, well-insulated homes with natural wood tone siding were recently priced at $80-100,000, with comfortable two-bedroom homes in good locations listed in the $60-$70,000 range. Condominiums and rental apartments were priced in proportion. Due to Cedar City's relative isolation, living costs were slightly above the national average. Some possibility exists for career employment in educational and government agency fields.

Drawbacks? The only flaw we found was that Interstate 5 runs right through the city.

Scores: Urban 10. Climate 4. Elevation 4. Terrain 5. Awareness 4. Nutrition 2. Fitness 5. Stress 1. Mind 4. Social 2. Volunteer 1. Spiritual 2. Care 3. Total Healthfulness: 47.

Information: CoC, Box 1007, Cedar City, UT 84720 (801-586-5124). P&R, Box 249, Cedar City, UT 84720.


**CHAPEL HILL, NC.** Population: 45,000. Urban Stress: EST 2.1. Elevation: 450'. "This is the place for intellectual activity as well as physical fitness," is how the Chamber of Commerce introduces Chapel Hill in its retirement brochure. Home of the University of North Carolina (UNC), Chapel Hill is a high energy community where, regardless of age, almost everyone seems to be a bicyclist, walker, swimmer, or tennis buff. At the same time, this exquisite college town offers a bewildering array of intellectual and cultural enrichment.

Together with nearby Durham and Raleigh, Chapel Hill forms the famous Research Triangle Park, a dynamic R & D metropolis with an overall population of 600,000. Despite the thriving growth, Chapel Hill has retained its academic ambiance. The intelligentsia still gather in coffee shops for poetry readings and discussions, bookshops abound, and every kind of New Age and alternative human potential movement flourishes.

Chapel Hill has more Ph.D.'s than any other U.S. city and has the highest educational level in America. As a result, the prosperous, upscale residents tend to be individualists with open minds, and intellectual liberalism is the only status symbol. All this has drawn a steady stream of retirees, causing Chapel Hill to become an ageless community in which the interaction of the generations has clearly enhanced the quality of life. The crime rate is low. And the climate is mild and four-seasonal, with a mere five inches of winter snow.

Recreational bicycling on rural county roads is extremely popular. Both Chapel Hill and the adjoining smaller town of Carrboro share an extensive bikeway system. For seniors, the parks department maintains a year around program of Senior Games, with clinics in tennis and other fitness activities. Both senior lapswimming and a Masters swim program are scheduled year around at the Community Center Pool. Chapel Hill also has 21 public tennis courts. Both the parks department and the Y actively program every kind of healthful activity, including a "Wellness Class for Retired People" and workshops on "Rejuvenation of Health." Meanwhile, commercial health and fitness spas, body shops, athletic and racquet clubs, and martial arts classes operate nonstop from early morning until late at night.

UNC's continuous program of concerts, plays, dances, and lecture events is augmented by an equally-active cultural program at nearby Durham's Duke University. Duke's "Learning in Retirement" program for those 50 and up includes many social lunches plus the opportunity to audit university classes at ten percent of the credit fee. At UNC, senior citizens can audit up to eight hours per semester without charge. Both universities offer a mind boggling array of continuing education courses. At UNC, three great libraries are open to the public, the North Carolina Symphony performs regularly, and dozens of retirees enroll in the weekend "Adventure in Ideas" seminars. Carrboro's art center promotes and teaches every form of the fine arts, while major galleries, museums, and repertoire theaters, plus the Moorehead Planetarium, provide constant opportunities for intellectual growth.

Community owned groceries like the Weaver Street Market help residents stay on a natural diet. From yoga to stretching and biofeedback, every kind of stress-management system is readily available. There's a New Generation Club for those over 50, and socializing is an integral part of many regular fitness and cultural happenings.

North Carolina has the nation's highest rate of volunteerism and Chapel Hill offers a plethora of volunteer openings, with the Retired Senior Volunteer Program handling the majority of demands for volunteers aged 60 and over. Besides all the usual churches, the free catalog *Change Works* lists scores of New Age and other spiritual paths.

Chapel Hill has one of the nation's highest doctor-patient ratios, and UNC's 600-bed Memorial teaching hospital spearheads an impressive list of Triangle medical centers, including Durham's V.A. hospital. Also available is a wide selection of wellness centers staffed by alternative health professionals. Although a wide choice of new and resale homes is usually on the market, housing costs recently averaged 33 percent above the national average, while living costs were also 10 percent above the average. Nonetheless, most residents feel that Chapel Hill is well worth the extra cost. Chapel Hill traditionally has a low unemployment rate and, though competition is keen, those with qualifications may find work in hi-tech, clerical or health care fields. An adequate bus service links most parts of the city, while Senior Citizen Cards are good for discounts at many establishments. The principal drawbacks appear to be lack of inexpensive housing, parking problems, and congested rush hour traffic.

Scores: Urban 9. Climate 3. Elevation 1. Terrain 3. Awareness 5. Nutrition 4. Fitness 5. Stress 4. Mind 5. Social 5. Volunteer 5. Spiritual 5. Care 5. Total Healthfulness: 59.

Information: CoC, Box 2897, Chapel Hill, NC 27515 (919-667-7075). P&R, 200 Plant Road, Chapel Hill, NC 27514 (919-968-2784).

**CLEARWATER, FL.** Population: 100,000. Urban Stress: EST 2.7. Elevation: 32'. It was a relief to leave busy Clearwater behind and to enjoy paddling my canoe across the wide intracoastal waterway. Gentle waves lapped against the bow as, with each paddle stroke, I drew closer to Caladesi Island, a virgin, undeveloped barrier beach island about two-and-a-half miles offshore. A last outpost of unspoiled Florida, Caladesi proved to be a jungle of raw mangrove swamp and cabbage palms.

I hid the canoe behind some bushes and walked around to the ocean beach. The tide was out. For three miles, the sandy beach stretched north, invitingly hard and easy to walk on. Gulls screeched overhead and sandpipers darted up and down the sands as I strode briskly to the island's north end and returned. Back in the canoe, it took 45 minutes more of vigorous paddling to return to the mainland.

In a single afternoon I'd paddled five invigorating miles and walked six brisk miles, giving myself a wonderful whole body workout. You won't find this health-building activity in any of Clearwater's publicity brochures. But I'd elect to live there just to enjoy this superb fitness activity each afternoon.

While some of Clearwater's drawbacks are all too apparent, the city does have several important pluses. The air is clear. The Recreation Department has some of the best adult fitness programs in Florida. There's lots of social life and volunteer work. And despite the endless miles of paved-over concrete, the neighborhoods are full of greenery: moss-draped oaks, exotic palms, and purple bougainvillea.

Its location on a breeze-swept isthmus between the Gulf of Mexico and Tampa Bay has made Clearwater Forida's most popular middle income retirement town. From downtown Clearwater, a palm-lined causeway leads across the inter-coastal to the island resort of Clearwater Beach, where plush motels and condominiums loom above two miles of powdery white beach. Meanwhile, Clearwater itself has burgeoned into Florida's eleventh largest city. From the downtown core of high-rises and department stores, busy roads radiate out to a sea of subdivisions and shopping malls. And beyond that, to the north, east and south, lies an almost unbroken 50 miles of megalopolis. So great has been the growth that land is running out. Traffic jams are routine and driving anywhere is often painfully slow.

Imposed atop the retirement boom has been a second boom as dozens of medical and hi-tech industries have moved into Clearwater. Nowadays, the population is a mix of younger, active, and affluent Midwestern retirees and younger professionals and executives. This combination makes for an extremely health-conscious population. As a result, Clearwater's residents have become very aware that a low-risk lifestyle can buffer them against the stresses of the city's growing pains.

In response, the Recreation Department has developed a very complete adult fitness program. To start with, the city has no fewer than seven *pars cours* heart exercise trails, each consisting of a one to a one-and-a-half mile trail lined by fourteen to twenty exercise stations. Twice weekly, a senior group fitness walks on the beach, while the Mild Striders hold winter walks for exercise.

A good tennis town, Clearwater has ten complexes, encompassing sixty-one courts. The McMullen complex, with seventeen courts and a pro shop, organizes adult teams, leagues, and tournaments. Although only one municipal and one Y pool are heated in winter, adults can lapswim every day in the year, or join in Masters swims. From dancersize to aerobics, martial arts, and rhythm n'exercise, the Recreation Department offers every type of flexibility, aerobic, and strength-building workout. Supplementing all this is Clearwater's huge Y—the world's largest single story Y— with a similar program of its own. For a change of pace, both ice and roller skating rinks are available.

While offering an extensive array of adult education courses, Clearwater tends to rely on neighboring Tampa and St. Petersburg (see) for top caliber symphony, opera, ballet, and visual arts. Nonetheless, the city's own Performing Arts Center and theater does stage a remarkable year around series of concerts, plays, and musicals, often featuring the Clearwater and Florida symphonies.

Nutritionally, we were impressed by the number of open air stands selling a tempting variety of fresh tropical fruits from South Florida. A quite adequate bus service covers Clearwater and also links the city to St. Pete and Tampa. Also helping to offset stress is the Recreation Department's extensive series of classes in yoga, and dance n'stretch. Again, the Recreation Department offers a host of social programs including square and ballroom dancing. And a thriving Senior Service Center places volunteers in a variety of jobs based on helping other retirees. Clearwater's three well-equipped hospitals are thoroughly capable of handling any emergency. The nearest V.A. hospital is in St. Petersburg, the nearest military hospital in Tampa (both an hour distant).

Thousands of new and resale homes are on the market, many in exclusive developments, some on waterfront, others in charming older neighborhoods. Recently, the median home price was $100,000 but a wide choice was available below this level. Also here is a huge assortment of less expensive condominiums, rental apartments, and mobile homes. Many mobile homes are in adult-only golf and country club type developments, often miles from downtown. Though competition for jobs is high among retirees, younger workers with qualifications often find a variety of career choices open in the medical and data processing fields.

Drawbacks? The beaches are crowded on weekends and parking space there is often hard to find.

Scores: Urban 6. Climate 4. Elevation 1. Terrain 4. Awareness 4. Nutrition 3. Fitness 5. Stress 3. Mind 3. Social 4. Volunteer 4. Spiritual 3. Care 4. Total Healthfulness: 48.

Information: CoC, Box 2457, Clearwater, FL 33517 (813-461-0011). P&R, Box 4748, Clearwater, FL 33518 (813-462-6532).

**COLORADO SPRINGS, CO.** Population: (area) 300,000. Urban Stress: ZPG 2.5. Elevation: 6,035'. Colorado Springs has always been a health and fitness town. Founded after the Civil War as a health resort for the affluent, the city's dry, bracing air soon made it a popular location for TB sanitariums. Nowadays, thousands of athletes train at the city's Olympic Training Center each year and Colorado Springs has hosted three U.S. Olympics Sports Festivals. Due to strong emphasis on outdoor exercise, "The Springs" has become headquarters for a dozen national sports associations, including the U.S. road and mountain bicycling associations. Although growing steadily, only clean industries are welcome. And ZPG ranked Colorado Springs among the five best cities of its size in the nation for urban stress.

From the Old World elegance of the Broadmoor Hotel to the terraced Victorian houses of Manitou Springs, from the tall firs of the Black Forest area to the sprawling subdivisions of Security, Widefield, and Fountain, residents enjoy an awe-inspiring panorama of mighty Pike's Peak towering overhead. Add in 42 miles of center-island flower beds and planters, lots of rock outcroppings, and tens of thousands of trees and you can appreciate why Colorado Springs has won eleven successive awards as "Tree City U.S.A." Its stimulating high-altitude and dramatic setting also earn it our highest ranking for elevation and terrain therapy.

Popular with retired military men and other retirees on-the- go, Colorado Springs has a youthful median age of 28, due no doubt to the presence of a large and highly mobile population of military personnel and workers in various hi-tech industries. Not surprisingly, since The Springs is home to several major army and air force bases, one-third of all residents are connected with the military and one in four has a college degree.

Frankly, we didn't find resources for fitness activities quite equal to those of Boulder 100 miles north. Colorado Springs nevertheless provides well-rounded opportunities for virtually every kind of physically-active recreation. Bicycle riding is popular, both in the city and on local roads, while miles of unpaved roads exist for mountain bicycling. Over 50 miles of nearby mountain trails provide splendid hiking in summer and cross-country skiing in winter. Both private and parks department pools offer ample opportunity for year around lapswimming, and we counted a total of 110 public and private tennis courts. Also here are three heart exercise trails, two huge indoor ice skating rinks, and a senior center with almost daily fitness classes and organized walks for those 50 and over. Most activities can be enjoyed in such inspiring locales as Palmer and Memorial Parks, Cheyenne Canyon, and among the red rock towers and spires of the Garden of the Gods.

Providing an abundance of intellectual stimulation are the extensive list of continuing education classes at the University of Colorado plus a wealth of musical and cultural events. The city's Performing Arts Center presents a steady flow of concerts, Broadway plays and dance productions, while Pike's Peak Center and the Broadmoor International Center host two or more annual operas and dozens of other plays and symphony concerts. From Shakespeare in the Park to the fine displays of western art at the Fine Arts Center, Colorado Springs offers an endless series of programs to stimulate the mind.

All the usual yoga, stretching, and stress-management courses are here, along with a city bus service to help reduce the daily stress of automobile driving. Two senior centers and dozens of organizations offer every type of adult social activity. Volunteers are needed for virtually everything, from food distribution programs to outreach work, and to coach and referee youth sports. Over 350 churches serve the city. And besides four general and two military hospitals, the city's parks department has classes in acupressure, herbalism, nutrition, massage, yoga, and other alternative health care systems. One directory for seniors, published by the Senior Information and Referral Agency, lists over 100 agencies that provide health care services to those 50 and over.

The mobile population is responsible for a fairly high turnover in new and resale homes, and we found home prices considerably lower than in neighboring Boulder. Recent median prices ranged from $70,000 for a three-bedroom, two-bath home near Fort Carson in the south, to $95,000 in more affluent neighborhoods. Vacancies were also plentiful in rental apartment complexes (average rent $540), many of which had their own pool, weights room and tennis courts. For years the cost of living has stayed three percent below the national average. The large military payroll insulates the economy from fluctuations and job openings are often available for the technically skilled.

Drawbacks? Despite the high sunshine rate, winters are long and cold, winds can be high, and a gray, high-altitude haze hangs over the city on winter days. The crime rate also seems somewhat above average.

Scores: Urban 7. Climate 4. Elevation 5. Terrain 5. Awareness 4. Nutrition 4. Fitness 5. Stress 4. Mind 5. Social 4. Volunteer 4. Spiritual 4. Care 4. Total Healthfulness: 59.

Information: CoC, Drawer B, Colorado Springs, CO 80901 (719-635-1551). C&VB, 104 South Cascade, Suite 104, Colorado Springs, CO 80903 (800-888-4748). P&R, 1401 Recreation Way, Colorado Springs, CO 80905 (303-578-6630).

**COLUMBUS, OH.** Population: 650,000. Urban Stress: ZPG 2.6. Elevation: 777'. Its expertise in high technology has transformed Columbus from a traditional rust belt manufacturing city into an energetic and dynamic center of the computer software business. Add in Ohio State University and six other four-year colleges, with their total 20,000 faculty and 80,000 students, and it becomes apparent that the educational level of the population is exceptionally high. That Columbus is, indeed, a city of prosperous, well educated (and, therefore, health-conscious) people is evident in the low crime rate, the spotless neighborhoods with their safe, tree-lined streets, the lack of large apartment complexes, and the splendid highway system that enables traffic to flow smoothly through the city without rush hour jams.

A major jogging and bicycling town, Columbus also rates highly for the brilliance of its intellectual and cultural opportunities. The terrain isn't terribly inspiring, but its urban stress level is far below that of most other cities of this size. The distinctly four-seasonal climate provides weeks of crisp, mild days in spring and fall. And even the warm, humid summer, and the chilly winter with frequent snow, seldom interferes with outdoor exercise. Despite being the home of several manufacturers of junk food and hamburgers, a high proportion of Columbus residents have upgraded their diet, while stores offer an enormous selection of fresh produce and exotic fruits.

An extensive pattern of bicycle and walking trails network the city and parks system, with 24 riverfront miles providing a wonderfully scenic route to fitness. Huge annual bicycle events like TOSRV (Tour of the Scioto River Valley) have earned Columbus the reputation of being a bicycle-friendly city. And as we have already discovered, being bike-friendly invariably confirms that a city is exceptionally health and fitness oriented.

In case of snow, for example, you can walk indoors at four athletic complexes. Daily lapswimming is available at, among other places, the parks department's indoor swim center, while in summer ten other pools offer daily lapswimming. Adult and senior aerobics and fitness classes are taught at most of the city's 25 recreation centers. And there are literally hundreds of opportunities for fitness activities of every imaginable variety.

To transform Columbus into a major center of the performing arts, the city has refurbished three traditional theaters and has built three others in the Wexner Center for Visual Arts. Now elegantly restored, the opulent Palace Theater is home of grand opera and Broadway plays, while the equally grand Ohio Theater features plays, concerts, and dance performances. Additionally, three thriving theater companies present a continuous series of plays. The widely acclaimed Columbus Symphony presents 100 concerts annually, and the Pro Musica has become a top chamber orchestra. Culture buffs will find a top caliber series of almost daily ballet, opera, dance, plays, and concerts. Add in a tremendous range of continuing education classes, and it becomes clear that Columbus provides unlimited opportunities to keep the mind stimulated and active.

Stress management classes and volunteer referral agencies are all here in abundance, together with singles groups and social get-togethers of every type for adults and seniors.

Besides all the usual places of worship, Columbus is well supplied with New Age churches and just about every other form of spiritual faith. A businessman's coalition for cost-effective health care has helped keep the cost of medical treatment below average. Led by the large Riverside Methodist, Columbus has twelve hospitals with over 5,000 beds and a total of 2,500 physicians.

The city's 160 hi-tech companies, together with the universities, state government, and financial institutions have helped Columbus to maintain a traditionally low unemployment rate and to offer a wide variety of career choices. The cost of living is moderate and home prices, though somewhat above average, are not yet excessive. An adequate bus service operates throughout the city. For anyone seeking a safe, health-conscious city in which to work and raise a family, Columbus would be difficult to equal.

Scores: Urban 7. Climate 3. Elevation 1. Terrain 3. Awareness 5. Nutrition 3. Fitness 5. Stress 3. Mind 5. Social 4. Volunteer 4. Spiritual 5. Care 5. Total Healthfulness: 53.

Information: CoC, Box 1527, Columbus, OH 43215 (614-221-1321 ) C&VB, 10 West Broad Street, Suite 1300, Columbus, OH 43215 (800-821-5784). P&R, City Hall, Room 127, 90 West Broad St., Columbus, OH 43215 (614-645-3333).

**CORVALLIS, OR.** Population: 50,000. Urban Stress: EST 1.7. Elevation: 375'. For anyone seeking a smaller, more relaxed college town, Corvallis ranks well above average on almost every factor affecting health. Located in the center of Oregon's fertile Willamette Valley, and surrounded by lush fir trees and greenery, this running and bicycling center is safe, immaculate and pollution-free. Historic homes and buildings line the orderly streets that lead over gentle hills to tree-shaded neighborhoods. Beautiful tree-clad parks border the placid river that flows through the city. Colorful hanging baskets adorn downtown, while bookshops abound and every block seems to have at least one natural foods store or a sports or bicycle shop. Wherever you go, the neat yards and academic flavor suggest that this is a quality town.

A city of verdant trees and lawns, Corvallis has a total of 50 parks and preserves, which isn't surprising in this exceptionally mild climate. Most of the annual 40-inch rainfall descends between November and March. But summer days are pleasantly warm and winters relatively mild. The lack of extremes is due to a gap in the Coast Range Mountains through which ocean winds penetrate all year, giving Corvallis the highest air quality in the Willamette Valley.

A popular retirement town, most of Corvallis' adults are nonetheless highly educated, affluent baby boomers who are extremely aware of the importance of wellness, fitness, and nutrition.

Ideally placed for fitness activities, Corvallis has over 60 miles of bicycle routes, while both city and county have advisory commissions on bicycling. Bicyclists told us of the great road-bike touring on local backroads, while others praised mountain bicycling opportunities in nearby McDonald Forest and in the Cascades. Almost weekly, thousands take part in runs of 10K, 20K, or marathons, and almost everyone seems to jog or walk for exercise. Miles of trails wind along the river and through the various city parks. Organized mass walks draw thousands of residents of all ages. And the nearby Cascades (an hour's drive away) are filled with scenic mountain hiking and cross-country ski trails. For upper body exercise, you can canoe on the river right in the city. Osborne Aquatic Center provides daily lapswimming throughout the year, while the parks department maintains several tennis complexes (most in high schools) open to adults. Both the parks department and the experimental college offer dozens of classes in every type of fitness and martial arts. Half a dozen private fitness centers and exercise spas flourish downtown.

Confirming the city's high level of nutritional awareness is the First Alternative, a large natural foods supermarket. The abundance of fresh, local produce is boosted by the

Sunday morning farmers' market. The Nearly Normal vegetarian restaurant guarantees tasty, well-prepared meals free of fat. And the area is so pollution-free that drinking water is minimally-treated and supplies are ample.

We found classes galore in yoga, stretching, and biofeedback, as well as in special stress-management workshops for seniors. One parks department class we watched was called "Yoga Relaxation for Seniors." Helping to minimize urban stress is a weekday citywide bus service. All downtown parking is free. And even during rush hour, you can drive across the widest part of the city in under fifteen minutes.

Home of Oregon State University (OSU), Corvallis is brimful of classes in every area of self-enrichment, education, and culture. Resident senior citizens can audit OSU classes at nominal cost. Added together, the continuing education programs of the University Summer School, the community college, the experimental college, and the parks department embrace every level of mental activity from studying astronomy to Buddhism, computers, cosmology, and right through the alphabet to zen. OSA also presents a continuous program of plays, lectures, ballet, and musical events, many starring nationally famous artists.

A Retired Senior Volunteer Program recruits those 60 years of age or older to help out at over 70 public agencies. There are never enough volunteers to fill the need. A thriving senior center organizes a constant round of dances, dinners and outings, making it difficult for any active person over 50 to experience loneliness. All major religious denominations are represented, and health care is provided by a 188-bed community hospital and 150 physicians. We found housing costs slightly above average, but there seemed an adequate supply of affordable homes, and rentals are often plentiful in summer. A small but steady demand exists for skilled workers in education, research and health care fields.

Scores: Urban 10. Climate 3. Elevation 1. Terrain 4. Awareness 5. Nutrition 4. Fitness 5. Stress 4. Mind 4. Social 3. Volunteer 4. Spiritual 4. Care 3. Total Healthfulness: 54.

Information: C&VB, 420 NW Second Street, Corvallis, OR 97330 (503-757-1544), P&R, 760 Southwest Madison Street, Corvallis, OR 97333 (503-757-6918).

**DAVIS, CA.** Population: 50,000. Urban Stress: EST 1.7. Elevation: 60'. Thirteen miles west of Sacramento, in California's Central Valley, lies Davis, a college town so dedicated to health and fitness that the city's publicity brochure proclaims, "Unique Lifestyle Keeps Davis Forever Young." This is no PR puffery. By minimizing dependence on fossil fuels and on the automobile, Davis' highly-educated citizenry have achieved a quality of life rarely equalled in any other U.S. city.

Bicycles outnumber cars and have become the number one mode of travel. Hundreds of citizens commute to work or school via the city's 40 miles of bike paths and lanes. With a total 40,000 bicycles, Davis has the highest ratio of bikes to people in the U.S. Bicycles are openly encouraged over cars and bicycling has become a way of life that is completely safe and pleasant.

The *raison d'etre*, and the driving force behind all this, is the University of California, Davis (UCD), third largest of the university's nine campuses. The air of learning pervades every corner of Davis, from the two mile Arboretum filled with trees and plants, to the sixteen rather quaint downtown blocks full of art galleries, bookshops, sidewalk cafes, boutiques, and sports shops. The tree-shaded streets, the parks and greenbelts, and the blooming redbud and acacias along the banks of Putah Creek provide a wealth of potential for terrain therapy. And though days and nights can be hot during the long summer—and most of the annual seventeen feet of rainfall comes in winter—spring and fall are beautiful and dry.

The presence of 20,000 students adds to the already high health awareness of Davis' population. Almost everyone seems dedicated to helping the environment by using alternative forms of both energy and transportation. Even youngsters who hold a driver's license willingly ride a bicycle to school.

Bicycling leads the fitness field. Road races and criteriums are popular and the famed Double Century (200 miles) ride draws several thousand bicyclists each spring. It takes three separate guidebooks to describe all the possible bike rides and tours in the area. The Davis Bicycle Club schedules frequent rides over *Cardiac Hill* and up Mount Diablo, among many other destinations.

Jogging and brisk walking rival bicycling in popularity. The Davis Running Club schedules frequent workouts and fun runs while the Dynamos Walk Club arranges regular 10K and 12K hikes. At least six pools schedule daily adult lapswimming in summer, with three heated pools remaining open all year. Or you could sign up for the Aquatic Masters program which offers eight structured swimming workouts each weekday. Both public and private tennis courts are available, including courts on the campus and at the Racquet and Fitness Club. Rounding out the exercise scene are the scores of low-impact aerobics classes offered by the parks department, Senior Center, and the university.

One of the nation's 25 top research universities, UCD and the city of Davis brim with activities to challenge the mind. Residents can pick from over 1,000 continuing education classes at UCD. A total of six theaters present an almost nonstop series of world class concerts, dance presentations, plays, musicals, and lectures throughout the year. A science center displays mind-expanding exhibits in the sciences for all ages. And all the culture of California's high-energy capital, Sacramento, is only 30 minutes away.

Confirming the high level of nutritional awareness is the twice weekly old-fashioned Farmers' Market, loaded with fresh fruits and vegetables and home-made bread. Together with three vegetarian restaurants, the town's dozen oriental,

Greek and Italian eateries serve healthful, low-fat gourmet meals. At least a dozen hatha yoga and stretching classes help residents beat stress. And the handsome Senior Center features regular parties and social events for those 55 and over. Another swift way for newcomers to meet the fit and healthy is to join the Davis Bicycle Club.

Ready to match volunteers with a diversity of needs is Davis' Volunteer Center, run by a full-time volunteer coordinator. Davis' 28 churches range from a Unitarian church to an Islamic Center plus scores of New Age and esoteric faiths. The Sutter Davis Community Hospital is well equipped to handle cardiac emergencies and there are 56 physicians, 8 chiropractors and an H.M.O. The hospital encourages the low-risk lifestyle through programs in wellness and health education.

This obviously healthful city appears to have only two flaws: the long, hot summers, and the inflated cost of homes. However, condominium living or apartment renting are less expensive alternatives. Also here is a deluxe retiree congregate living complex. Most job openings occur at the university and in agricultural research such as plant genetics.

Scores: Urban 10. Climate 3. Elevation 1. Terrain 3. Awareness 5. Nutrition 5. Fitness 5. Stress 4. Mind 5. Social 4. Volunteer 5. Spiritual 4. Care 4. Total Healthfulness: 58.

Information: CoC, 228 B Street, Davis, CA 95616 (916-756-5160). P&R, 23 Russell Boulevard, Davis, CA 95616 (916-756-3747).

**DURANGO, CO.** Population: 16,000. Urban Stress: EST 1.7. Elevation: 6,512'. If you've been turned off by the ferocious freeways, smog, and bigness of Denver, here is a relaxed health and fitness town in the kind of Colorado setting most people dream about. Encircled by spectacular mountains and the San Juan National Forest, Durango is nationally known as a major running, mountain bicycling and cross-country ski center. At least six top professional mountain bike racers call

Durango home. Almost everyone is into some kind of fitness activity. Air and water quality are good, the crime rate is low, and Durango is known for its safety, for its high quality of life, and for its strong focus on physical activity and health. Despite the million tourists who visit Durango annually, compared to Aspen or Vail it remains relatively unknown—an outpost of health and wellness isolated by the vastness of the Four Corners Region.

Its dramatic mountain setting—especially beautiful when blanketed with fresh snow, or arrayed in the gold and russet colors of fall—gives Durango the highest rating for terrain therapy. The constantly low humidity minimizes the effects of winter cold and the few hot summer afternoons that are part of Durango's stimulating four-seasonal climate. The average year sees 300 full days of sunshine while the average winter snowfall of 69" guarantees an abundance of deep powder snow for cross-country skiing.

Energetic, upbeat, enthusiastic, outgoing, easy-to-know, younger-than-average, generally well-educated, independent, and individualistic is how the citizens of Durango were described in a 1987 report on the city's health made by the graduate student nurses class of the University of Colorado School of Nursing. After interviewing over 400 residents, the nurses described Durango as having a laid-back, casual, low-stress lifestyle built around participating in physically-active sports and recreations. They reported finding a very high citizen awareness of the benefits of exercise, nutrition and other health-promoting behaviors. The nurses were also impressed by the large number of healthy active Durangoans aged 65 and over. Of the total population in 1987, 37 percent were single and 47 percent were married. The nurses' report revealed that many talented people have chosen to live in Durango including younger retirees, professional people, and artists.

From Durango, the Colorado Trail reaches 482 miles northwest to Denver, offering superb hiking and mountain bicycling. It's just one of a huge choice of old mining roads and railroad beds that are so challenging both the state and national mountain bike championship races have been held here. In winter, the same roads and trails are thronged by cross-country skiers. Five area lakes offer still-water canoeing for upper body exercise. The parks department provides daily summer lapswimming and there are sixteen tennis courts.

Surprisingly, for such a small town, Durango has several quality theater companies where you can enjoy a variety of plays. Occasional presentations of the Four Corners Opera and the San Juan Symphony are given at Fort Lewis College. And there's an annual writers' fair. But beyond the summer season melodrama presented in Durango's historic downtown, it's a long drive to any really sophisticated big city culture.

Durango's uncontaminated drinking water is minimally treated and four small healthfood stores are available. The 55 Plus Center sponsors a series of social potlucks, dances, and outings for both singles and couples. Demand for volunteers far exceeds the supply with scores of interesting openings available at local health care agencies.

Included among Durango's 40 churches is a temple of the Baha'i faith. In their report, the nurses noted that many people are involved in spiritual growth even though not affiliated with any church.

Because they serve the far-flung Four Corners Region, Durango's two hospitals offer more sophisticated health care than might be expected in a city this size. One hospital provides monthly seminars in various aspects of the low-risk lifestyle. Also available is acupuncture and massage therapy.

We found home prices somewhat above average in cost, with a good supply of new and resale homes normally available. The fact that Durango's economy is tourist driven results in wages being seventeen percent lower than in Denver. If you must work, we advise obtaining a firm job commitment at an acceptable remuneration before planning to move here.

Drawbacks? Job openings are relatively few and people who start a business to enable them to live here experience a high failure rate. A gray haze of suspended particulates hangs above the city on cold winter days—however, air quality remains relatively good. Some drunk driving results from the large number of downtown bars. Fortunately, most of the piles of still-radiating uranium tailings left over from mining days have now been removed.

Scores: Urban 10. Climate 4. Elevation 5. Terrain 5. Awareness 5. Nutrition 5. Fitness 5. Stress 3. Mind 2. Social 3. Volunteer 3. Spiritual 3. Care 3. Total Healthfulness: 56.

Information: CoC, Box 2578, Durango, CO 81302 (303-247-0312). P&R, 949 East Second Avenue, Durango, CO 81303 (303-247-5622).

**EAU CLAIRE, WI.** Population: 60,000. Urban Stress: EST 1.9. Elevation: 800'. If your idea of health is to spend the day gliding on cross-country ski trails glistening in the winter sun, then to laugh your head off at a comedy in an elegant dinner theater—or to enjoy a symphony concert or to be inspired by a play—Eau Claire may be for you. Fitness fever is so rampant in this northern Wisconsin university city that thousands of residents welcome snow shoveling as a chance to enjoy yet another aerobic and strength-building exercise. Relatively uncongested, totally safe, and with an enviably-low crime rate, this city of tree-lined streets and parks offers an enticing year around array of health-enhancing activities for both body and mind.

Eleven thousand college students keep the community spirit youthful and help to power community support for a fitness-based lifestyle. Although the January temperature averages only 12°, winter is the favorite season for outdoor fun and recreation. Thousands strap on their blades and ice skate daily at the city's seventeen supervised open air skating rinks, while adult ice hockey leagues abound. Cross-country ski trails are so numerous that to list them all fills an entire brochure. Starting in mid-December, groomed trails are maintained at most city parks and golf courses and some are lighted for after-dark skiing. Tower Ridge Park alone has over eleven miles of maintained trail. And a few miles outside the city are limitless miles of secluded woodland trails. Wisconsin is also a hotbed of cross-country ski racing, and you'll find a host of races to whet your appetite. As gateway to the huge Indian Head Recreation Area, Eau Claire has easy access to a vast region of lakes, streams, and state and national parks.

In summer, residents keep fit by brisk walking, jogging, bicycling, canoeing, and playing tennis. Strenuous canoe paddling can be found on a choice of nearby lakes and rivers. A network of low-traffic bicycle routes (each described in a separate Parks and Forest Department brochure) lead from Eau Claire to a variety of county parks; a typical ride is 50 miles round-trip. Tennis buffs find a pro shop and five indoor courts at the Y Tennis Center plus numerous other courts in city parks. Lapswimming is available at four indoor high school pools, plus the Ys Olympic pool and, in summer, at several scenic lake beaches. Completing the fitness picture is a splendid Y with 27 Nautilus machines and a long list of fitness activities; and the Athletic Club with another swimming pool, aerobics classes, and a dedication to making fitness a lifestyle for everyone.

Cultural activity is led by the University of Wisconsin, Eau Claire (UWEC) which occupies a handsome riverbank campus. UWEC's Artist Series features symphony and chamber music concerts with world class soloists, while its Forum Series invites a steady stream of outstanding speakers, A host of other plays and concerts are presented on university stages or at Eau Claire's restored State Theater. Over 17,000 residents make learning a lifelong venture by enrolling in the university's many credit and non-credit continuing education and outreach programs. For the scientifically-inclined, the Planetarium offers a series of mind-provoking lectures.

Despite the city's cheese factories and meat packing plants, thousands of residents prefer a low-fat diet and prefer to shop at Mother Nature's Foods or to dine at a growing number of restaurants with extensive salad bars. You can laugh away your stress at several comedy clubs or enroll in a variety of yoga, flexibility or biofeedback classes. Adult singles clubs cater to all ages, and the United Way recruits volunteers for hundreds of positions with a variety of service agencies. Eau Claire's 65 churches include a Jewish synagogue and several non-denominational places of worship. But most of the interest in New Age churches, the human potential movement, meditation groups, and eastern philosophies seems limited to the university population.

Together, the 310-bed Luther Hospital (with comprehensive cardiac center) and the 344-bed Sacred Heart Hospital, plus 175 physicians, provide an exceptionally high standard of health care. A variety of alternative healing techniques is provided by the city's sizeable number of chiropractors.

From charming Victorians to modern ranch-style houses, comfortable homes recently sold for around $90,000 new and $80,000 for resales. Many new condominiums and rental apartments were priced in proportion. A growing hi-tech industry usually offers a choice of careers for those who are qualified.

Drawbacks? The city does have some industry, including a paper mill that recycles paper.

Scores: Urban 9. Climate 3. Elevation 1. Terrain 4. Awareness 5. Nutrition 3. Fitness 5. Stress 2. Mind 4. Social 3. Volunteer 4. Spiritual 3. Care 4. Total Healthfulness:50.

Information: C&VB, 2127 Brackett Avenue, Wagner Complex, Eau Claire, WI 54701 (800-344-3866). P&R, 1300 First Avenue, Eau Claire, WI 34703 (715-839-5032).

**EUGENE, OR.** Population: 110,000. Urban Stress: ZPG 2.1. Elevation: 425'. Home of the University of Oregon (UO) and the state's second largest city, Eugene combines the relaxed air of academia with the high energy of a major health and fitness center. Riverbank walks and bicycling and jogging trails meander through hundreds of acres of tall oaks, spruce, and maples and through manicured rose and rhododendron gardens. The scores of mountain bikes parked outside every cafe and many buildings testify that thousands prefer the two-wheeled, non-polluting form of transportation. And, indeed, Eugene has several dozen miles of bicycle routes, trails, and paths on which you can pedal for miles beside the Willamette River, and also reach most points in the city.

In this Mecca of physical fitness, world class athletes share the Prefontaine Trail, and a dozen others, with local walkers and joggers. Hiking trails lead to the summit of Spencer Butte (2,065'). And it's only 45 minutes drive to Willamette National Forest in the nearby Cascade Range where you can hike, cross-country ski, or mountain bicycle over hundreds of miles of old logging roads and mountain trails.

At least five 25-meter heated pools offer daily lapswimming for adults and seniors, including the lively Swim Park Center. And for upper body exercise you can paddle a canoe through Alton Baker Park's three-mile canal. Beside all this, the parks department operates several fitness centers with weight machines and aerobics classes. Like most big state university centers, Eugene provides every type of fitness activity from martial arts to yoga and exercise dancing for everyone of every age. There are 22 public lighted tennis courts and numerous organizations offer frequent hikes, runs, and road and mountain bike rides. Fitness is a way of life for almost everyone.

Permitting outdoor exercise year around is the temperate climate with its mild, dry summers and brisk, rather rainy winters. A mix of highly-educated professionals, and millworkers from the adjoining forest products town of Springfield, combine to make Eugene a place where everyone can share the same sane, satisfying and healthful lifestyle.

Spearheading opportunities for mental activity is the auditing Program at UO through which anyone 65 and over may audit university classes. Four mind-stimulating museums

(Art, Science, Natural History, and a Planetarium) are housed in Museum Park, while Eugene's Symphony, and Opera and Ballet companies, are all housed in the elegant Hult Center for the Performing Arts. The Center features a year around extravaganza of top rung musicals, concerts and plays. From its flourishing art center to an Experimental College (a free school with hundreds of courses) to an extensive program of parks department classes in virtually every major subject, Eugene provides exceptional opportunities for lifelong cultivation of the mind.

Eugene's Vegetarian Restaurant serves a variety of tasty fat-free dishes, while Lane County publishes its own weekly buyer's guide to sources of fresh fruits and vegetables. Many restaurants feature natural foods dishes and we found eight natural foods stores. From yoga to Buddhism and meditation groups, from Rolfing to foot reflexology, Eugene offers virtually every type of stress management at minimum cost. Two senior centers sponsor frequent trips, dinners, and social activities for retirees. And organizations like the Y, library, and university list hundreds of opportunities for selfless service in outreach programs, hospitals and nonprofit and public agencies, often with extensive free training.

Every mainstream church is here, together with virtually every New Age church and human potential movement from t'ai chi to kundalini yoga. An important regional medical center, with a 432-bed general hospital and 450 physicians, Eugene is also home to some of the nation's top licensed health professionals in the alternative healing arts. The only serious drawback we encountered was seasonal air pollution from field burning in the Willamette Valley. The university is the largest employer, but Eugene is also an important medical and professional center. A choice of homes and rentals is normally available at generally affordable prices.

Scores: Urban 9. Climate 3. Elevation 1. Terrain 4. Awareness 5. Nutrition 5. Fitness 5. Stress 5. Mind 5. Social 4. Volunteer 5. Spiritual 5. Care 5. Total Healthfulness: 61.

Information: C&VB, Box 10286, Eugene, OR 97440 (800-547-5445,or in Oregon 800-452-3670). P&R, 22 West 7th Avenue, Eugene, OR 97401 (503-687-5333).

**FAYETTEVILLE, AR.** Population: 45,000. Urban Stress: EST 1.8. Elevation: 1,450'. Why have so many people been willing to take a pay cut to be able to live in Fayetteville? The answer: because Fayetteville is a small, safe, friendly town with charming, tree-lined neighborhoods, and a high level of terrain therapy, plus freedom from urban pollution, traffic jams, crime, and exorbitant living and housing costs. Simultaneously, as home of the University of Arkansas, Fayetteville offers the intellectual enrichment, cultural diversity, health awareness, and fitness opportunities of a much larger city. It's entirely possible to retire to the simple life here while exploring the boundaries of human knowledge through auditing tuition-free classes at the university. In fact, many professors who taught at the university here have returned to Fayetteville to retire.

Almost every house has a scenic view of trees, a meadow, hill, or park, while in spring, the historic district is framed by masses of blooming dogwood and redbud. Adding to Fayetteville's livability is the four-seasonal climate which is free of most extremes and is less humid than in most Midwestern areas. We were disappointed by the number of people who still smoked. But the majority of residents consist of young professionals and younger, affluent retirees. And both groups are noticeably more health conscious than the general population.

Though not a major bicycle town, Fayetteville does have a city-wide bicycle route system. With a bike route map, you can bicycle all over town on low traffic roads. There's great canoe paddling and warm-season swimming in rivers and lakes a few minutes drive from town, or in larger Beaver Lake also nearby. You can also swim at the university. Walking and running trails exist at several city parks. You can also hike on several hundred miles of trail in nearby Ozark National Forest. In addition, the parks department offers rhythmic aerobics, water exercises, adult basketball, tennis, and strength-building exercise training for adults.

Residents over 60 can audit any university course tuition-free or attend the many continuing education classes. Featured on the stage of the combined city-university Fine Arts Center are at least 69 concerts and nine top-caliber plays annually, plus celebrity lectures and exciting visual arts shows. The Music Festival of Arkansas features three weeks of classical music and jazz each summer, while the University Fine Arts Concert series presents the North Arkansas Symphony with celebrity guest artists during winter.

An encouraging sign of the move to a high-fiber diet are the piles of home-grown vegetables and fruit sold thrice-weekly at the summer-long Farmer's Market. Helping to buffer life's stresses are Fayetteville's very reasonable living and housing costs, while a hospital run Center for Exercise teaches a relaxing flexibility course. If you enjoy country western dancing, Fayetteville abounds with lively night spots. For something quieter, the Community Adult Center sponsors social events, cards and educational programs for men and women 55 and over. We didn't see any central volunteer agency but the Retired Senior Volunteer Program welcomes retired volunteers.

Nor, despite Fayetteville's 14,500 students, did we see any New Age church other than Unity. Supplying Fayetteville's medical care needs are two modern hospitals with a total 400 beds and a V.A. hospital with 187 beds.

Virtually every type of housing is available, from refurbished Victorians to suburban family homes, five-acre ranchettes and luxury condominiums, all recently priced at around 15 percent below national average housing costs. Fayetteville also ranks high in affordability with a recent cost of living index some 11 percent below the national average and with medical care costs around 30 percent below the national average. The most frequent employment openings occur in the educational and health care fields.

Scores: Urban 10. Climate 4. Elevation 1. Terrain 5. Awareness 4. Nutrition 3. Fitness 4. Stress 3. Mind 4. Social 3. Volunteer 2. Spiritual 3. Care 3. Total Healthfulness: 49.

Information: CoC, Box 4216, Fayetteville, AR 72702 (501-521-1710).

**GAINESVILLE, FL.** Population: 90,000. Urban Stress: EST 2.3. Elevation: 100'. Far from the drugs, crime, hoopla, hi-rises, and congestion of South Florida, the bicycle-friendly university center of Gainesville offers a high quality lifestyle that combines both intellectual stimulation and fitness activities. A leader in health care for mature adults, Gainesville is home of the University of Florida's Center for Exercise Science, where dozens of studies have validated the benefits of exercise for older Americans. Combining freedom from air pollution with a relaxed pace, this northern Florida city offers active retirement at costs that almost anyone can afford.

A city of trees, flowers, lakes, and rivers, Gainesville makes a worthwhile contribution to terrain therapy. Just about any fitness activity not requiring snow or mountains is available, and the area has some of the best still-water canoeing in America. It's the only city in Florida where bicycles are an important component of the lifestyle and the city actively promotes alternative forms of transportation. There are several bicycle clubs and many pros train here in winter. Gainesville has 77 miles of streets approved for bicycling and 10,000 bicyclists commute to work daily. Scores of nearby backroads are popular for recreational bicycling, police patrol on bicycles, and bike parking is mandatory at all new developments. Canoeing is enjoyable on dozens of lakes and rivers, while lapswimming and tennis are widely available. There's a mile-long heart exercise trail, miles of scenic, wooded walking and jogging trails, an active Y, and a dozen health and fitness clubs. You'll find square dances galore, plus impact-free senior aerobics classes. Meanwhile, North Florida's Regional

Medical Wellness Center specializes in fitness for mature adults and promises a supportive atmosphere.

Its seductive, down-to-earth flavor makes Gainesville a paradise for active retirement. The highly educated, younger than average population mingles with the Fifty-Plus set, providing a strongly supportive background for a low-risk lifestyle. And the snow-free, four-seasonal climate, with its azure skies and omnipresent sunshine, makes outdoor exercise pleasant and comfortable most of the year.

As Florida's largest university town, Gainesville provides a rich cultural milieu. Residents over 60 can audit university courses tuition-free and the university libraries are open to all. The three-quarter round Hippodrome Theater presents over 400 plays, concerts and dance events annually, while the Miracle on 34th Street, a state of the art cultural complex, includes an art museum with monthly traveling exhibits and an 1,800-seat performing arts hall. A monthly guide lists hundreds of events by such groups as Dance Alive, the Florida Chamber Orchestra, the Civic Ballet, and three repertory theater companies. An enormous choice of continuing education courses is available.

Its 35,000 students and 3,400 faculty demand high nutritional standards that are met by the big Mother Earth natural foods market and by other stores with names like "Homespun" and "Natural." Every type of stress-management training is available. Adult social life is augmented by the Golden Gators and the Thursday Lunch Group, while singles clubs flourish for all ages. A central volunteer agency has hundreds of openings to choose from and dozens of others are available through the Retired Service Volunteer Program and the Older Americans Council.

Gainesville boasts 93 mainline churches plus a wide representation of New Age churches and virtually every branch of esoteric and eastern philosophies, from sufi to zen and yoga.

Gainesville's four big hospitals provide an unsurpassed range of medical care facilities and include a V.A. hospital, the Shands University Teaching Hospital, and two acute care hospitals. A total 875 physicians give Gainesville the highest doctor-patient ratio in Florida. There are inexpensive Health Maintenance Organizations, while the North Florida Regional Medical Center combines mainstream medical care with holistic alternative healing methods.

Both housing and living costs were recently just below the national average. With economic growth propelled by the university and hi-tech and medical research, the economy is strong and growing. Although this is a low wage area, newcomers with skills are often able to eventually find work.

Scores: Urban 8. Climate 3. Elevation 1. Terrain 3. Awareness 5. Nutrition 4. Fitness 5. Stress 4. Mind 5. Social 4. Volunteer 5. Spiritual 5. Care 5. Total Healthfulness: 57.

Information: CoC, Box 1187, Gainesville, FL 32602 (904-336-7100). C&VB, 10 Southwest Second Avenue, Suite 220, Gainesville, FL 32601 (904-374-5210). P&R, Box 490, Gainesville, FL 32602 (904-374-2120).

**GREEN VALLEY, AZ.** Population: 16,000. Urban Stress: EST 1.7. Elevation: 2,900'. Known for its clear skies and technicolor sunsets, this smog-free Southern Arizona retirement resort lets you enjoy healthful exercise year around. True, during summer you might want to exercise early in the day, but the sun shines 85 percent of the time and the higher elevation keeps summer temperatures several degrees cooler than in Tucson, 25 miles north. Traffic is unhurried and dozens of residents go everywhere in Green Valley by bicycle.

Established in 1964, Green Valley is an unincorporated community of 5,000 acres located on the flat Santa Cruz Valley floor. Covering an expanse seven by two miles in area, Green Valley is split down the center by I-19. Approximately 9,500 residences line the quiet streets that surround two large shopping centers and several smaller plazas. To minimize yard work, most lots are fairly compact, with the homes and townhouses often only a few yards apart. Hence many homes have privacy walls. Yards are gravel with cactus gardens. Most homes are of white stucco with flat or pitched red-tiled roofs. Ruling the entire community, and rigidly enforcing standards, are 32 powerful neighborhood associations. The result is that Green Valley is one of the best kept communities in the Southwest with an enviably low crime record.

Don't expect a lot of verdure but to the east are breathtaking views of the Santa Cruz Mountains while on the west are a series of copper mine slag heaps that blend imperceptibly with the desert landscape. Virtually the entire population is retired. And though you won't find many vegetarians, you often do see 70-year-old men jogging or bicycling. Considering the age level, many residents are confirmed fitness buffs.

Fitness activities are provided by five recreational centers, each with an exercise room, heated swimming pool, and tennis courts. In return for an annual fee of $189 per household, all facilities are for the exclusive use of residents. Three annual tennis tournaments and several men's and women's leagues, including the Green Valley Girls Team, are played on the eleven lighted clay tennis courts. Altogether, nine swimming pools serve the community and the Aquabelles, a women's precision swim team, has been featured in several national magazines. Weekly hikes are held by the Hiking Club, frequently in Madera Canyon, an oak woodland wilderness webbed by 70 miles of trail. Scores of local four-wheel drive roads and tracks provide challenging mountain bicycling and you can also bike to the summit of Mount Hopkins, site of the Whipple Observatory.

Clear, star-filled skies are so routine that several astronomical observatories are located here. Thus, among intellectual activities, it's not surprising to learn that the Sonora Astronomical Society has 250 Green Valley members. Also available are classes at an off-campus branch of the University of Arizona, and also at nearby Pima Community College. Additionally, Green Valley has its own 30,000 volume library and a Cultural Arts Coalition that sponsors chamber music concerts, locally-produced plays, a writers group, and a great books discussion group. A Green Valley branch of the Association of University Women testifies to the high level of education here. Then, too, all the cultural facilities of Tucson, including its famous symphony, are only 25 freeway miles distant.

Three large social centers help dispel loneliness. Square, round, and ballroom dancing groups flourish, and there are active newcomers and singles groups. We were assured that unlimited opportunities exist for volunteers willing to teach adult literacy, with dozens of other openings available through Green Valley service organizations. Seventeen mainline religious denominations were recently represented, plus an interesting metaphysical study group.

Several of these same churches operate wellness clinics aimed at promoting spiritual, mental, and physical health. A 60-bed allopathic health care center serves Green Valley, along with an emergency clinic and physicians in the most needed specialties.

A wide choice of new and resale homes and townhouses is normally available at prices slightly above the national average. Also available is a 175-unit full-service rental apartment complex with health care included.

Drawbacks? Air conditioning is essential for the long, hot summer afternoons. Many homes seem distressingly alike. The captive shopping clientele contributes to higher prices. And you should stay well away from I-19 and its noise.

Scores: Urban 10. Climate 4. Elevation 2. Terrain 4. Awareness 4. Nutrition 3. Fitness 5. Stress 2. Mind 2. Social 5. Volunteer 4. Spiritual 2. Care 3. Total Healthfulness: 50.

Information: CoC, Box 566, Green Valley, AZ 85622 (602-625-7575).

**HUNTSVILLE, AL.** Population: 175,000. Urban Stress: ZPG 2.5. Elevation: 700'. Home of the U.S. Army's Missile Command and Marshall Space Flight Center, plus the second

174

largest concentration of research industries in America, this north Alabama city combines the natural beauty of the Old South with the rocket and missile programs of the bold New South. Huntsville begins with its historic district of dogwood-lined streets bordered by antebellum homes. From this relaxed core it unfolds into a modern, fast-paced city on-the-move, steadily growing in all directions yet, through its beautification program, continuing to offer a satisfying and enriching quality of life. Despite having become the South's Silicon Valley, Huntsville remains a city of beautiful parks and trees. Located in the foothills of the Tennessee Valley, it lies close to the Tennessee River and its many adjoining lakes.

Drawn by its hi-tech economy, Huntsville has over 700 residents with non-medical Ph.D.'s, while the number of engineers exceeds 6,000. Add this affluent, highly-educated populace to the verdant environment and warm, snow-free climate, and you have all the ingredients for producing one of the most health-conscious cities in the South.

From the grassy two to three mile loops of Huntsville's Cross Country Running Park to other miles of fitness trails and on to the city's splendid heart exercise trail, Huntsville bristles with opportunities to become and stay fit. Twenty different exercise stations line the two-mile heart trail, equivalent to an hour's workout at a gym. During the rather humid summer (or at any time of year) you can swim laps at the Brahan Springs Natatorium or at a choice of other outdoor and indoor pools. Or you can swim from beaches at three large lakes within an hour's drive; or you can canoe-paddle on all three lakes plus the Tennessee River itself.

Tennis anyone? Included among Huntsville's 89 courts is a fine parks department tennis center with ten Rubico and six laykold courts (all lighted) and a pro shop. Similar facilities exist at the private Racquet Club and at the Athletic Club. Among the parks department's many programs is Men's Over 35 Basketball, while private martial arts, fitness and health clubs abound, several with their own swimming pools. For a change of pace, both roller and ice skating rinks are here.

For a real intellectual workout, many adults enjoy visiting NASA's Space and Rocket Center with its 60 hands-on displays of rocket and space equipment, including an opportunity to sample weightlessness, and a Spacedome Theater with total immersion projection. Through Alabama A&M and the University of Alabama-Huntsville (UAH), a tremendous choice of extension courses is available for adults. Equally rich in the performing arts, Huntsville's Art Council, Inc., gets you involved through frequent chamber music and symphony concerts, plays and musicals, and ballet and grand opera, all staged in the Von Braun Civic Center or in UAH. Also here is a well-stocked museum of art showcasing many famous prints and featuring touring arts exhibits.

While all the usual stress-management techniques are readily available, Huntsville also has a Comedy Club where you can laugh away the day's stress and tension. Meanwhile, the Pearly Gates natural foods restaurant offers healthful eating and the Garden Cove produce center supplies every type of natural food, produce, and whole grain in bins.

The big Senior Center serves all retirees with continuing education, travel trips, and frequent social events. It also recruits men and women 55 and over for the area's many volunteer openings that include unusually interesting positions in museums, art galleries, and other institutions that keep history and culture alive in Huntsville. Twenty-eight Christian and two Jewish places of worship cater to all mainline religions.

Huntsville's four hospitals (1,100 beds) plus 360 physicians (with over 40 specialties) has made it the regional health center of northern Alabama. With housing and living costs hovering close to the national average, Huntsville recently had a variety of resale homes listed from $70-$100,000, plus many more elegant residences in top neighborhoods from $100,000 up. Many homes have large pine-shaded lots and wide, green lawns. A score of modern apartment complexes offer two-bedroom unfurnished units at $400-$500 monthly, some with tennis courts, swimming pools, and fitness centers.

Huntsville normally has a variety of hi-tech employment and associated job vacancies in service occupations, but actual availability of openings is tied to the vagaries of federal spending.

Scores: Urban 7. Climate 3. Elevation 1. Terrain 4. Awareness 5. Nutrition 5. Fitness 5. Stress 4. Mind 4. Social 4. Volunteer 4. Spiritual 3. Care 4. Total Healthfulness: 53.

Information: C&VB, 700 Monroe Street, Huntsville, AL 35801 (800-225-6819 in AL; 800-843-0468 out of state). P&R, Box 308, Huntsville, AL 35804 (205-532-7418).


**KERRVILLE, TX.** Population: 26,000. Urban Stress: EST 1.7. Elevation: 1,646'. Decades ago, the Rockefeller Foundation ranked Kerrville as one of the five healthiest places in America. Their selection was based on such inherent factors as the warm, dry climate and the city's location in the heart of the panoramic Texas hill country. Due in part to the publicity which followed, this riverside resort has grown to become the most popular residential and retirement town in Texas, with possibly the highest quality of life in the state.

The air is pure, the water uncontaminated by agricultural run-off. For 50 miles around, this pleasant city is surrounded by limestone hills mantled by juniper and live oaks, and slashed by shade-dappled rivers lined by tall cypress trees. There is little congestion, no parking meters and the crime rate ranks among the nation's lowest. Kerrville has a splendid Olympic-sized swimming pool, 25 tennis courts, miles of hiking on state park trails and backcountry roads, and absolutely the finest year around, open road bicycle riding in the entire Sun Belt. Kerrville has tremendous potential to become one of the nation's leading centers of the health and fitness culture.

But most residents still eat a high-fat diet, and the majority prefer soft, easy living to exercise. Even though retired bicycling couples are moving here from New York and New

England, not a mention of the area's wonderful year around bicycling appears in any promotional literature. We found a mere two lanes reserved for lapswimming at the Olympic pool while the rest is used for frolicking and goofing off.

Nevertheless, Kerrville has such undeniable potential for fostering the low-risk lifestyle that, despite the lack of community and peer support, it scores a surprisingly high 50 for total healthfulness. Actually, you can find other health-conscious residents. The local bicycle club hosts weekend rides through the hills. You can join a group of seniors who have secured the Olympic pool for an hour of lapswimming three times a week in summer. Weekly hikes are offered by the Trailblazer Walk Club. Each Easter sees a marathon run and a three-day rally of 1,500 bicyclists, with a choice of daily rides through the hills. And plans are afoot to host an annual Senior Games.

Most fitness activity is sponsored by affluent health professionals, and by retirees who comprise 22 percent of the populace. Hundreds of younger retirees walk around the neighborhoods each morning, and some do try to follow a low-risk lifestyle. You can meet them at the Dietert Center, a multi-purpose retirement organization that holds social functions, places people in volunteer openings, and offers classes and get-togethers for everyone over 50.

The area's great bicycling begins 15 to 20 miles from the city (you drive out by car). Here, hundreds of miles of paved, low-traffic country roads web the wooded hills. The riding is for experienced bicyclists able to go 25-50-75 miles a day. Actually, you can ride for days, staying overnight at motels, and ranging as far as Big Bend National Park 400 miles west.

Join the Dietert Claim and you can lapswim in the 50-meter pool three times weekly in summer for just $5 a month. Or you could distance-swim in one of three pools in the Guadalupe River which meanders through the city. A health club has a heated 20-meter pool for winter swimming.

Kerrville has its own state park, with three others within an hour's drive, all with scenic hiking trails. The city's H.E.B. tennis complex and nineteen other courts provide lessons and scheduled tournaments. You can exercise the upper body by canoe paddling on three local lakes. And the parks department and local health clubs offer a choice of aerobic dance and exercise classes.

Intellectual enrichment is provided by a very complete adult education program, plus a handsome modern library. There are music festivals at Quiet Valley Ranch. The Performing Arts Society sponsors six events annually, from the Austin Ballet to chamber music, symphony concerts and Broadway musicals. And the Point Summer Theater stages three meritorious productions annually in the riverside Point Summer Theater.

Kerrville's traditional cowboy image discourages many from cutting down on steaks and other hi-fat western foods. But local apples and peaches are abundant. And at least one restaurant has an outstanding salad bar. Yoga, stretching, and other stress-management training is available. An active U-nity Church is included among Kerrville's 50 mostly mainline Protestant places of worship. And quality medical care is provided by a 175-bed community hospital, a 286-bed V.A. hospital, a cadre of 50 physicians skilled in most specialties, and a holistically-oriented cardiac rehabilitation center. A military hospital exists in San Antonio, 75 miles away.

A big draw is that living costs recently averaged 3 percent below the national average, while home prices have been depressed for several years. Recently, every type of home, condominium, mobile and manufactured homes, and rental apartments were available at very reasonable cost, including several self-contained communities for seniors aged 55-62 and over. Part-time jobs for retirees in stores and restaurants were also available. But for working adults, most better-paying jobs were limited to the health-care field.

Drawbacks? Kerrville has excellent resources for healthful living but lacks strong community support. The city is also dedicated to economic growth, thereby destroying the very qualities that are drawing retirees to settle here.

Scores: Urban 10. Climate 4. Elevation 2. Terrain 5. Awareness 3. Nutrition 2. Fitness 5. Stress 2. Mind 2. Social 3. Volunteer 4. Spiritual 3. Care 4. Total Healthfulness: 49.

Information: CoC, 1200 Sidney Baker, Kerrville, TX 78028 (512-896-1155). P&R, 800 Junction Highway, Kerrville, TX 78028 (512-257-7300).

**LA CROSSE, WI.** Population: 55,000. Urban Stress: EST 1.9. Elevation: 650'. If you're willing to view snow shoveling as part of your fitness program, this relaxed river town in west Wisconsin offers a cornucopia of opportunities to stay fit and healthy. Scores of residents aged 60 and over actively ice skate, ride mountain bicycles, and go cross-country skiing by day, then dance the night away or enroll in mentally-stimulating college classes.

Nestled between the Mississippi and forested bluffs, La Crosse is filled with parks webbed by hiking and cross-country skiing trails. Both Viterbo College and the University of Wisconsin, La Crosse (UWLC) provide outstanding opportunities for adult education plus an inspiring cultural program. Filled with natural beauty—and with clean air and a low crime rate—La Crosse also scores well for terrain therapy, nutrition, stress management, volunteer opportunities, and medical care.

With miles of riverside parks, and a 1,600-acre forest for its centerpiece, La Crosse blazes with brilliant foliage in fall. No one claims it's tropical: temperatures in January hover between 7° and 25°, and freezing temperatures occur from October 16 until April 25. But the city's largely German and Norwegian population thrive in this clear, cold weather.

A review of fitness activities begins with limitless miles of hiking and jogging trails, all within the city limits. You can hike for miles through Hixon Forest or continue on up to enjoy the stunning views from the 560' heights of Grandad Bluff, all without leaving town. A state-maintained bicycle trail starts from the city and connects with a 225-mile state-wide bike trail system that takes most people four days to cover. Good road bicycling can also be found on scores of county lanes and rustic roads. A similar network of superb flatwater canoeing rivers provides hundreds of miles of scenic paddling for upper body fitness.

In winter, golf courses and parks come alive with cross-country skiers and you'll find superb trail systems in Hixon Forest, Bluebird Spring Recreation Area and scores of other city and county parks. Besides several heated indoor 25-meter pools for year around lapswimming, during summer there's fine outdoor swimming from sandy river beaches. Tennis can be enjoyed year around at UWLC, and in summer at fourteen outdoor municipal courts. And a truly mind-blowing array of courses and classes for lifelong adult fitness is available at the Y, the parks department and UWLC.

Outstanding also is UWLC's Adult Fitness Unit, which offers a complete low-risk lifestyle based on aerobic, strength-building, and flexibility exercises combined with nutrition and stress management. Throw in eleven outdoor ice skating rinks (with adult ice hockey leagues) plus three roller skating rinks, and you have some idea of the extent of fitness opportunities in this clean, uncongested northern city.

Presented on the stages of Viterbo College and UWLC is an exciting winter series of plays, concerts, lectures, film, ballet, and opera. A strong art community is focused around the Pump House Regional Art Center, source of more visual arts, theater, and dance performances. And capping it all is a tempting assortment of evening classes in the arts and humanities offered to the public by UWLC.

Exemplifying the city's awareness of nutrition is the 500 Club in which a dozen participating restaurants serve tasty meals each containing no more than 500 calories. With its own Stress Management and Biofeedback Institutes (provided by hospitals and UWLC) La Crosse offers every type of relaxation skill, including rolfing and a course entitled *Wellness Through Touch and Massage.*

Opportunities for social contacts range from folk and ballroom dancing classes to adult singles groups and numerous square dancing events. Unlimited volunteer work is available at hospitals, the Y's, and at dozens of charitable organizations and service clubs.

Three large clinics and hospitals provide affordable, high-quality medical care. Between them, UWLC and Lutheran Hospital also offer a series of health education workshops and a *Seniors on the Move Fitness Program* designed to facilitate the low-risk lifestyle.

Housing of all types is readily available while both housing and living costs hover close to the national average. La Crosse has traditionally enjoyed a low unemployment rate with most new jobs being in hi-tech and the services sectors.

Scores: Urban 9. Climate 3. Elevation 1. Terrain 5. Awareness 5. Nutrition 4. Fitness 5. Stress 4. Mind 5. Social 3. Volunteer 4. Spiritual 2. Care 5. Total Healthfulness: 55.

Information: C&VB, Box 1895, Riverside Park, La Crosse, WI 54602 (608-782-2366). P&R, City Hall, La Crosse, WI 54601 (608-789-7533).


**LAS CRUCES, NM.** Population: (area) 85,000. Urban Stress: EST 2.2. Elevation: 3,900'. With its gentle mix of Hispanic, Native American, and Anglo cultures, this southern New Mexico city lures hundreds of early retirees each year. They come primarily to live in the dry, smog-free desert air and to seek a second career in the area's robust hi-tech economy. In the process, they reap a variety of subtle environmental and lifestyle health benefits.

Seen from a hilltop driving south on Interstate-25, Las Cruces appears as an oasis in the desert—a wide swathe of greenery spread across the Mesilla Valley floor and framed by the needle-sharp peaks of the Organ Mountains. At closer quarters, Las Cruces becomes a vibrant, modern city with wide, clean streets and an impressive mall, all clustered around the campus of New Mexico State University (NMSU) and ringed by a host of space age industrial plants.

But Las Cruces is also a city of two distinctly different socio-economic groups: first, approximately 12,000 affluent, well-educated residents who are employed at the university, at nearby White Sands Missile Range, and at various research plants; and second, the less-educated remainder who are responsible for Las Cruces' low per capita income. Helping to maintain the very youthful average age level are some 12,000 students enrolled at NMSU.

Las Cruces' proximity to the Mexican border gives it a strongly bilingual culture. Most middle class residents, of course, live in well-kept neighborhoods of modern, single story homes with rock or grass lawns and at least a splash of greenery. With only 8.5" of rain annually, irrigation is essential for any kind of verdure. Nonetheless, the city has launched a landscaping and beautification program. And from virtually every location, you can enjoy the vividly-colored sunsets and the compelling views of the 9,000' peaks of the Organ Mountains.

Although summer afternoons are undeniably hot, the sun shines on 350 days annually and nights are invariably cool. We found the best walking on two foothills hiking trails at Aguierre Springs Recreation Area seventeen miles out. However, many residents walk or run daily and the Mesilla Valley Track Club promotes frequent fun runs, biathlons, and triathlons. The Sun Country Striders Walk Club holds weekly hikes.

Most keen tennis players belong to the Las Cruces Tennis Club, which hosts many USTA and SWTA tournaments, while others play on courts in several city parks. Lapswimming is available at one city pool and at a lake beach in summer. For winter swimming, you must join a private club. And the Munson Senior Center promotes senior slimnastics and aerobics classes.

The strong cultural presence of NMSU is the main driving force behind Las Cruces' three performing arts theaters, the city's series of major chamber music and symphony concerts, and the presentations of ballet, drama, comedies, and musicals. The perennially clear skies make astronomy a popular pursuit, Retirees may enroll in any NMSU class for $62 and receive full credits. Meanwhile, Dona Ana Community College offers an enormous choice of continuing education classes in virtually every area of academic and vocational studies.

A large farmers' market and a natural foods store supply fresh local produce and whole grain breads. Munson Senior Center helps retirees overcome stress by teaching meditation and stretching techniques, while the Road Runners bus service provides an alternative to the stress of driving. Two thriving senior centers offer all residents 50 and over a variety of social activities, ranging from square and ballroom dances to tours and parties. The same centers recruit senior volunteers, as does the Retired Senior Volunteer Program which annually assigns 800 volunteers to 90 different agencies.

While Catholic churches predominate, virtually every Protestant church is also represented plus a variety of New Age and New Thought churches and groups in the campus area. A 286-bed acute care hospital plus 108 physicians representing 24 specialties, provide a high level of medical care. A small military hospital exists at White Sands.

Compared to the national average of 100 percent, medical costs in Las Cruces were recently 102 percent, housing 108 percent, living costs 102 percent, and utilities only 80 percent. A wide selection of homes is usually available, ranging from large homes in prestigious neighborhoods at $100-$120,000 to comfortable modern homes elsewhere at $70-$80,000, plush townhouses and condominiums from $55-$85,000, and a variety of rental apartments and mobile homes priced in proportion. Most job opportunities occur at the university and in the dynamic hi-tech economy.

Scores: Urban 8. Climate 4. Elevation 3. Terrain 4. Awareness 3. Nutrition 3. Fitness 3. Stress 2. Mind 4. Social 3. Volunteer 3. Spiritual 3. Care 3. Total Healthfulness: 46.

Information: C&VB, 311 North Downtown Mall, Las Cruces, NM 88001 (800-343-7827). P&R, 575 South Alameda, Las Cruces, NM 88005 (505-526-0668).


**LOS ALAMOS, NM.** Population: 22,000. Urban Stress: EST 1.8. Elevation: 7,410'. Anyone seeking a Shangri-La of healthful living, tucked away in the spectacular mountains of northern New Mexico, might well consider Los Alamos. That's exactly what the federal government did in 1942 when seeking a secluded hideaway for the top-secret atomic bomb project.

An entire federal city called Los Alamos was built atop a series of fingerlike mesas, with stunning views of the Rio Grande 1,700 feet below. In 1957, Los Alamos was thrown open to the public and the federally-built houses and city services were acquired by the residents.

At that time, Los Alamos consisted of small homes, duplexes, and quadruplexes scattered around the government research labs. A few years later, custom-built homes had occupied all the remaining land. All further expansion then took place in White Rock, another community 500' lower and 12 miles distant over a winding mountain road. A modern city of quality homes, motels, and stores that looks out over cliffs to a series of spectacular mountain ranges, White Rock today is home to one-third of the area's residents.

Still powering the economy is the Department of Energy's National Laboratory and a series of hi-tech research firms. With the exception of retirees, now numbering 11 percent of the area population, virtually all other residents consist of affluent, highly-educated scientists and researchers and their families. This profile explains the city's strongly health-conscious attitude, its preference for fitness activities, the city's high degree of safety, and its low crime rate, and the overall high quality of life.

Surrounded by rich, red mesas and dramatic vistas, Los Alamos is known for its pure air, spectacular sunsets, and turquoise skies. Its high elevation contributes to a statistically lower risk of heart disease. And though snow falls during the dry, sunny winter, the cool summers, and invigorating spring and fall seasons encourage outdoor activity throughout the year.

Surrounded by forested mountains, wilderness areas and National Monuments, the entire region is webbed with trails for hiking and cross-country skiing, with plenty of trails in National Forests and at several nearby monuments for mountain bicycling. A running club holds regular fun runs and several annual marathons. Many older adults also participate in the 500-Mile Walk Club. In Los Alamos and White Rock are: eighteen parks, some with tennis courts; two heart exercise trails; and the unique Larry R. Walkup Aquatic Center, the highest Olympic-sized swimming pool in the nation. Besides daily adult lapswimming, the center offers a Masters Swim Training program with regular meets. You can also ice skate in winter at an outdoor rink.

For major cultural events, most residents drive to Santa Fe (see), 35 miles distant. However, Los Alamos has a well-stocked 85,000 volume library, the Bradbury Science Museum with hands-on displays, a two-year campus of the University of New Mexico where retirees may audit classes, and the Fuller Lodge Art Center which showcases regional art.

The city's Senior Center sponsors a *Staying Healthy After Fifty* program. And scores of volunteer programs are always open, ranging from teaching literacy to working in the hospital. Besides the usual mainline churches, Los Alamos is home to a pioneering Zen Center. And the local 88-bed hospital and 38 physicians can handle virtually any emergency situation.

Although taxes have been traditionally low, home prices have risen somewhat above the national average—a situation that could change rapidly should the National Laboratory ever close. The original federally-built homes are more affordable, of course. But the most popular homes today are three-bedroom, two-bath ranch style houses or solar adobes. Another less expensive alternative are townhouses, or even modular or mobile homes. Most middle income retirees are usually able to find affordable housing. Since everything must be trucked in, the cost of living usually hovers a few percent above the national average. Skilled workers in hi-tech research fields may be able to find employment in Los Alamos, but opportunities in other fields are few.

Scores: Urban 10. Climate 4. Elevation 5. Terrain 5. Awareness 4. Nutrition 2. Fitness 5. Stress 2. Mind 2. Social 3. Volunteer 4. Spiritual 3. Care 3. Total Healthfulness: 52.

Information: CoC, Box 460, Los Alamos, NM 87544 (505-662-8105). P&R, Box 30, Los Alamos, NM 87544 (505-662-8170).

**MADISON, WI.** Population: 187,000. Urban Stress: ZPG 1.7. Elevation: 845'. Known as the Midwest's Bicycle Capital, Madison has more bicycles than cars, an unfailing indication that the city is a bastion of the health and fitness culture. Yet Madison also ranks as one of America's most livable cities. Its astonishingly beautiful setting on an isthmus rimmed by sapphire lakes provides a constantly high level of inspiring terrain therapy. The intellectual impact of the University of Wisconsin (UW), one of America's top ten state universities, guarantees a rich fund of stimulating music, drama, dance, and arts activities, plus exceptional opportunities for adult education. Five general hospitals, the university medical school, and 600 physicians make it a world class medical center. And its metro bus system helps minimize dependency on the automobile.

Free of slums and racial imbalances, and with one of the nation's consistently lowest crime rates, Madison is full of friendly, affluent, well-educated, health-conscious people. Despite the obvious prosperity, however, ostentation is ridiculed, and housemaids and chauffeurs are virtually unknown. Instead of expensive cars, high performance bicycles and community service are the keys to prestige. No one gives a second glance at women in saris or men in African robes. The population is sophisticated and cosmopolitan and extraordinarily supportive of every aspect of a low-risk lifestyle.

Despite a roller-coaster climate that ranges from 35° below in winter to the humid 90°s in summer, the city officially recognizes bicycles as a viable means of transportation. Over 140 miles of bike paths web the city and meander on picturesque routes around lakes. Throughout summer, over 100,000 trips are made by bicycle every day instead of by automobile, helping keep the air clean and the streets uncongested. From the city, a labyrinth of low-traffic dairy farm roads fans out all over Wisconsin, providing magnificent bicycle touring, while extensive mountain bicycling is available an hour away in Kettle Moraine Forest.

Madison abounds with opportunities for every kind of fitness activity including year-around lapswimming at a total of seven heated indoor pools. In winter, 25 miles of superbly-groomed trails (lighted at night) take you gliding on skinny skis through the city, and there are over 50 indoor and outdoor ice skating areas, 82 public tennis courts, and great opportunities for canoeing and rowing on the city's four lakes. Madison so abounds with every type of exercise activity that any fitness buff is guaranteed to strike rich pay dirt here.

Madison's exceptional resources for intellectual stimulation begin with the huge public and university libraries, and include an elegant Civic Center theater for the performing arts. Meanwhile, on campus are the Elvehjen Museum of Art and the Madison Art Center. The annual Festival of the Lakes features top drama, dance, and music performances plus visual art exhibits. Madison is also nationally known for its full season of symphony performances, its own opera and ballet companies, and at least twelve theater groups, producing everything from full-scale musicals to modern experimental theater.

A unique one-of-a-kind city filled with beautiful parks and trees, Madison also boasts a sixteen-block Mall-Concourse lined by ethnic restaurants and cafes where street musicians and jugglers and other fun happenings hold sway each noon.

The same exceptional standards apply to every other factor that contributes to a low-risk lifestyle. On every score, Madison ranks as one of America's healthiest and most livable cities.

Though not exorbitantly priced, the cost of homes and rentals runs about 20-30 percent above the national average. The university and state government are the main employers. But though the economy is dynamic and expanding, competition for jobs is quite intense. Hundreds of residents have taken pay cuts to be able to move here from big, polluted cities.

Scores: Urban 10. Climate 3. Elevation 1. Terrain 5. Awareness 5. Nutrition 4. Fitness 5. Stress 4. Mind 5. Social 4. Volunteer 4. Spiritual 5. Care 5. Total Healthfulness: 60.

Information: CoC, Box 71, Madison, WI 53701 (608-256-8348).For P&R write: Madison School Community Recreation, 1045 East Dayton Street, Room 120, Madison, WI 53703 (608-266-6070).

**MELBOURNE, FL.** Population: 60,000. Urban Stress: EST 2.8. Elevation: 20'. As computer and electronics plants replace the once-dominant Cape Kennedy space industry, Melbourne has become a hi-tech city of affluent baby boomers with a sprinkling of early retirees. Although Melbourne is full of busy traffic, and is growing steadily, it is far removed from the frenzied pace and overbuilding of South Florida. Located on Florida's Upper East Coast, where much waterfront property is federally-owned and safe from development, the Melbourne area has earned a reputation for its exceptional quality of life.

Today, Melbourne is a hub city for a strip metropolis of subdivisions, golf and country club developments, and mobile home parks that reach south for miles to Palm Bay and north for more miles to Titusville. From these mainland towns, causeways reach east across the broad Indian River (intercoastal waterway) to a string of barrier beach islands flanked by 32 miles of sunbleached sands. On these beach islands are several beach resorts plus Kennedy Space Center, Patrick Air Force Base, Merritt Island National Wildlife Refuge, and the Canaveral National Seashore with its thirteen miles of virgin beach. Throw in two great rivers, two huge lakes, and over 800 miles of canoeable waterfront, and you have a vast recreational area brimming with opportunities for staying fit and healthy. Housing costs are still reasonable, and among all hi-tech cities in America, Melbourne recently reported the lowest living costs.

Rich in subtropical growth and with hundreds of miles of scenic waterfront, the Melbourne area provides a significant level of terrain therapy. With an average temperature of 61° in January and 82° in August, the climate is among the most equable in Florida.

Four city parks have exercise trails, with walking and jogging trails in six others. Inviting hiking trails wind through Merritt Island Wildlife Refuge. And at low tide, you can walk or jog for miles along the relatively uncrowded beaches.

Although public tennis courts and swimming pools are available, most fitness buffs prefer to enroll in the Pines Resort and Tennis Club (30 laykold all-weather courts and a 25-meter swimming pool) or the American Lifestyle Club (Olympic-sized swimming pool) while military retirees play tennis at Patrick Air Force Base. Though not generally considered a good bicycling city, Melbourne has bicycle trails along many streets and thoroughfares. Canoeing, of course, is excellent and you'll find literally hundreds of miles of good paddling, from the St. John's River to huge Mosquito Lagoon and on to a wilderness canoe trail through the city.

Opportunities to cultivate the mind focus on Melbourne's six-story performing arts center where plays, musicals, concerts, and dance productions are presented. Other plays are presented at the Ensemble Theater. Appearing frequently are the upbeat East Coast Dance Theater, the Brevard Symphony, and the Space Coast Philharmonic. Science buffs enjoy programs at the Space Coast Science Center and at Cocoa's Planetarium. Available for auditing by retirees are classes at Cocoa's University of Central Florida, while science-oriented Melbourne offers a wide assortment of adult education courses.

Among nutrition pluses, Melbourne is home of the famous Indian River citrus, several restaurants have extensive salad bars, and regular workshops are offered in nutrition. With its many square, folk, and ballroom dance clubs, adult social clubs and the Brevard Adult Singles Club, Melbourne provides an abundance of opportunities for social contacts.

Along with volunteer organizations like the Retired Senior Volunteer Program, the area is full of service clubs in need of help.

Led by Melbourne's 528-bed Holmes Regional Medical Center, half a dozen hospitals and 600 physicians provide every type of allopathic medical treatment. Military retirees use the hospital at Patrick Air Force Base. Meanwhile, 44 chiropractors provide a variety of alternative healing techniques.

Worth looking at is the city of Titusville (pop. 40,000), some 20 miles north of Melbourne, a less congested and more relaxed community near Canaveral National Seashore and with its own health and fitness clubs, community college, swimming pools, and its own volunteer clearing house.

Every type of housing is available, from plush waterfront and fairway homes to comfortable ranch style homes, townhouses, condominiums, and mobile home parks, all at prices appreciably lower than in South Florida. Property taxes, water and sewage rates have long been below average while many businesses give discounts to retirees.

Drawbacks? Melbourne's proximity to teeming Orlando intensifies crowding at some beaches and at beach parking on weekends.

Scores:  Urban 6. Climate 4. Elevation 1. Terrain 4. Awareness 4. Nutrition 2. Fitness 4. Stress 1. Mind 3. Social 3. Volunteer 4. Spiritual 3. Care 4. Total Healthfulness: 43.

Information: Melbourne CoC, 1005 East Strawbridge, Melbourne, FL 32901 (407-726-7321). Titusville CoC, 2000 South Washington, Titusville FL 32780 (305-267-3036). Melbourne P&R, 1515 South Sarno Road, Melbourne, FL 32935 (407-242-6529).


**MINNEAPOLIS-ST. PAUL, MN.** Population: (area) 2,300,000. Urban Stress: ZPG Minneapolis 3. St. Paul 2.8. Elevation: 750'. When you see all the joggers, walkers, and cross-country skiers in the Twin Cities, it comes as no surprise to learn that Minnesotans have the nation's longest life expectancy. Half the population of Minnesota lives in the Twin Cities and the majority are avid fitness and culture buffs. Trails for running, walking, or ski-touring wind for dozens of miles through a series of parks, around lakes and along riverbanks, and in winter you can even admire wildlife as you ski on trails through the famed Minneapolis Zoo. Throw in a vigorous and sophisticated cultural life, with an extravaganza of opera, symphony, theater, and educational opportunities, and you'll understand why St. Paul, as well as larger Minneapolis, have won a score of City Livability awards.

Both sibling cities—they're located elbow-to-elbow on opposite sides of the Mississippi—have transformed their former rundown milling areas into charming riverside parks and arty neighborhoods of ethnic restaurants and funky bars. Residential sections are clean, safe, and attractive and the crime rate is among America's lowest. The only drawback we found was rather severe carbon monoxide pollution, something difficult to avoid in a metropolis this size.

A trendy and aggressively modern business, hi-tech and finance center, Minneapolis is a vigorous industrial city with a skyline of glass-walled hi-rises. But despite the flat terrain, many of its industries—along with the huge state university campus—are tucked away unobtrusively among the city's 22 lakes and 150 parks. Smaller St. Paul climbs from river bluffs up tree-lined avenues to hills terraced with a mix of old and new sections. Its location as Minnesota's capital has kept St. Paul vibrant and contemporary yet reserved and dignified. It, too, has twenty parks with a total 83 lakes. Both cities have miles of glass-enclosed, climate-controlled pedestrian walkways that link all important buildings without having to walk outdoors.

Twin-Citians are best described as liberal-minded with an upbeat mood and a brisk, upscale lifestyle in which fitness is taken for granted. They are avid recyclers of glass and aluminum and a city ordinance bars all non-recyclable food packaging. Few cities are more supportive of a pro-health lifestyle.

The miles of riverside trails, parks, and lakes inspire worthwhile terrain therapy despite the generally unimpressive scenery. Depending on season, you'll find limitless opportunities to hike, bike, jog, or ski cross-country on over 100 miles of trails that wind around lakes and through secluded parklands to a scenic river gorge. In winter, several big parks and golf courses offer cross-country ski rentals, groomed trails and warming houses, while skaters take over dozens of lakes. St. Paul alone has several hundred public tennis courts and you can lapswim year around at a choice of pools. Throughout the year, the various parks departments and Ys offer an unbelievable variety of exercise and fitness classes.

To benefit from all this, of course, you must enjoy being outdoors in cold weather. There's ample snow throughout the long, severe winter when midday temperatures often hover around 12°F. But midsummer days can be humid.

Home of the University of Minnesota, America's largest state university located on a single campus, Minneapolis is well supplied with natural foods stores and stress-management classes. Volunteer opportunities are legion. The parks department alone recruits hundreds of adults and seniors to help rehabilitate the physically-handicapped and for clean-up and beautification programs. Likewise, numerous organizations provide constant opportunities for dances and social get-togethers for all age levels. Virtually every mainstream and New Age church is here while eastern philosophies and human potential movements are also well represented. Also, both cities have excellent accessibility to high quality hospitals and doctors.

Yet it's in opportunities for intellectual activity that the Twin Cities really excel. The cultural scene is vigorous, with an abundance of corporate-subsidized and, therefore, very affordable world class opera, ballet, symphony, and theater productions. Home of the Minnesota Orchestra, the St. Paul

Chamber Orchestra, three opera companies, a dozen theater companies producing both classical and original works—plus such famous theaters as the Guthrie and Crawford Livingston—the Twin Cities present a continuous bill of top-flight cultural fare. Add in the outstanding Walker Art Museum, St. Paul's Science Museum, and the Ordway Music Theater plus a wealth of campus activities, and the scope for intellectual activity is almost limitless.

Along with the university, big insurance and computer firms keep the economy exceptionally stable. The unemployment rate is usually low, with an above-average choice of career opportunities. Housing and rentals are plentiful, especially in four adjoining suburban cities known as North Metro Minneapolis.

Scores: Urban 5. Climate 3. Elevation 1. Terrain 3. Awareness 5. Nutrition 4. Fitness 5. Stress 4. Mind 5. Social 4. Volunteer 4. Spiritual 4. Care 5. Total Healthfulness: 52.

Information. *Minneapolis:* C&VB, 1219 Marquette Avenue, #300, Minneapolis, MN 55403 (612-348-4313). P&R, 310 South Fourth Avenue, Minneapolis, MN 55145 (612-348-2142). *St. Paul:* C&VB, 600 NCL Tower, 445 Minnesota Street, St. Paul, MN 55101 (800-627-6101). P&R, 24 West Fourth Street, St. Paul, MN 55102 (612-292-7400).

**MISSOULA, MT.** Population: 80,000. Urban Stress: EST 2. Elevation: 3,210'. Powered by all the energy and vitality of a major university, Missoula is an exceptionally health-conscious town surrounded by the mountain wilderness of western Montana. The wide, clean streets were made for bicycling and almost every downtown facility has bicycle parking. This isn't surprising when you learn that every other resident owns a bicycle, and the city supports a strong community bicycle program. As in every bike-friendly city, Missoula's widespread interest in bicycling indicates strong underlying community and peer support for living the low-risk lifestyle.

Missoula's inventory of healthful assets begins with the city's beautiful riverfronts, renovated historic core, and colorful flower gardens. An upbeat city with lots of elbow room, Missoula earns a high score for terrain therapy. All around, towering national forests and dramatic mountains provide a winter backdrop of snow, trees, and frozen rivers, and in summer the mile-deep valleys are rich with sunfilled meadows.

Missoula's long, cold winters are responsible for its freedom from big city woes and urban crunch. The winter snowfall of 49" ensures superb cross-country skiing on dry powder snow. And sheltering mountains are responsible for the almost perfect months from May to September. Epitomizing Missoula's warm, friendly, frontier spirit is its almost classless society. Loggers, wranglers, and truck drivers live next door to prominent writers and artists and others from all walks of life. Enlivening the perennially youthful scene are 10,000 students attending the University of Montana (UM).

Its location at the hub of five valleys gives Missoula access to unlimited miles of dirt roads and trails for summer hiking and mountain bicycling, and for Nordic skiing in winter. Road bicycling is also reportedly good. You can pick from an enormous variety of mountain trails for day hikes. Cross-country skiers can choose between the expertly-groomed Nordic trails at ski resorts like Marshall or Snow Bowl—mere minutes from downtown—or rugged trails through Lolo Pass, Pattee Canyon, or Lower Rattlesnake Wilderness areas.

For upper body fitness, a string of beautiful blue glacial lakes provide exhilarating still-water canoeing within fifteen minutes of the center. Thirty-five parks department tennis courts cater to tennis buffs, while the Y and Sports Medicine Fitness Center each have a 25-meter heated lapswimming pool with weight rooms and indoor running tracks. All welcome drop-ins. Additionally, residents use the university pool and tennis courts.

196

A modern comprehensive university, UM arranges a dynamic succession of cultural events. From the Riverfront Summer Theater in a big-top tent to the MT Repertory Theater and the MCT Community Theater, Missoula's stages come alive with summer entertainment. And throughout the year, there are lectures and concerts by nationally-recognized personalities.

All the usual yoga and stretching exercise classes exist to offset the effects of stress. Missoula's nutrition awareness is evident in the summer season Farmers' Market and in the popularity of whole wheat and sprouts sandwiches, available even in some fast food eateries. Due to the youthful age level, residents told us that the fellowship of fitness activities was the best way to meet new people. Obviously, Missoula is not your average retirement city. But for active seniors-on-the-go, it can be an exciting and stimulating place to live.

With a ratio of one physician to every 400 residents (two-and-a-half times the national average) Missoula is home to three hospitals that together can handle everything from open heart surgery to kidney dialysis. The Y also presents a series of lectures on living the low-risk lifestyle.

Housing costs remain a smidgen above the national average as does the cost of living. Meanwhile, job openings occur mostly in connection with the university and in medical fields, or in the wood products industry. The only criticism we heard concerned the noisy presence of snowmobiles on national forest roads in winter. Fortunately, there aren't too many on weekdays.

Scores:   Urban 9. Climate 3. Elevation 3. Terrain 5. Awareness 5. Nutrition 3. Fitness 5. Stress 2. Mind 3. Social 3. Volunteer 3. Spiritual 3. Care 4. Total Healthfulness: 51.

Information: C&VB, Box 7577, Missoula, MT 59807 (406-543-6623). P&R, 100 Hickory Street, Missoula, MT 59801 (406-721-7275).

**MOAB, UT.** Population: 4,700. Urban Stress: EST 1.7. Elevation: 4,020'. Scoring tops for Urban Stress, Terrain Therapy, and Fitness Activities, Moab is a small, quiet, stress-free Mormon town in the heart of southeast Utah's spectacular Canyonlands country. In a verdant valley beside the Colorado River, Moab is surrounded by vividly colored red rock walls and rugged canyons while, to the east, the snow-capped La Sal Mountains tower above a vast wilderness of lakes, streams, and lush meadows bordered by the firs and aspens of Manti La Sal National Forest.

Once a rip-roaring uranium mining town, Moab's fame today rests on its exceptional mountain bicycling. Often called the Fat Tire Capital of the West, thousands of mountain bicyclists from all over the world come here to ride such legendary trails as the 10-mile Slickrock Trail, the 35-mile Porcupine Rim Trail, and other world class trails that lead through a wonderland of mesas, canyons and high desert terrain. Add in hundreds more miles of backcountry roads and single track trails in Arches and Canyonlands National Parks, and in the La Sal Mountains, and you begin to understand why so many fitness and bicycling enthusiasts are buying retirement homes in the area. Not only are these challenging trails available for bicycling, but they are equally suited for hiking and, in winter, for cross-country skiing. For good measure you can canoe and swim on quiet stretches of the Colorado River. Also here are tennis courts and a good adult lapswimming center. For anyone who loves to bicycle over naked slickrock, or to hike or tour-ski, this dry desert town offers a supremely healthful lifestyle.

Living here already are a health-conscious assortment of conservationists and river runners, plus fugitives of all ages from Denver, Los Angeles, and other stress-torn big cities. Although predominantly Mormon, Moab has more churches of other denominations per capita than any other Utah city, including the non-denominational Moab Christian Center. We also encountered a surprising number of people who followed New Age and New Thought philosophies.

Moab is also beginning to draw its share of painters and other artists, some lured here by the University of Utah's fine arts college. Incidentally, the college offers a splendid choice of classes in Southwest Native American art and craftwork. Otherwise, the biggest cultural event is the annual music festival that accompanies the famous Fat Tire Festival at the end of October. And though many people follow a low-fat diet, they must depend on the produce sections of several local supermarkets for their fruits and vegetables.

Not that there's much stress, here but for yoga, biofeedback and other stress-management techniques, you're usually on your own. And, since the Mormon Church operates its own welfare system, volunteer openings may be harder to locate. Again, the story is that early pioneers found Moab so healthful that they had to shoot somebody to start a cemetery. True or not, the city is served today by a small but well-equipped 36-bed hospital, several capable physicians and two chiropractors. Nowadays, sports injuries tend to be the most common medical problem. And, of course, the crime rate is low.

Most fitness buffs get together at Don Amigo's Mexican Restaurant before setting forth on their mountain bikes for Hoorah Pass, Poison Spider Mesa, Gemini Bridges or any of the other fearsomely-named destinations tucked away in the awesome vastness of the sandstone ledges that reach away to the east of Moab.

Haulage costs to this isolated locale make food prices slightly above average. But recently, home prices were still at soothing levels and the best three-bedroom, two-bath, two-car garage homes sold at $60-$70,000, with many others for considerably less. Many homes here use passive solar heating. Don't look for job openings, but any new business venture in the sports and outdoor recreation fields seems to stand an above-average chance of success.

Drawbacks? Summer afternoons can be quite hot, so most people exercise early in the day.

Scores: Urban 10. Climate 3. Elevation 3. Terrain 5. Awareness 4. Nutrition 3. Fitness 5. Stress 1. Mind 1. Social 2. Volunteer 1. Spiritual 2. Care 3. Total Healthfulness: 43.

Information: CoC, 64 South Main Street, Moab, UT 84532 (801-259-7531).

**MOUNT DORA, FL.** Population: 7,800. Urban Stress: EST 1.8. Elevation: 184'. It's hard to imagine being able to live healthfully in high-stress Orlando, a Central Florida boom town obsessed with growth and corporate profits and bristling with freeways filled with kamikaze drivers. But amazingly, only 25 miles north of this crowded and congested metropolis is the laid-back, lakeside resort of Mount Dora, a relaxed old-fashioned town that is the very antithesis of restless, rootless Orlando. Best of all, you can live healthfully in low-stress Mount Dora, and simply drive into Orlando for a few hours whenever you need to sample its big city culture or resources.

Perched on a high bluff overlooking the broad expanse of Lake Dora, the town of Mount Dora is one of the prettiest, safest, most livable, and most healthful small towns in Florida. Picturesque, gingerbread-adorned Victorian homes, and more recent ranch-style houses, line hilly streets shaded by gnarled, moss-bearded oaks. Although Mount Dora is gradually becoming a bedroom community for Orlando commuters, it remains peaceful, serene and low-key—a delight to anyone prone to stress. Herons, egrets, and ibis cruise overhead and one of the city's parks preserves twelve acres of wetland teeming with bird and animal life.

While it isn't yet filled with joggers, bicyclists, and vegetarians, Mount Dora's demographics show that 27 percent of the population consists of well-heeled retirees from the Midwest and Northeast, while another 16 percent are aged 30-44 and consist mainly of affluent young professionals who commute to Orlando. Despite the 45-minute daily commute, these baby boomers prefer Mount Dora, not only for its laid-back lifestyle and ever-present natural beauty, but also for its pure air and drinking water, and its high elevation. Even during the long, hot summers, fresh breezes filter through the trees, modifying the summer humidity, and making winters crisp and zestful.

Every morning during our recent visit, we watched a 70-year-old retiree paddle a kayak the six-mile length of Lake Dora as part of his cardiovascular fitness schedule. And we can personally vouch for the splendid canoeing. We took our seventeen-foot Grumman between the tall cypresses of the Dora Canal and on out into a scenic chain of lakes linked by tree-bordered rivers and waterways.

Dozens of people daily walk or jog the four beautiful miles around Lake Gertrude. Indicative of Mount Dora's high level of health awareness is the city's twenty-station heart exercise trail which contains 32 different exercises and five heartbeat check points. The active local bicycle club organizes bicycle tours of all lengths on Central Florida's backroads, and each fall the city sponsors a three-day bicycle festival with daily rides. A new Y heated outdoor pool provides several weekly adult lapswimming sessions. There are six tennis courts. And Mount Dora has a basketball league for adults over 29.

Culturally, Mount Dora is known for its Ice House Theater, one of the best players groups in Florida. The town also sponsors a community concert series and an annual art show. Should you ever feel uptight, there are yoga classes to help you unwind. Making friends is easy in this small community. And Mr. A.M. Liverwright, of the Chamber of Commerce, assured us that volunteer opportunities are available in a wide range of activities. A well-equipped small hospital is available four miles away. Or, within an hour, one can be at the huge Orlando Regional Medical Center, a major teaching hospital.

Available in Orlando is a choice of aquatic centers and swimming clubs, a dozen top private tennis clubs, and more miles of hiking and jogging trails. With its cultural life funded by the well-heeled United Arts Foundation, Orlando's various theaters and performing arts centers stage a long winter season of topflight ballet, opera, Broadway plays, musicals, symphony and chamber music concerts, and visual arts exhibits. For continuing education, Orlando's Valencia Community College offers retirees a choice of dozens of noncredit courses in almost every subject.

Normally, Mount Dora has scores of attractive homes for sale, with charming two to three bedroom homes recently priced at $65-$100,000 and luxurious condominiums from $55,000 up. Hundreds of residents prefer living in mobile or manufactured homes in some of the area's large adult-only parks, many of which have extensive recreational and social activities. Rental apartments are also usually available. While Mount Dora itself has few employment openings, Orlando traditionally offers a wide choice of career opportunities.

Scores: Urban 10. Climate 4. Elevation 1. Terrain 5. Awareness 4. Nutrition 3. Fitness 4. Stress 2. Mind 2. Social 3. Volunteer 4. Spiritual 2. Care 3. Total Healthfulness: 47.

Information: CoC, Box 196, Mount Dora, FL 32757 (904-383-2165). P&R, Box 176, Mount Dora, FL 32757 (904-383-2141).

**PARADISE, CA.** Population: 35,000. Urban Stress: EST 1.8. Elevation: 1,800'. Younger couples with children—refugees from the big smogbound California cities—are moving into this peaceful retirement town in northern California's Sierra foothills. Retirees, too, continue to relocate in Paradise, creating a fairly steady population growth. But Paradise still manages to retain its small town flavor. A town of rustic homesites tucked away under tall pines in a park-like setting, Paradise is relatively free from serious crime and also from smog, fog, and congestion.

Above the valley fog and the worst of the summer heat, its elevation is also low enough to escape almost all winter snow. On a ridge rising 2,000' higher are the three historic suburbs of Magalia, Stirling City, and Inskip, now filled with retirees. In spring, the air is fragrant with apple blossoms, and all around are mountains, canyons, streams, and lofty pines.

Notwithstanding the influx of younger couples, the city's economy is solidly based on retirement checks. With a median age of 48, half the population is retired. Nowadays, of course, an increasing number are affluent, active early retirees, many lured here by the opportunity to stay fit in such a healthful environment.

Great walking is everywhere, from Bille and Coutolenc Parks in the city to forested trails in Feather River Canyon and Lake Oroville State Recreation Area. (In winter, residents cross-country ski on frozen Lake Oroville and canoe on it in summer.) Close to downtown is a jogging and heart exercise trail plus an outdoor swimming pool (with adult swim hours and swim-and-trim classes) and eight public tennis courts. More racquetball and swimming is available at a private health club. And the parks department offers low-impact aerobics, dancercize, and strength-building exercise classes.

For continuing education classes, most residents drive 14 miles to California State University in Chico. During June, however, Paradise hosts a monthlong arts festival with guest soloists and concerts, plays, and ballet by regional performing groups.

Since California ranks as the nation's most nutrition-conscious state, many Paradise residents raise organically grown vegetables and fruits. Apple orchards abound. And local Chinese and Italian restaurants serve a distinctly low-fat cuisine. It's difficult imagining anyone becoming stressed in Paradise but, just in case, the parks department provides a chance to relax through classes in t'ai chi and yoga.

From hobby clubs to the active Senior Singles group and the thriving Adult Activity Center, the parks department provides abundant opportunities to socialize at get-togethers and dances of all types. To help shut-ins, or to provide meals-on-wheels, volunteers are constantly needed throughout the community. Catering to spiritual needs are 29 churches of all principal denominations. And health care is provided by a 109-bed hospital, 32 physicians, 10 chiropractors, and an osteopath.

While housing costs are far below those in southern California, an elegant home still costs $250,000. Most retirees should count on spending $100-$120,000 (recent prices) for a comfortable middle class home. Smaller homes sell from $70,000. Over 1,500 mobile and manufactured homes are located in Paradise, with prices from $55-$70,000. In the same price range are many new condominiums and rental apartments. Living costs are close to the national average. The parks department offers job training for residents 55 and over, but opportunities for full-time career employment are few.

Drawbacks? The mercury exceeds 90° on some 65 summer afternoons annually and falls below 32° on some 32 days each winter.

Scores: Urban 10. Climate 3. Elevation 2. Terrain 5. Awareness 4. Nutrition 3. Fitness 4. Stress 2. Mind 2. Social 3. Volunteer 3. Spiritual 2. Care 2. Total Healthfulness: 45.

Information: CoC, 5587 Scottwood, Paradise, CA 95969 (916-877-9356). P&R, 6626 Skyway, Paradise, CA 95969 (916-872-6393).


**PENSACOLA, FL.** Population: 70,000. Urban Stress: EST 1.9. Elevation: 60'. To this easygoing West Florida city, the booming growth of South Florida is anathema. The lack of high rises, and the city's many blocks of historic homes, reveals Pensacola's preference for a relaxed pace and its own stable rate of growth. Built between bayous where red cliffs and golden bluffs face huge Escambia Bay, Pensacola is one of Florida's hilliest cities. To the south, east, and west, a total 32 miles of powder white beaches line spindly barrier islands, all accessible by car yet preserved for posterity in a National Seashore. The air is pure, congestion is mild, and this laid-back city in the sun has been the retirement choice of thousands of former military men.

Settings for homes range from waterfront to wooded hills with views of the Gulf. And with a green sheath of moss-festooned oaks and magnolias shading the older sections, Pensacola offers a worthwhile measure of terrain therapy. Although a hurricane can be expected every eight years, Pensacola enjoys mild winters and warm, moderately humid summers, with a total 343 sunny days each year. While it isn't a hi-tech capital bursting with Ph.D.'s, the existance of the Everyman Natural Foods Coop, and a flourishing cultural life, indicates an above-average awareness of health, nutrition, and fitness needs. The ambiance is Southern and relaxed and ex-military retirees outnumber civilian senior citizens.

Pensacola's involvement with fitness is evident in the annual running events which range from a 10K run in May to a marathon each December and a fantastic 50-mile American Cancer Society run each February. For several hours at low tide, you can walk, jog, or run along miles of undeveloped beach, all easily accessible by car. The Pensacola Bicycle Club also organizes Sunday morning rides on backroads around nearby Milton and you can always ride the bike path along the Fort Pickens Road to the beach. Led by Spott Tennis Center, the city's 34 public tennis courts are used for tournaments for all ages. However, many tennis buffs prefer to play at private clubs like the Racquet Club or the Fitness Club. As with tennis, many swimming enthusiasts also prefer to swim at private clubs like Cordova Park or Scenic Heights Swim Club. Also available are active Ys.

When it comes to canoe paddling for exercise, Pensacola is a standout. Not only is canoeing great on the many back bays, but at Tomahawk Landing (close to nearby Milton) canoeists can access a series of clear, springfed rivers lined by white sandbanks that wind for dozens of miles through the solitude of Blackwater River State Forest.

Led by the Arts Council of Northwest Florida, Pensacola stages a year around series of plays, musicals, and concerts featuring several top regional dance and players groups plus the surprisingly talented Pensacola Symphony. Chamber music concerts are presented at historic Christ Church with most other presentations held in the handsomely restored Saenger Theater. The Museum of Art, housed in a former jail, hosts touring exhibits and also sponsors the Great Gulf Coast Art Festival each year. Also available is a wide choice of adult education classes, while senior citizens may audit certain classes at the University of West Florida.

Helping residents alleviate stress are the eight-week Relaxation and Meditation Seminars held at Baptist Hospital Health and Wellness Center, while a county transit bus service, with senior discounts, makes weekday driving unnecessary for many.

The Leisure Department's active Over-55 Club sponsors frequent social events, including a Mardi Gras Ball for seniors, held each January. With three large hospitals and a Navy hospital, Pensacola has become the medical center of West Florida.

From refurbished eighteenth and nineteenth century homes in the city's historic districts to comfortable suburban homes, condominiums, and townhouses, Pensacola offers a wide choice of housing options, all available at some of Florida's lowest prices. Many are on waterfront, or in wooded subdivisions, and you'll find many attractive complexes of rental apartments. Likewise, the city's cost of living has long been among the lowest in the South. And while most of the better employment openings occur in medical care and educational fields, Pensacola has traditionally enjoyed a low unemployment rate.

Scores:   Urban 9. Climate 4. Elevation 1. Terrain 4. Awareness 4. Nutrition 4. Fitness 4. Stress 3. Mind 4. Social 3. Volunteer 3. Spiritual 3. Care 4. Total Healthfulness: 50.

Information: C&VB, 1401 East Gregory Street, Pensacola, FL 32501 (800-874-1234 outside Florida; 800-343-4321 in Florida). P&R, Box 12910, Pensacola, FL 32521 (904-435-1770).

**PORTLAND, OR.** Population: (area) 1,400,000. Urban Stress: ZPG 3.2. Elevation: 175'. Since 1970, a major renaissance has given Portland an elegantly-restored downtown, one of America's best transit systems, a dynamic hi-tech economy, a rich cultural life, and dozens of lush parks, greenbelts, gardens, and fountains. Nowadays, Portland constantly receives accolades for its quality of life. And it offers a lifestyle almost identical to that once available in San Francisco—but which no longer exists in California.

In the mild, damp climate, lawns and trees stay green all year. Forested parks reach almost into the center and include the largest wilderness park in a U.S. city plus hundreds of acres of rose and rhododendron gardens, a beautiful arboretum webbed by 10 miles of trails, and miles of riverside parks. Snowcapped Mount Hood is visible from almost every neighborhood. Providing exceptional livability, this combination gives Portland the highest score for terrain therapy.

Of the energetic, active but relaxed and younger-than-average population, 47 percent are baby boomers and 8 percent younger retirees, while 18 percent exercise daily (compared to a national average of under 8 percent), 33 percent own a bicycle, and 12 percent play tennis regularly. Although maligned for its drizzling winter days, Portland's annual rainfall of 37" is less than that of many eastern cities and the climate is free of almost all extremes. The air is clean and so is the water in the Willamette River which flows through the city.

A network of 140 miles of hiking and bicycling trails encircle the city, linking every major park and recreation area and providing limitless opportunities for fitness exercise. Lapswimming is available year around at three indoor pools and in summer at eleven more. The parks department maintains a splendid system of 115 outdoor tennis courts plus the Portland Tennis Center. Bicyclists find miles of safe backroads in adjoining Washington County, while mountain bicycling opportunities are legion. It's an hour's drive to a choice of grand hiking and cross-country skiing trails in the Cascades. And the parks department offers dozens of exercise classes for seniors and adults, as well as organized bike rides, canoe trips, back country hikes, cross-country ski trips, and even climbs of major peaks.

Portland is famed for its unusually pure drinking water, its many oriental restaurants serving gourmet low-fat cuisines, and its abundance of organically-grown fruits and vegetables. Nutritionally-aware Portlanders purchase four times as much food from natural food stores as do people in traditional cities. The parks department offers scores of stress-management classes in yoga, stretching, and meditation.

Contributing to Portland's wealth of mind-stimulating activities are the Oregon Symphony and the Oregon Symphony Pops orchestras plus several top baroque and chamber music orchestras. The city is alive with companies practicing the thespian arts, and Portland has its own opera association and two top ballet companies. The result is an almost continuous series of performances on the four stages of the city's lavish Center for the Performing Arts. Focusing attention on the visual arts, and also providing art instruction, is the Oregon Art Institute, the largest gallery in the Northwest. A science museum and planetarium provide additional thought-provoking activity, while both the parks department and the various continuing education programs provide a tremendous assortment of study opportunities.

Scoring at least average for social activities, volunteer openings and for its many paths to spiritual growth, Portland is a standout for quality of health care. Not only is the city home of the Oregon Health Sciences Institute with its medical school and teaching hospitals, but it also has 22 acute care hospitals and one of the highest doctor-patient ratios of any large U.S. city. Under Oregon's progressive medical laws, licensed alternative health care practitioners can practice as primary health care providers. As a result, Portland is also home to accredited colleges of chiropractic, naturopathic and oriental medicine, and massage. There are over 400 chiropractors and 150 naturopathic doctors.

Utilities are inexpensive, medical and housing costs affordable, and the cost of living is among the lowest of any major West Coast city. Portland usually enjoys a low unemployment rate and its Silicon Corridor offers a choice of hi-tech careers.

Unfortunately, all is not quite perfect. Recently, crime and drugs were a major problem, while there had been gang violence which included racial skinhead activity.

Scores: Urban 4. Climate 3. Elevation 1. Terrain 5. Awareness 4. Nutrition 5. Fitness 5. Stress 4. Mind 5. Social 3. Volunteer 3. Spiritual 3. Care 5. Total Healthfulness: 50.

Information: CoC, 221 Northwest Second Avenue, Portland, OR 97209 (503-228-9411). C&VB, 26 Southwest Salmon, Portland, OR 97204 (503-222-2223). P&R, 1120 Southwest Fifth Street, Room 502, Portland, OR 97204 (503-796-5193).

**PRESCOTT, AZ.** Population: 30,000. Urban Stress: EST 1.8. Elevation: 5,389'. Located midway between desert heat and mountain chill, this popular summer resort has long been a haven for people with asthma or allergies. The reason is that hundreds of square miles of tall Ponderosa pines surround Prescott, filtering the air so that neither pollen nor pollution exist. Along with its neighboring communities— Prescott Valley and Chino Valley—Prescott is experiencing steady population increase. But so far, it has not been overwhelmed by brushfire growth.

From the tree-shaded town square and historic district, Prescott's streets wind up steep hills past hundreds of homes tucked away on spacious lots beneath tall pines. As a result, Prescott still offers the rich quality of small town life far from choking traffic fumes and urban sprawl. With its miles of rolling pineclad hills, and a spectacular backdrop of buttes and mountains, its dazzling fall colors and zestful mountain air, Prescott scores high for terrain therapy, elevation, and climate. Days are bright, dry, and sunny and the four distinct seasons range from an invigorating winter with a total 24" of snow, to warm summer days with invariably cool nights.

All this has drawn hundreds of refugees from smog-filled Phoenix and Los Angeles, including a high proportion of early retirees in their fifties. Add in the student bodies from three local colleges and you have a high-energy population with a pronounced preference for an active lifestyle.

All this is evident in a small County Health Department publication that gives a complete rundown on where to find every type of fitness activity in Prescott. For example, there's splendid mountain bicycling on four-wheel-drive roads in a huge expanse of adjacent National Forest land, while the Chain Gang Bicycle Club holds weekly rides at which beginners are welcome. Hiking trails web the same National Forest, with cross-country skiing in winter at higher elevations. Close to town, you can hike to the top of Thumb Butte or Granite Mountain. And three hiking groups organize a series of brisk fitness walks and longer half and all-day hikes. Also here is a race walk clinic, and a roller skating rink for the young at heart.

Five swimming pools offer adult lapswimming, either year around or during summer, and six tennis complexes (some private) provide challenging play with an organized summer tournament. Runners can join the Trailblazers Run Club and participate in a marathon in May, a 10K run in September, and even a Man-Against-Horse Race. The Y, the Racquet Club, the Sheraton Health Club, and the parks department provide dozens of adult exercise classes, including aerobics, strength-building, and flexibility programs. You can also canoe in summer on nearby Lynx Lake and on other neighboring mountain lakes.

Prescott's long love affair with the arts has culminated in the location here of two top museums: the Phippen Museum of Western Art, and the Smoki Museum, filled with Southwestern Native American ceramics and artifacts. Yavapai Community College sponsors a Friends-in-Concert series with regular performances by well-known soloists, quartets, and dance groups, while the Elks Opera House hosts symphony concerts and regional opera. For mental gymnastics, Yavapai College offers free tuition to anyone over 65 and Prescott College features adult degree programs that many retirees consider quite demanding. Also available is a stimulating series of adult education courses, as well as others offered by the parks department.

Meanwhile, Yavapai Regional Medical Center shows how to beat stress with a general fitness program that includes stretching with t'ai chi (a mind-calming martial art), taught in yang-style classes. Also, we found, Prescott's health-conscious population is keenly aware of the need to follow a low-fat diet. Frequent square and round dances are held by clubs and adult centers and there are plenty of social get-togethers with potlucks and bus tours all over the Southwest.

211

From meals-on-wheels to hospital work, volunteer opportunities are wide open. Most mainline churches are represented. And Prescott's 135-bed Regional Medical Center, together with the 217-bed Whipple V.A. Hospital, provide state of the art medical care, including most medical specialties. Two orthopedists cater to sports injuries, while five osteopaths and 25 chiropractors offer an alternative to allopathy.

Scores of homes for sale are usually listed, many on pine-shaded view lots. Patio homes, townhouses, and condominiums are also widely available, plus mobile homes and rental apartments. Both housing and living costs recently hovered close to the national average. Although Prescott has several light industries, competition for job openings is quite intense.

Scores: Urban 10. Climate 4. Elevation 4. Terrain 5. Awareness 5. Nutrition 3. Fitness 5. Stress 3. Mind 3. Social 3. Volunteer 3. Spiritual 3. Care 4. Total Healthfulness: 55.

Information: CoC, Box 1147, Prescott, AZ 86302 (602-445-2000). P&R, Box 2059, Prescott, AZ 86302 (602-445-5881).


**PROVIDENCE, RI.** Population: 175,000. Urban Stress: ZPG 3. Elevation: 80'. Once the sleazy crime capital of the New England mob, Providence has been transformed into a highly-livable center of education, banking, and health care. The home of 5 four-year colleges and universities, it supports a flourishing cultural and arts community. Prodded by powerful Brown University and the Rhode Island School of Design (RISD), Providence has revitalized its downtown and restored entire neighborhoods of eighteenth century homes. In place of run-down slum areas, tree-bordered streets now wind up through neatly manicured parks to College Hill and the quiet squares of the elegant east side. Overlooking this renaissance is the white marble dome of the state capital, symbol of the steadily declining crime rate and of a statewide effort to rid Rhode Island of toxic waste.

In this wholesome setting at the head of Narragansett Bay, Providence is known for its good lifestyle and health-conscious attitude. While not enthusiastic about aerobics or yoga, the city's strongly ethnic Portuguese and Italian population prefers a Mediterranean diet in which cholesterol-cutting olive oil plays a key role. The variable weather pattern lets you ski cross-country or ice skate in winter, and it's just right for brisk walking or bicycling in summer.

Many adults and seniors are really into fitness here. In Providence alone, we found nineteen senior exercise, dancer-cize, walking, and cardiovascular fitness clubs. Almost every larger park has trails, and in early morning or late evening hundreds of people also take brisk walks on golf course cart trails. In winter, these same trails are used for Nordic skiing. Entire snow-covered parks and golf courses also become exercise grounds for cross-country ski aficionados, while thousands enjoy ice skating on park lakes. Low-impact aerobic classes are held at most colleges and senior centers. The Community College of Rhode Island offers a special Over 60 Dance and Fitness Program. From the Masters Swim and Senior Olympics swim training programs at Brown University, senior and adult lapswimming is available at a variety of outdoor and heated indoor pools, along with weights rooms and strength-building exercise classes. You can canoe on the Seekonk River or bicycle over a variety of 20 to 35 mile backroad loops. The Narragansett Bay Wheelmen organize weekly rides. And tennis is available at a variety of parks and private clubs.

Leading the city's smorgasbord of intellectual activities are the splendid opportunities for seniors to audit college and extension courses without charge. All residents 60 and over may audit classes at state colleges or the University of Rhode

Island; and extension courses are available at both the university and Providence College. Many Elderhostel courses are also offered here. Rounding out the Providence cultural scene are several top repertoire and ballet companies plus the Rhode Island Philharmonic, all performing regularly at the Providence Performing Arts Center or on other city stages. Meanwhile, the dynamic RISD presents a series of top caliber visual arts exhibits and activities.

Providence's T'ai Chi Center provides a traditional method for managing stress. Several senior centers host a variety of social activities, as well as recruiting volunteers for service work. Besides several hospitals with state of the art treatment, Providence has several Health Maintenance Organizations and we noticed a number of chiropractors practicing a variety of natural healing systems.

Realtors customarily list a wide choice of homes, townhouses and condominiums at costs that range from 10 to 20 percent above the national average. Rental apartments are available in the same range. The city's traditionally low unemployment rate indicates a choice of career openings for qualified workers in the financial, educational, and health care fields.

Drawbacks? Several people told us that the school system could be better.

Scores: Urban 5. Climate 3. Elevation 1. Terrain 3. Awareness 4. Nutrition 3. Fitness 5. Stress 3. Mind 4. Social 3. Volunteer 3. Spiritual 4. Care 4. Total Healthfulness: 45.

Information: C&VB, 10 Dorrance Street, Providence, RI 02903 (401-274-1636). P&R, One Resevoir Avenue, Providence, RI 02907 (401-785-9450).


**REDDING, CA.** Population: 65,000. Urban Stress: EST 1.8. Elevation: 550'. A bright, modern, wholesome town with clean air, Redding lies among oak-dotted hills beside the Sacramento River at the northern tip of California's Great

Valley. The setting reminds you more of the Pacific Northwest than California. On three sides lie the rugged mountains of the Shasta-Cascade Recreation Area, a vast natural playground that includes two of California's highest mountains, Lassen National Park, two state parks, two national forests and two beautiful rivers—the Trinity and Sacramento.

As supply center for this far-flung area, Redding has become an important regional medical center with other services far beyond those of most cities of this size. Several years ago, it was ranked by one well-known guidebook as one of America's four best cities in which to live. Homes are far less costly than in Southern California. And though growing steadily, the city's announced goal is to ensure a fine quality of life even 50 years into the future. The only drawbacks appear to be hot summer afternoons and a rather limited choice of intellectual activities.

Many residents are well educated fugitives from smog-plagued Southern California who took a cut in pay for the privilege of living here. Others are affluent, younger retirees who came to enjoy the active lifestyle of the great outdoors. Within an hour's drive of Redding is some of the best mountain and road bicycling, cross-country skiing, mountain hiking, and lake swimming and canoeing in the West. In the city itself, you can run, walk, or bicycle for six miles beside the river on the scenic Sacramento River Trail. The parks department maintains 25 tennis courts, mostly lighted, and two public swimming pools. But most adults prefer to swim at the heated 25-meter pool of a local health club. Both the Y and the parks department each operate a separate Fitness-for-Seniors, low-impact, twice weekly exercise class. The city's low humidity helps alleviate the summer afternoon heat, but the rest of the year the mostly snow-free climate seems ideal for outdoor activity.

We wish Redding had as many opportunities to exercise the mind as the body. Although the city may one day become home for a campus of the University of California, at present cultural activities are limited to locally-produced concerts, plays, and fine arts activities at Shasta College plus similar regional presentations staged at the Old City Hall Performing Arts Gallery.

Like most Californians, Redding's citizens are well informed on nutritional matters, as evidenced by the salad bars, and the low-fat meals offered by several oriental restaurants. Stretching exercises and basic stress-management techniques are taught by the Y, parks department, health clubs, hospitals, and by the city's 22 chiropractors. Also helping to alleviate the stress of driving is the city's surprisingly efficient six days a week bus service.

Several hundred area retirees live outside Redding, in such historic former gold mining towns as Dunsmuir, Yreka, Trinity Center, McCloud, and many more. Each of these larger communities, together with Redding itself, has an active senior center offering low-impact exercise classes and social activities. All mainline churches are here, but we were unable to locate a central volunteer agency.

With two hospitals and 175 physicians providing the latest in cardiac and cancer care techniques, Redding offers the best medical care in northern California. As this was written, most realtors listed a variety of homes priced below $100,000, with two-bedroom apartments renting for around $475 a month. Shasta Hills Estates was one of the most attractive of several retirement living developments. Also here were many small mobile home parks, but few seemed to cater to adults-only or to offer luxury living. Through owning its own utilities, Redding has kept its cost of living slightly below the state average. The crime rate has been consistently below average for a city this size.

Scores:  Urban 10. Climate 3. Elevation 1. Terrain 5. Awareness 4. Nutrition 3. Fitness 5. Stress 3. Mind 2. Social 3. Volunteer 2. Spiritual 3. Care 4. Total Healthfulness: 48.

Information: C&VB, 747 Auditorium Drive, Redding, CA 96001 (916-225-4100). P&R, 814 Parkview Avenue, Redding, CA 96001 (916-225-4095).

**ST. PETERSBURG, FL.** Population: 260,000. Urban Stress: ZPG 2.8. Elevation: 16'. Since 1885, when the American Medical Association pronounced St. Petersburg as the healthiest place on earth, the Sunshine City has enjoyed a robust reputation as a health and retirement resort. Partly that's because it once recorded 700 consecutive days of sunshine, and even today an average of 361 sunny days occur each year. But since the 1960s, St. Pete has grown in mega-leaps to become a savvy city with an upbeat mood—not only a prime spot for active seniors on-the-go but also a great place for anyone to live and work.

With a median age of 45.8, the population today is somewhat younger and more affluent than it was in the sixties. Put together tens of thousands of young, well educated baby boomer professionals with as many younger, prosperous retirees, and you have an exceptionally health-conscious population. Nowadays, thousands of St. Petersburg residents are dedicated to living a low-risk lifestyle.

When you look behind the crowded freeways and the tourist facade, St. Pete scores well on most aspects of health. From its handsome waterfront that showcases the five-story pier and the mammoth Bayfront arena-theater complex, St. Pete unfolds through futuristic downtown blocks into a vast 58 square mile sea of suburbs dotted with manicured parks, golf courses and lush, subtropical foliage. Although 90 percent of all land is developed, you don't get the impression that it is all paved over. Summers are long and hot, of course, with frequent afternoon thunderstorms. But the warm, stable climate is generally ideal for outdoor activities.

Distance swimming is the favorite summer exercise. The city's Leisure Department operates a total of twelve outdoor swimming pools with another—the Olympic-sized North Shore pool—heated and open all year. Most pools have lap lanes and feature daily adult lapswimming with Masters Swimming and also competitive swimming for adults. Equally popular from May to October are lifeguard patrolled swimming beaches on the ocean or in calmer bay waters. Four running clubs sponsor a weekly run that includes a major triathlon. There are four heart exercise trails, plus miles of wooded hiking trails in city and county parks. Canoe paddling is enjoyable on a choice of sheltered waterways. St. Pete's bicycle club hosts a Sunday morning ride. And a 35-mile railroad bed is being converted into a hiking and walking trail.

Including St. Petersburg Tennis Club there are 73 public lighted courts, plus many private complexes, one with 45 courts. The Leisure Department's Walking Club sponsors daily walks for adults of all ages. Rounding out the fitness scene are the dozens of exercise classes held daily by the Leisure Department. We particularly liked the Total Fitness class that includes 10 minutes of flexibility, 25 minutes of aerobics and 25 minutes of strength-building exercise. Facilities like these have helped thousands of residents to remain fit and active into their eighties and nineties. For example, the Kids and Kubs softball team is composed exclusively of men aged 70 and over.

Spearheading opportunities for intellectual discovery and enrichment is a unique hands-on Science Museum and Planetarium, while Haslam's bookstore, Florida's largest, is a Mecca for book lovers and writers. A culturally vibrant city with a dynamic arts community, St. Pete presents a monthlong spring Artfest jam-packed with daily theater and dance performances, symphony concerts and visual arts exhibits. Throughout the year, the huge Bayfront Theater stages similar topflight fare, while four professional stock companies offer everything from Shakespeare in the Park to experimental theater. Also here are two major art museums, while the Florida Symphony presents a full Masterworks season. Dozens of retirees audit or take degrees at the University of

South Florida. And 25,000 adults are enrolled in the city's three vocational schools and its extensive adult learning program.

Fortunately, on St. Pete's breezeswept Pinellas Peninsula location, the air is always clear. And many residents help their nutrition by raising organic vegetables and subtropical fruits.

Although the Leisure Department offers a variety of stretching and yoga classes to help manage stress, and St. Pete has an adequate city bus service, statistics have shown a disturbingly high level of alcoholism, divorce, crime, and suicide. The fact is that, behind the golf courses and gleaming malls, over one-fourth of St. Petersburg consists of lower socio-economic neighborhoods in which so many homes have deteriorated that they pay virtually no property taxes. All this has helped shrink the city's tax base at a time when it is under a heavy tax burden to finance needed new infrastructure. Also worth knowing is that in the most rapidly growing northern sectors of the Pinellas Peninsula, the infrastructure remains inadequate and roads are jammed. Moreover, beaches and beach parking are often badly congested on weekends and the federal government has repeatedly warned of a severe hurricane threat to thousands of low-lying waterfront homes built on dredged-up sand *fingers* in the intracoastal waterway. None of this need affect a middle class lifestyle, but it's something every newcomer needs to know.

In St. Pete you can dance the night away to big band music or participate in a round of social events through singles groups or Leisure Department centers. Its two volunteer recruiting agencies—the Volunteer Action Center and Pinellas Opportunity Council for Seniors—plus an unlimited choice of other openings, gives St. Pete the highest score for volunteer opportunities. And the city's huge Bayfront Medical Center, a teaching and research institute plus the 670-bed V.A. hospital, 900 doctors and many other hospitals providing specialized surgery and care, give the city the highest ranking for health care.

The median home price is $100,000. From charming older close-in homes to small and medium-sized ranch style homes in quiet suburban neighborhoods, out to square miles of mobile home parks, every type of housing is available. The dozens of discount houses and malls help keep living costs exactly at the national level. Explosive growth in hi-tech plants, and in service industries, has kept St. Pete's unemployment rate low and job prospects favorable.

Scores: Urban 6. Climate 4. Elevation 1. Terrain 4. Awareness 4. Nutrition 3. Fitness 5. Stress 3. Mind 5. Social 4. Volunteer 5. Spiritual 3. Care 5. Total Healthfulness: 52.

Information: CoC, Box 1371, St. Petersburg, FL 33731 (813-821-4069). Leisure Department, 1450 16th Street North, St. Petersburg, FL 33494 (813-893-7441).

**SAN ANTONIO, TX.** Population: 1,100,000. Urban Stress: ZPG 3.5. Elevation: 700'. In acknowledging its rich bi-cultural heritage, one swiftly learns that at least 20 percent of the adult population of San Antonio is functionally illiterate. An estimated 217,000 adults are unable to read printed health advice and the majority live on the city's south and west sides in sprawling lower socio-economic neighborhoods that surround several of the city's huge military bases. Due to differences in language and culture, interest in health, fitness and nutrition is almost entirely confined to the better-educated, more-affluent one-third of San Antonio's population who live in the northern half of the city. Here are clean hi-tech industries, huge medical centers, universities, gleaming office towers, and relatively safe, well-kept middle class neighborhoods. It is here that the health and fitness culture endures.

Don't look for crowds of bicyclists, but the two large Sun Harvest natural foods supermarkets, the well-used natatorium and tennis centers, and the crowds of walkers and joggers in McAllister and other parks are visible signs of San

Antonio's persistent interest in following the low-risk lifestyle. Home to many thousands of military retirees, and to some 40,000 active military personnel, plus thousands of students, San Antonio is understandably a city of energetic and younger-than-average people, many of whom are intensely interested in staying healthy.

Free of polluting smokestacks and smog and with high quality drinking water, this ninth largest U.S. city is very adequately supplied with most of the resources needed for healthful living. The long, hot summer days make exercising before breakfast almost mandatory. But the sun shines on 300 days each year. And whether for retired military personnel or civilians, this major medical research center is superbly equipped to supply any needed form of medical treatment.

You can hike or jog along a historic trail that links four still-active colonial mission-churches, or you can do either in McAllister and other parks, or in nature retreats such as Freidrichs Park, all webbed by trails and handy to north side residents. Fifteen area Volksmarch clubs hold weekly walks and sanctioned events. Available year around is adult lapswimming in the city's northside natatorium, as well as at several indoor Y pools, and at two fine school pools open to adults on evenings and weekends.

A top tennis town, San Antonio is home of the McFarlin Tennis Center, base for the city's professional racquet team plus another 85 or more public courts, and countless others in private clubs. More than a score of community centers, together with Y branches and private athletic clubs and spas, offer every imaginable type of exercise class, in every category from strength-building to flexibility and stress-management. Good bicycling is available for those willing to drive into the adjoining hill country, while the San Antonio Wheelmen's Club holds group rides every summer evening and on weekends.

Nor is San Antonio short on intellectual activity. Ten colleges and universities, plus an extensive series of adult education courses cover the field from literature to astronomy. An active Performing Arts Association presents artists of international caliber in three annual operas together with ballet, Broadway plays, musicals, concerts, lectures, and avante garde experimental theater. The city's nationally-acclaimed symphony orchestra presents fourteen concerts each winter. Two major art museums—one with instruction—spearhead a renaissance in southwestern art. And you'll find a wealth of stimulating lectures and workshops in every field of human potential.

Besides its two natural foods supermarkets, northside San Antonio's restaurants are moving into menus for their nutrition-conscious clients. It's rare to find one that does not offer a low-fat, low-cholesterol dish. Drinking water is also almost completely free of agricultural run-off. Virtually every kind of stress-management training is available, while the award-winning 77-route city bus system helps thousands avoid the stress of driving. Two senior centers, and the many community centers, provide activities through which adults and seniors can make social contacts. A large United Way Volunteer Center matches thousands of altruistic men and women to an unlimited number of volunteer openings.

Although predominantly Catholic, San Antonio is well supplied with churches of every denomination and has a growing number of New Age and New Thought churches and groups. Leading the city's outstanding medical care facilities is the huge university Health Science Center with its teaching hospital. Clustered around are a dozen other top general hospitals, plus 5,000 physicians, a V.A. hospital, and two military hospitals, one of which is the U.S. Army's teaching and research hospital.

For years, San Antonio has ranked among the least expensive large U.S. cities, and housing costs also recently ranked somewhat below average. A huge choice of homes was recently available at $75-100,000 and up, with townhouses, condominiums, and rental apartments in the same cost range. Its steady growth of 20,000 new residents annually has made the Alamo City an opportune area for small entrepreneurs. For working adults, most career openings are in health care, defense, and other hi-tech fields. For other type jobs, bilingual ability may be needed.

Drawbacks? Wilting summer afternoon heat, crowded rush hour freeway traffic, poorly paved streets, a disturbingly high crime rate (mostly on the south and west sides), and a possible future water shortage, plus widespread predicted poverty among poorly-educated south and west side minorities, are the most commonly heard concerns. We weren't impressed by the city's flat, paved-over terrain and it was often quite a long drive to various fitness facilities.

Scores: Urban 3. Climate 3. Elevation 1. Terrain 2. Awareness 4. Nutrition 5. Fitness 5. Stress 3. Mind 5. Social 3. Volunteer 5. Spiritual 5. Care 5. Total Healthfulness: 49.

Information: CoC, Box 1628, San Antonio, TX 78296 (512-229-2104). P&R, Box 839966, San Antonio, TX 78283 (512-299-8480).


**SAN DIEGO, CA.** Population: 1,100,000, Urban Stress: ZPG 3.2. Elevation: 411'. "The sports and fitness capital of the U.S.," was how *Sports Illustrated* magazine recently described San Diego. Indeed, this beach, university, and Navy town ranks tops in fitness resources and health awareness. Free of frost, snow, high winds, or heat waves, the summery climate permits outdoor exercise year around. And according to the Convention and Visitors Bureau, the number of people who exercise regularly is more than twice the national average. San Diego also rates high for its world class theater and other mind-stimulating pursuits, for its extensive social networks for those over 50, for its unlimited volunteer openings, and for its three teaching hospitals and other top-caliber medical care options.

Twenty miles across, the sprawling city embraces cliffs, hills, mesas, canyons, and miles of beaches, all enhancing its potential for terrain therapy. It was for these reasons that the famous La Costa Health Spa was located here.

But to enjoy all these admittedly health-building assets does require some trade-offs.San Diego's smog and ozone contamination have been among some of California's worst. Home prices run 60 percent above the national average. And the freeways are so filled with hectic traffic throughout the day that many drivers over 50 have to take defensive driving courses to survive.

Its casual lifestyle and near-perfect climate have made San Diego so perennially popular for retirement that 20 percent of the populace is aged 55 or over. Most are active, affluent retirees-on-the-go. Add in a flourishing population of prosperous baby boomers and you have the high-energy source that is behind San Diego's reputation as a health and fitness city.

Bicycling, the best indicator of a city's involvement with fitness, is so popular that the famous *7-11 racing team* trains here each winter. Over 200 miles of bikeways network the city, and San Diego has its own bicycle coordinator. Car parking areas are being turned into more bicycle lanes. Buses, trolleys, and ferries are beginning to carry bicycles during non-rush hours. Hundreds more miles of bike lanes and paths take you roaming over the county's extensive highway system and through its parks. Huge Anza Borrego State Park offers limitless miles of canyon terrain for mountain bicycling. And if you show up at Carlos and Annie's Cafe in Del Mar around eight in the morning, you'll usually find a crowd of bicyclists assembling for the ride to Dana Point and back.

Brisk walking and jogging are equally popular. Over 200 runs and triathlons are held annually, while the thousands of miles of trails range from beach and cliff walks to a historic downtown walk and on to challenging hill and mountain hiking farther out. Among half a dozen thriving walking clubs,

*Walkabouts* schedules around 150 organized walks a month in the city's most scenic areas. Over 1,200 tennis courts and 350 racquetball courts are available. You can swim at nine ocean beaches in summer and at a score of heated pools in winter. Or you can join the University of California's noon workouts for the Masters swim program. For still more upper body exercise, you can canoe on several lakes.

Spearheading San Diego's cultural riches are its many top-caliber theaters. Together, they program an almost continuous series of professional opera, ballet, Broadway plays and musicals, symphony concerts, and a Shakespeare festival. Four art museums showcase frequent touring exhibits. Nine science museums and the famous Museum of Man stimulate intellectual inquiry. Scores of *fun* classes are featured by the Access Organization. Literally thousands of continuing education courses are held in every field of academic endeavor. And deserving special mention is State University College's Educational Growth Program designed to further lifelong learning for those aged 55 and over.

Home vegetable gardens flourish year around in the warm, sunny climate. Along with dozens of oriental restaurants, Jimbo's and Kung Foods vegetarian restaurants provide tasty, low-fat meals for San Diego's predominantly health-conscious populace. From yoga and biofeedback to t'ai chi and A Course in Miracles, stress management and human potential courses abound. Many people prefer to avoid the stress of driving by using the city's extensive bus and trolley system.

Providing unlimited opportunities for companionship, at least for those over 50, are the city's 120 senior centers and groups. Both the local *Senior World* newspaper and the slick *Senior Life* magazine are often filled with articles on health and fitness. And the city's vast Senior Citizens Service Organization constantly needs hundreds of volunteers to continue its outreach programs for older residents throughout San Diego County.

So many churches exist in San Diego, including many little-known denominations, that it takes a special directory to list them all. Its teaching hospitals together with 35 general hospitals, two military hospitals, a V.A. hospital and 4,000 physicians, are responsible for San Diego's emergence as a major medical research and cancer treatment center. Among the many HMOs and other options is a large Senior Citizens Medical Center run by Scripps Hospital. Helping offset the high cost of medical treatment in California is a wide assortment of special health insurance plans.

Although the cost of living was recently 16 percent above the national average, anyone who can pay cash for a home will not find other costs excessive. The median home price was recently $165,000. Renting an apartment or purchasing a mobile home are somewhat less expensive options. For those who are qualified, employment openings in the hi-tech and health care fields are usually good.

Scores: Urban 4. Climate 5. Elevation 1. Terrain 4. Awareness 5. Nutrition 4. Fitness 5. Stress 4. Mind 5. Social 5. Volunteer 5. Spiritual 5. Care 5. Total Healthfulness: 57.

Information: CoC, 110 West C Street, Suite 1600, San Diego, CA 92101 (619-232-0124). C&VB, 1200 Third Avenue, Suite 824, San Diego, CA 92101 (619-236-1212). P&R, 5201 Ruffin Road, San Diego, CA 92123 (619-565-3600).


**SANTA FE, NM.** Population: 80,000. Urban Stress: EST 2.1. Elevation: 7,000'. Known for its rambling adobe homes with corner fireplaces and piñon fires, this art and literary haven has grown to become the nation's second largest art market and an exuberant center of the performing arts. Over 150 art galleries, smart restaurants, luxury accommodations, and $250,000 homes fill the City's historic east side. In the process, however, all the infrastructure and the supporting service businesses have sprouted on the less desirable west side. Here, four miles of tacky roadside commercialism borders four-laned Cerillos Road and the traffic is horrendous.

The city's crime rate is something less than desirable. Dust storms are common in spring. Tourists are everywhere. And many lower-echelon workers cannot afford to live in Santa Fe at all.

Nonetheless, in 1987 the City Livability Awards Program named Santa Fe the "Most Livable Small City" (under 100,000) in America. And if you can overlook such blunders as Cerillos Road, you'll find the rest of Santa Fe a stimulating place to live or retire. Behind the adobe facades, the art galleries and gourmet restaurants, the city emerges as an affluent, health-conscious community with top ranking scores in the majority of health-enhancing lifestyle factors.

The elevation is invigorating; the air is clean and clear; the climate dry, brisk, sunny, and four-seasonal; and the Southwestern lifestyle is a blend of noncomformity, intellectualism, and liberal thinking. The city fairly bristles with alternative health therapies, stress management courses, and holistic healing practitioners and institutes. Worthy of mention: the International Institute of Chinese Medicine; Jay Scherer's Academy of Natural Healing; the Southern College of Life Sciences; the Southwest Acupuncture College; a wonderful chiropractic center offering a variety of whole person therapies; the Academy of Massage and Advanced Healing Arts, specializing in bodywork and reflexology; and the splendid Ten Thousand Waves Japanese spa which provides everything from shiatzu to Rolfing in a restful mountain setting.

Yoga, zen, and New Age churches seem as popular as mainstream religious denominations. And confirming the city's strong preference for natural living are such institutions as the Marketplace natural foods store, and the Natural Cafe, specializing in vegetarian and seafood cuisine.

For such an arty town, Santa Fe has a rich array of fitness activities. Close to the city, on Baldy Mountain, are limitless square miles of national forests labyrinthed with scenic trails for brisk walking and mountain bicycling in summer, and cross-country skiing on deep powder snow in winter. Two local ski-touring clubs also maintain extensive systems of groomed trails. The Santa Fe Striders, a strong running club, hosts a weekly fun run and several challenging runs each year. Four large racquet clubs augment the city's 27 public tennis courts, making Santa Fe a worthwhile tennis town. Three heated indoor, and one outdoor, municipal swimming pools provide extended periods of adult lapswimming year around. You can also swim at nearby Cochiti Lake beach, or canoe on several local lakes. Dozens of challenging single and double mountain bike tracks are within easy reach, while the Sangre de Cristo Cycling Club hosts bicycle road rides and races.

Complementing these terrific health and fitness resources is one of the most event-filled cultural schedules in America. Santa Fe's world class opera features five to nine productions each summer, including many world or American premieres. Clustered around the opera is a host of dance, ballet, and theater companies, plus chamber music groups and symphony orchestras, many giving almost daily performances. No fewer than twelve different plays are performed each summer in the Shakespeare in the Park series. The Santa Fe Symphony, the Orchestra of Santa Fe, the Desert Chorale, and the Theater of Music are just a few of the many top cultural groups that perform frequently. Besides six major art museums, dozens of art classes and workshops are offered in all the fine arts. Also here is a fine choice of adult education courses, plus seminars in many human potential subjects.

Santa Fe's popularity has boosted housing costs to where a traditional pueblo-style adobe home is as costly as a home in Southern California. Nonetheless, most moderately-affluent retirees can still afford a frame and stucco home with tan adobe exterior and a flat roof. More reasonable still are some condominiums and townhouses. And once you have a roof overhead, living costs are not exorbitant. Because so many younger residents have taken a pay cut to live in Santa Fe, the job outlook is not too encouraging.

Scores: Urban 9. Climate 4. Elevation 5. Terrain 4. Awareness 5. Nutrition 4. Fitness 5. Stress 4. Mind 5. Social 3. Volunteer 2. Spiritual 4. Care 5. Total Healthfulness: 59.

Information: C&VB, Box 909, Santa Fe, NM 87501 (800-777-2489). P&R, 737 Agua Fria Road, Santa Fe, NM 87501 (505-984-6860).

**SEATTLE, WA.** Population: (area) 2,000,000. Urban Stress: ZPG 3.3. Elevation: 200'. Consistently ranked by quality-of-life surveys as America's most livable big city, Seattle also scores high on almost every issue affecting health. Squeezed into an hourglass shape between Puget Sound and Lake Washington, central Seattle has no room to sprawl. Instead, city fathers concentrated on making the existing area more viable and livable. Although dramatic new hi-rises are burgeoning downtown, waterways, forests, and lakes extend into the heart of the city. Miles of perpetually verdant salt and freshwater shorelines reveal picturesque harbor views with backdrops of snowclad Mount Rainier and the Olympic Mountains glistening in the sun. Miles of trails lead through parks and greenbelts, and scores of charming residential districts occupy wooded or waterfront settings.

All this gives residents a strong bond with the outdoors. Thousands, in fact, show up at work in L.L. Bean clothing and hiking boots. Well-mannered, well-educated, and polite, with a median age of 33, the predominantly affluent baby boomer population has become a potent political force with enough clout to ensure that fitness activities and public transit receive at least as much attention as providing for more cars and freeways. Progress this far has included over 100 miles of bicycle trails, a special Bicycle Guide Map showing city-wide bicycle routes, and the best Metro area bus system in America. Today, 10 percent of all downtown parking must be for bicycles, and Seattle has its own bicycle coordinator.

Recycling, another unfailing indicator of a population's strong health awareness, has spread citywide. We were told that many residents deliberately drive older but well-kept cars to discourage the automobile from becoming a status symbol. Library statistics show Seattle as having the highest level of literacy and book readership among large U.S. cities. And though many winter days are admittedly damp and gloomy, the climate is mild all year with cool summers, not-too-cold winters and few, if any, extremes.

With its pure drinking water and abundance of fresh salmon and halibut (high in healthy omega-3 fatty acids and taken from unpolluted waters), Seattle ranks high in nutritional awareness. Mountains of fresh produce, fish, and seafood crowd the open stalls in its picturesque Pike's Place Market while scores of local restaurants specialize in low-fat fish and seafood dishes, or in high-fiber Italian, Chinese, and Japanese cuisines. Seattle is also known for its fine whole grain breads.

Seattle has so many fitness activities that it takes a 284-page Sport Source directory to list them all. Among large U.S. cities, Seattle is the undisputed best metro area for bicycling. Bicycles are considered part of the city's transportation system and all ferries and some buses carry bicycles, while police patrol on mountain bikes. Although bike trails are shared with walkers and joggers, hundreds of bikers pedal the 12-mile Burke-Gilman Trail daily, following the shores of Lake Washington and continuing out to connecting trails that continue on for 30 or 40 miles through a wonderland of lakes and forests. Alternatively, in 30 minutes you can take your bike on a ferry to a choice of quiet island roads; or you can ride a scenic 78-mile road loop through Snohomish and Monroe; or you can explore limitless miles of old logging roads on a mountain bicycle.

The same extensive trails system is available for walking or jogging, plus other fitness walking trails along the downtown waterfront. Adult lapswimming is available daily year around at eight or more public pools. Tennis buffs find fitness on the city's 151 public courts and at the splendid Tennis

Center. It's just a two hour drive to a choice of three great national parks with exciting hiking and cross-country skiing. Opportunities for canoe paddling and sliding-seat rowing are abundant. And through the Ys and parks department, there are literally hundreds of classes in everything from senior aerobics to martial arts and t'ai chi, plus senior Sunday walks and Volksport hikes.

Cultural and intellectual activities are highly valued and strongly supported. With at least four top theater companies, Seattle ranks second only to New York in live theater performances. Its symphony orchestra is world renowned, while six major operas and six ballets are staged annually in the Seattle Center Opera House. Visual arts activities center around Seattle's Art Museum and two smaller art museums. Other cultural events are presented at the University of Washington. You'll also find literally hundreds of classes offered by the city's continuing education program.

Seattle ranks equal to, or better than, average for stress management classes, volunteer openings, opportunities for social activities, and for its choice of churches and other spiritual paths. The city's 26 general-acute and four special purpose hospitals, plus 3,000 physicians, make Seattle one of the best diagnostic and medical treatment centers in the U.S. So many medical centers and teaching hospitals exist, plus a fleet of paramedic-manned emergency vans, that Seattle is considered the safest city in the world in which to have a heart attack.

Affordable homes for sale have been numerous in outlying suburban areas, though they tend to be rather a long, congested commute from downtown. Living costs are generally close to average with utilities usually below average. Employment opportunities are centered around software, computers, the university, and biotechnology.

While far superior to most other cities of its size, Seattle suffers from congested traffic and freeways, while crime, slums, and pollution still cause problems.

Scores: Urban 4. Climate 3. Elevation 1. Terrain 5. Awareness 5. Nutrition 5. Fitness 5. Stress 3. Mind 5. Social 4. Volunteer 4. Spiritual 4. Care 5. Total Healthfulness: 53.

Information: CoC, 1200 One Union Square, Sixth and University, Seattle, WA 98101 (206-461-7200). C&VB, 520 Pike Street, Suite 1300, Seattle, WA 98101 (206-461-5800). P&R, Dexter Avenue North, Seattle, WA 98109 (206-684-4075). For rental video newcomer's kit: MacPherson's Realtors, 12733 Lake City Way N.E., Seattle, WA 98125 (800-426-1662).

**SILVER CITY, NM.** Population: 12,000. Urban Stress: EST 1.8. Elevation: 6,000. Anyone seeking a relaxed, uncomplicated lifestyle might well consider this picturesque mining town in southwestern New Mexico. In past decades, its mile high altitude and dry, invigorating climate made it a natural location for TB sanitariums. Spread across mountain foothills on the continental divide, historic Silver City still offers unusual potential to the health aficionado. Scores of couples have fled America's big, polluted cities to retire here. The mountain air is clear and cool, the quality of life is high, and immediately north lies vast Gila National Forest with over 1,500 miles of trails for hiking, mountain bicycling, and cross-country skiing.

One of few really small towns in this book, Silver City nonetheless supports a natural foods coop and a healthfood store, while support for conservationism seems unusually high. This surprisingly enlightened attitude emanates from the faculty and student body of Western New Mexico University (WNMU), a small but excellent state-supported four-year institution. Many educated retirees, and a sprinkling of younger couples, round out a general picture of the populace.

Though everything but the scenery is on a small scale, Silver City offers a surprising assortment of fitness activities. For $25 per semester, any resident could recently have purchased an activity card allowing full use of all fitness facilities at the university, including a heated swimming pool with senior swimming and water aerobics. Although many people fitness-walk through the city's historic sections, forest hiking trails begin a few miles out. The city's annual Scott Nichols Bicycle Tour includes 32 different races held during a five-day period and draws top bicycle racers from across the Southwest. By driving away from the city, we found good road bicycling on quiet mountain roads, plus unlimited mountain bicycling on forest tracks and backroads. Half a dozen city tennis courts and a municipal pool are also popular with retirees. We heard few complaints about lack of opportunities for exercise.

Normally included among WNMU's enrollment are at least 50 full-time students aged 50 or over. From computers to karate, a wide range of continuing education classes is also available. And performances by guest soloists or regional orchestras and players groups are presented regularly at WNMU's Fine Arts Center. Silver City residents may also use the university library.

Stress-management classes in t'ai chi, a way of achieving inner stillness through outward motion, are given at WNMU. Through hobbies, fitness activities, conservationism, or outdoor recreations, most newcomers soon meet a circle of new acquaintances. Volunteers are always needed to teach literacy. Through the influence of WNMU, many local people have become interested in natural healing systems and techniques. The 88-bed general hospital can handle any emergency. And the city's 32 physicians represent all major specialties.

Don't look for career openings here. But for many newcomers, the very reasonable cost of new homes is a pleasant surprise. Many of the better homes in and near town, some on three to five acres, were recently priced at $100,000 or less and for under $70,000 we saw traditional adobes with viga ceilings and corner fireplaces that would have cost three times as much in Santa Fe. The only drawbacks seemed to be the fairly steady traffic on US 180 which runs through the city and location of a large open pit mine and smelter some 10 miles east. We were assured that no fumes ever reach Silver City.

Scores:   Urban 10. Climate 4. Elevation 4. Terrain 5. Awareness 3. Nutrition 3. Fitness 5. Stress 3. Mind 2. Social 3. Volunteer 3. Spiritual 3. Care 3. Total Healthfulness: 51.

Information: CoC, 1103 North Hudson Street, Silver City, NM 88061 (505-538-3785). WNMU, Box 680, Silver City, NM 88062 (505-538-6011).


**SUN CITIES, AZ.** Population: 64,000. Urban Stress: EST 1.6. Elevation: 1,000'. Begun in the 1960s and, with over 40,000 residences completed, older Sun City and its adjoining twin, Sun City West, form the world's largest and most successful controlled-age community. Currently, one member of every household must be 55 or over and no children under eighteen may live at home. As a result, the Sun Cities have the nation's lowest per capita crime rate and one of the lowest levels of urban stress. The entire community is immaculate, safe, and free of noise. Both the residents and the community leadership strongly support the low-risk lifestyle. No fewer than eleven recreation and exercise centers provide very complete facilities for swimming, tennis, and every fitness activity, while nutrition classes urge residents to follow a low-fat diet.

Many residents report achieving a higher level of fitness than at any prior time in their lives. In fact, a 1982 study by University of Arizona psychologists found that Sun Citians lead more fulfilling lives, both physically and emotionally, than people of similar ages living elsewhere. Seventy-eight percent of Sun Citians rated themselves in excellent or good health, compared to only 69 percent in the average city. Volunteerism is a way of life, and the Sun Cities have the most diverse array of adult social and other activities of any U.S. city this size.

With the exception of the searingly hot summer afternoons, the warm, dry sunny climate encourages outdoor activity at most other times. Although the flat terrain and the many rock lawns are uninspiring, all utilities and garbage cans are underground, all community services are topnotch, and the Sun Cities have become a model for urban planners.

Although originally designed as a golf and country club community, interest in golf is reported to be steadily declining. Nowadays, the Sun Cities' slogan is "A Sun City Lifestyle is a Healthy One." From Sun City's huge Bell Recreation Center, with its Olympic-sized pool, to Sun City West's Beardsley Center, with another huge pool, the eleven recreation centers offer splendid opportunities for lapswimming, jogging or brisk walking, racquetball, tennis, weight training, and aerobics. Each fitness center is designed to promote a sound cardiovascular warm-up program and there are daily classes in yoga and jazzercise. You can bicycle almost anywhere, and the Crestview Bike Club organizes regular rides. If that isn't enough, you can join the Dance Fitness Club, the Energetic Exercise Club, the Racquet Association, or a choice of square and tap dance groups. For all this, the annual recreation center fee was recently $106 in Sun City West and $70 in Sun City.

Spearheading cultural inspiration is the 7,200-seat Sundown Center for Performing Arts, the nation's largest single level theater. Operated by Arizona State University, the theater annually features over 100 performances, ranging from musicals to lectures, classic films, dance ensembles, plays, an annual pop series by the Phoenix Symphony, and frequent concerts by the 90-piece Sun City Symphony. For academic studies, Arizona State University operates a Sun Cities branch campus, while each Sun City has a well-stocked library. Additionally, intellectual clubs flourish: from great books groups to others studying computers, astronomy, and cosmology. Adding to it all are the theaters, concerts, art galleries and museum of Phoenix, just 15 miles away by freeway,

The almost endless round of social events, from coffee get-togethers to bridge and dance clubs, makes loneliness almost impossible. Newcomers find a huge choice of active singles groups, a women's social club, and a thriving western square dance club with beginners classes. Dozens of other activities are largely based on meeting people and building relationships.

The choice of volunteer openings is bewildering. Besides referral agencies like Sunshine Services and Lending Hands—which sponsor community and people-to-people projects—a group of 440 volunteers called the "Prides" clean all public streets and areas, 2,000 volunteers work in Sun City hospitals, and 250 others form the sheriff's posse, responsible for the Sun Cities' exceptionally low crime rate. Additionally, 26 service clubs need volunteers for work outside the Sun Cities, including teaching Native Americans on local reservations.

Don't look for New Age churches. But the Sun Cities do have two non-profit hospitals with a total 557 beds, plus another 104-bed hospital in adjacent Youngtown. There is a 24-hour paramedic service, two medical clinics, a cardiac institute, a V.A. hospital in Phoenix, and a military post just 10 miles away.

All housing consists of bright, spacious, energy-efficient single family, or garden or patio homes, with an average price tag of around $110,000. Many cost less, of course, and resales are available. All have sewers. The average Sun Citian is aged 70 and few, if any, residents are employed. Sun City West is somewhat more affluent and upscale than Sun City.

Among drawbacks are the long, hot summers, congested highways leading into Phoenix, a lack of parks, and the distance (20 miles) from the nearest natural recreation area. Also, as Sun Citians tend to abandon golf for more fitness-oriented activities, recreation centers and pools can become crowded at times.

Scores: Urban 10. Climate 3. Elevation 1. Terrain 2. Awareness 4. Nutrition 4. Fitness 5. Stress 3. Mind 4. Social 5. Volunteer 5. Spiritual 2. Care 4. Total Healthfulness: 52.

Information: CoC, Box 1705, Sun City West, AZ 85372 (800-341-6121; in Arizona 800-453-7167; in Phoenix 975-2270).

**TALLAHASSEE, FL.** Population: 135,000. Urban Stress: ZPG 2.4. Elevation: 50'. A busy state capital and university center that has preserved its Southern charm, Tallahassee has been ranked by several surveys as one of America's safer and more livable cities. Zero Population Growth ranked it as having one of the nation's lowest levels of environmental stress. So far, no one seems to have considered this north Florida city as particularly healthful. Yet Tallahassee has considerable potential for living a low-risk lifestyle. For example, the economy is based on government and academic employment, two fields which have drawn thousands of affluent, well-educated baby boomers. Add in 35,000 college students and some early retirees, and you have an overall population that, statistically at least, has a high level of health awareness.

That this is true is evident by Tallahassee's 65 miles of bikeways, plus several *pars cours* heart exercise trails and 30 public tennis courts. For year around lapswimming, most adults use private pools. There are plenty of gyms, fitness centers, and exercise classes, and thousands of people take daily brisk walks. And opportunities for canoe paddling abound in the area's many lakes and rivers.

Most residents exercise early in the day to avoid the hot, humid summer afternoons. But fall, winter and spring are ideal. And Tallahassee's historic, tree-canopied streets and gardens—ablaze in spring with dogwood, camellias, and roses—supply a steady source of terrain therapy.

Tallahassee's two major institutions of higher learning— Florida State University and Florida A&M—provide a steady program of cultural fare. The Tallahassee Symphony, the Civic Ballet, and the Florida State Opera perform regularly in Ruby Diamond Auditorium, while five talented players groups present drama, comedies, and musicals throughout winter. Thousands of residents keep their minds honed by signing up for courses in the city's extensive adult education program. Others find inspiration in the university's distinguished lecture series.

The university area is a rich source of classes and workshops in human potential and stress-management subjects. Here, also, are several natural foods stores, groups who are into natural healing therapies, and others who follow eastern philosophies. Mainstream churches, predominantly Southern Baptist, also include four Catholic and two Jewish places of worship. Tallahassee's Memorial Medical Center and its Community Hospital, together with 300 physicians, have earned the city a solid reputation as a regional medical center.

While close-in housing can be fairly high, the suburbs are full of reasonably-priced homes, condominiums, and rental apartment complexes plus outlying mobile home parks. Due to Tallahassee's predominantly younger population, adult-only developments are few and your neighbors are likely to have children. A comfortable suburban home recently cost $80-100,000 with smaller homes from $65,000 and smaller townhouses from $55,000. Many developments outside the city use septic tanks.

In Tallahassee's stable government and university-based economy, unemployment has traditionally been low and a choice of career opportunities is usually available for qualified adults in education, government employment, and hi-tech fields,

Scores: Urban 7. Climate 3. Elevation 1. Terrain 4. Awareness 4. Nutrition 3. Fitness 4. Stress 3. Mind 4. Social 3. Volunteer 3. Spiritual 3. Care 4. Total Healthfulness: 46.

Information: C&VB, 100 North Duval, Tallahassee, FL 32301 (800-628-2866). P&R, 912 Myers Park Drive, Tallahassee, FL 32301 (904-222-7529).


**TUCSON, AZ.** Population: (area) 800,000. Urban Stress: ZPG 3.5. Elevation: 2,400'. For decades, Tucson's dry, warm air had earned it a reputation for healthfulness. But when the city was chosen for the site of Canyon Ranch, the Rolls Royce of health spas, Tucson's natural salubrity was confirmed. Each year, thousands of people from all over the world flock to this plush fitness vacation resort to learn to live the low-risk lifestyle.

Fortunate are those who choose to live or retire in Tucson, for they can enjoy the same climate and the same enviable lifestyle every day in the year. Once a winter resort, brush-fire growth has transformed Tucson into a dynamic, sprawling metropolis covering almost 550 square miles of desert and foothills. Tens of thousands of newcomers have arrived in recent years to work in the burgeoning hi-tech plants that ring the city. And though Tucson suffers from air pollution, a perennial water shortage, heavy rush hour traffic, and above-average rates of crime, suicide, divorce, and alcoholism, for a city this size it also has many commendable pluses.

Tucson has more sunshine than any other U.S. city. Only three other U.S. cities of under one million population have such a full complement of the performing arts. For years, it has been one of the best cities for job openings. It has been a

239

longtime favorite city for retirement. And with its city-wide network of bicycle paths, Tucson is filled with enticing fitness opportunities.

True, ugly power lines tower above miles of new subdivisions that are encroaching on the northern foothills. Yet most neighborhoods are verdant with native desert landscaping and a ring of distant mountains encircles the city. To escape the wilting midday heat of summer, you may have to take your daily 5-mile walk or jog at sunrise. But from fall through spring, Tucson enjoys month after month of mild, dry, sunny weather.

Over 40 percent of the population are prosperous baby boomers and another 10 percent are younger, affluent retirees. Add in 31,000 students enrolled at the University of Arizona, and you have an exceptionally well-educated energetic and health-conscious population. The median age is 32.

A network of bicycle paths leads through quiet streets and byways all over the city, while outside Tucson good bicycling can be found in Saguaro National Monument and Sabino Canyon. Two large Arizona bicycle clubs sponsor frequent group rides, and the annual 100-mile Tour de Tucson—America's largest city perimeter ride—draws thousands of bicyclists.

Among the more than 400 public and private tennis courts, we were particularly impressed by the park department's 24-court Randolph Tennis Center and by the courts in Himmel and Reid Parks. Seven thriving recreation centers are each equipped with jogging or heart trails, weight rooms, and gymnasiums, and some have indoor jogging tracks for use in summer. Various parks department classes teach martial arts, senior fitness, sweat-and-swim techniques, body contouring, and aerobic dancing for adults. The five parks department pools each offer several daily hours of adult lapswimming, and the Club 100 presents awards to those who rack up total distances of 25, 50, or 100 miles. The Southern

Arizona Hiking Club organizes weekly hikes. Or you can drive out a short distance and find miles of beautiful desert hiking trails in a series of parks and canyons in the Santa Catalina Mountains.

Tucson will keep your mind stimulated with a host of nationally-recognized cultural events and non-credit study courses. Presenting a long string of winter season performance in the splendid Community Center Theater is the highly-acclaimed Tucson Symphony; a professional opera company; the professional resident Arizona Theater company; the Ballet Arizona company; and the Southern Arizona Light Opera. Adding zest to the theater scene are experimental theater productions at the Invisible Theater. More lectures, classic films, and chamber music concerts are presented by the university. Two major art museums showcase western art. And you can study almost any subject through the non-credit courses of the university's continuing education program.

For stress management, the parks department offers year around classes in yoga, t'ai chi, and aquaflex stretching. The Volunteer Bureau matches adults to volunteer openings. And most adults find unlimited social opportunities through the many senior clubs (open to all over 50) and the popular round and square dances that culminate in an annual festival.

Home of the 300-bed University Medical Center teaching hospital, plus eleven other community hospitals, 1,500 physicians, a V.A. hospital, seven HMOs, and a military base hospital, Tucson provides exceptionally good medical care. A wide choice of flat-roofed pueblo-style new and resale homes are available at affordable cost and you'll normally find a huge choice of rentals, many in deluxe apartment complexes. Also here are scores of outlying mobile home parks. Living costs are about average and inexpensive evaporative coolers are often preferred to refrigerated air. For active retirement, you might consider Sun City Vistoso, a new fitness-oriented version of the Sun Cities (see) located 11 miles north of downtown. A city-wide bus service is available.

Most drawbacks have already been mentioned. A ring of copper smelters, plus auto exhausts, form a steady source of air pollution, while non-renewable underground water resources are being steadily depleted. Eventually, yard and golf course watering may be banned.

Scores: Urban 3. Climate 4. Elevation 2. Terrain 3. Awareness 5. Nutrition 3. Fitness 5. Stress 3. Mind 5. Social 4. Volunteer 4. Spiritual 3. Care 5. Total Healthfulness: 49.

Information: CoC, Box 991, Tucson, AZ 85702 (602-792-2250). C&VB, 130 South Scott, Tucson, AZ 85701 (602-624-1817). P&R, 900 South Randolph Way, Tucson, AZ 85716 (602-791-4873).

**WEST PALM BEACH, FL.** Population: (area) 500,000. Urban Stress: EST 3. Elevation: 13'. West Palm Beach today is the flagship city for over twenty adjoining mainland communities plus the aristocratic resort of Palm Beach, which is located on a spindly 14 mile long barrier island. Together, they comprise the Palm Beaches, one of Florida's wealthiest and fastest-growing metropolitan areas. Amid all the emphasis on golf and polo, and on the elegant luxury of Palm Beach, health and fitness receive scant attention in publicity brochures. In fact, the city of Palm Beach once tried to prohibit joggers from running without wearing a shirt and, more recently, they tried to ban tennis ball machines. So how important, really, is health and fitness in these playgrounds of the rich and famous?

You may not hear much about fitness resources, but the fact is that the area's sheer wealth has provided a bounty of trails, tennis courts, parks and lakes, and some of the finest municipal swimming pools in the nation. Behind the towering hi-rises—some 30 stories high—that block access to beaches and overwhelm public facilities, are a dozen parks and wilderness preserves with superb walking and canoeing. This is a great place for tennis. And despite poor bicycling, opportunities for keeping fit abound.

In Palm Beach, you can still find rakish coconut trees and masses of purple bougainvillea pouring wildly over pink walls. But elsewhere, outside the public parks, the presence of congested freeways and boulevards, and massive shopping malls and hi-tech plants and the endless miles of flat, paved-over, look-alike suburbia is almost overwhelming. Nonetheless ocean breezes keep the air constantly pure, and tens of thousands of retirees manage to enjoy relaxed living in quieter communities like Lake Worth, Lantana, and Jupiter. Summers are long, hot and humid, of course, and most people exercise in the cooler early morning hours. By contrast, winters are perfect for spending the entire day outdoors.

With 30 percent of the population retired, affluent baby boomers and active retirees are the force behind the growing interest in health and fitness. Presence of the big Healthy Harvest natural foods supermarket, together with Esser's Health Ranch, and natural foods eateries with names like *Alive and Well*, confirm the high level of nutritional awareness. Thousands of residents grow papaya, mango, guavas, avocadoes, pineapples, and citrus in their backyards.

Miles of scenic lakeside trails web the parks, you can walk or jog on Lantana beach (recently still free of hi-rises), or you can hike up Palm Beach's Lake Trail through the manicured estates of the ultra-rich. With a canoe, you can paddle up the intracoastal, waterway a mere dozen feet from the backyards of pedigreed Palm Beach scions, or on a choice of lakes and rivers, or through Loxahatchie Wildlife Refuge. For serious swimming, there are four 50-meter pools with daily lapswimming and three are heated in winter. Some have Masters programs with daily competitive speed swimming for adults. A total of over 1,200 tennis courts includes more than 60 complexes with unlimited opportunities for day or night play. We found a delightful heart exercise trail in a Lake Worth park. Bicycling is admittedly poor, but local cyclists manage to ride in the exclusive suburb of Wellington on weekdays and on Highway A1A along the ocean early on Sunday mornings.

From top-caliber symphony concerts to the Ballet Florida, Miami City Ballet, grand opera, and scores of professional plays, mind-inspiring culture flourishes during the winter tourist season. Norton Art Gallery showcases a world class permanent art exhibition, with futuristic art displayed at Lake Worth's Lennon Art Foundation. Rounding out the intellectual scene are the hundreds of adult education classes offered by Palm Beach Community College, while a science museum and planetarium stimulate interest in cosmology and physics.

From yoga to biofeedback and t'ai chi, every type of stress-management technique is available, while one of Florida's better bus services relieves residents from the stress of driving. Among numerous opportunities for adult social activities are the regular ballroom dancing sessions at Lake Worth's oceanfront casino. Virtually every religious denomination is represented, including several very active Unity churches, and one of the largest metaphysical bookshops in the South. And while the Palm Beaches lack any outstanding hospitals, excellent health care is available everywhere.

An explosion of new hi-tech industry, with corresponding fast growth in employment, has sent home prices soaring in recent years. Among less expensive housing alternatives are thousands of condominium apartments, hundreds of rental garden apartments, and at least 50 well-equipped mobile home parks, many restricted to older adults.

In addition to some of the drawbacks already mentioned is the deafening jet aircraft noise over some of the older sections of the city. Parking is expensive at beaches and virtually unobtainable on weekends. Some beaches are eroding. Freeways are crunched with cars. Drugs, crime, and break-ins are commonplace. And there are square miles of lower socioeconomic neighborhoods that are unsuited to retirement.

Scores: Urban 5. Climate 4. Elevation 1. Terrain 4. Awareness 4. Nutrition 4. Fitness 5. Stress 3. Mind 4. Social 4. Volunteer 3. Spiritual 3. Care 4. Total Healthfulness: 48.

Information: CoC, 401 North Flagler Drive, West Palm Beach, FL 33401 (407-833-3711). C&VB, 1555 Palm Beach Lakes Boulevard, Suite 204, West Palm Beach, FL 33401 (407-471-3995). P&R, 2700 Sixth Avenue South, Lake Worth, FL 33461 (407-964-4420).

# FOR FURTHER READING

Ahlquist, J.E., Sibley C.G. "Phylogeny of the Hominoid Primates as Indicated by DNA-DNA Hybridization." *Journal of Molecular Evolution,* No 20, 1984: pp 2-15.

Barnwell, G. "Your Contribution to Global Warming." *National Wildlife,* Vol 28, No 2, Feb-Mar 1990: p 53.

Baruch, Grace; Barnett, Rosalind. *Lifeprints.* McGraw Hill, (New American Library; Signet), 1985.

Black, Dean, Ph. D. *Health at the Crossroads.* Tapestry Press, 1988.

Brenner, B.M., et al. "Dietary Protein Intake and the Progressive Nature of Kidney Disease." *New England Journal of Medicine,* No 307, 1982: pp 652-659.

Borysenko, Joan, Ph. D. *Minding the Body, Mending the Mind.* Addison Wesley, 1987.

Brookes, Warren T. "The Global Warming Panic." *Forbes,* Dec 25, 1989.

Burkett, D.P. ; Towell, H.C. *Western Diseases: Their Emergence and Prevention.* Harvard University Press, 1981.

Capra, Fritjof. *Looking Glass Universe: Science, Society and the Rising Culture.* Bantam, 1982.

Carpenter, Betsy. "A Faulty Greenhouse." *U.S. News,* Jan 1, 1990: p 52.; "The Greening of the Church." *U.S. News,* Nov 27, 1989: p 66.; "Living With Our Legacy." *U. S. News,* April 23, 1990: p 60.; "Secrets of the Sea." *U. S. News,* Aug 21, 1989: p 48.

Cooper, Kenneth H, M.D., M.P.H. *Aerobics Program for Total Wellbeing.* Bantam, 1988.

Dahlberg, F, editor. *Woman the Gatherer.* Yale University Press, 1981.

Devall, W., Sessions, G. *Deep Ecology: Living as if Nature Mattered.* Peregrine Smith, 1985.

Diamond, Jared (professor of physiology, UCLA School of Medicine). "Dawn of the Human Race." *Discover,* May 1989.

Dychtwald, K. *Age Wave.* J.P. Tarcher, 1989.

East-West Journal's editors. "The Best and Worst Places to Live—rating the healthful cities." *East-West Journal,* May 1989: p 47.

Easterbrook, Gregg. "Cleaning Up Our Mess." *Newsweek,* July 24, 1989: pp 26-40.

Eaton, S. Boyd, M.D.; Konner, Melvin J., M.D., Ph. D.; Shostak, Marjorie. "Stone Agers in the Fast Lane: Chronic and Degenerative Diseases in Evolutionary Perspective." *American Journal of Medicine,* No 84, 1988: pp 739-749.; *The Paleolithic Prescription.* Harper & Row, 1989.

Ferguson, Marilyn. *The Aquarian Conspiracy: Personal and Social Transformation in the 1980s.* J. P. Tarcher, 1980,

Ford, Norman D. *Where to Retire on a Small Income,* 26th revised edition, Harian Press, 1985.; *Best Rated Retirement Cities and Towns.* Consumer Guides, 1988.; *Formula for Long Life,* 3rd revised edition. Harian Press, 1985.; *Lifestyle for Longevity.* Para Research, 1984.; *Good Health Without Drugs.* St. Martin's Press, 1977.; *Sleep Well, Live Well.* Zebra Books, 1985.; *Keep on Pedaling—the complete guide to adult bicycling.* Countryman Press, 1990.

Fuchs, Victor. *The Health Economy.* Harvard University Press, 1986.

Harmon, Willis, Ph.D. *Global Mind Change.* Knowledge Systems, Inc., 1988.

Heaney, R.P. "Calcium, Bone Health and Osteoporosis." *Journal of Bone and Mineral Research,* No 4, 1986: pp 225-301.

Gilbert, Susan. "America Washing Away—wrecking the nation's finest beaches." *Science Digest,* Aug 1986.

Inlander, Charles B.; Lowell, S. Levin. *Medicine on Trial.* Prentice Hall, 1988.

Keys, Ancel. *Seven Countries: a Multivariate Analysis of Death and Coronary Disease.* Harvard University Press, 1980.

Lang, Susan S. "The World's Healthiest Diet (Chinese Diet Study)." *American Health,* Sept 1989: p 105.

Levine, Robert. "In Search of Eden: City Stress Index." *Psychology Today,* Nov 1988: p 53.

Lovelock, James E. *Gaia: a New Look at Life on Earth.* Oxford University Press, 1979.; *The Ages of Gaia.* Norton, 1988.; "Geophysiology: a New Look at Earth Science." *Bulletin of the American Meterological Society,* Vol 67, No 4, April 1986: pp 392-397.

McLoughlin, Merrill with Carpenter, Betsy et al. "Our Dirty Air." *U. S. News,* June 12, 1989.

Mendelsohn, Robert S. *Confessions of a Medical Heretic.* Contemporary Books Inc., 1979.

Money Magazine's editors. "The Best Places to Live." *Money Magazine,* Aug 1987: p 34.

Ornish, Dean, M.D. *Stress, Diet and Your Heart.* New American Library, Signet Books, 1983.; *Dr. Dean Ornish's Program for Reversing Heart Disease.* Random House, 1990.

Paffenbarger, R. S. et al. "Physical Activity, All-Cause Mortality and Longevity of College Alumni." *New England Journal of Medicine,* No 314, 1986: pp 605-613.

Pelletier, Kenneth. *A New Age: Problems and Potentials.* Robert Briggs Associates, 1985.

Pena, Nelson; Fremont, James. "How the Bike Can Save L.A.—and your town, too." *Bicycling,* Aug 1990: pp 32-38.

Perlmutter, Cathy. "Reverse Heart Disease Naturally." *Prevention*, May 1990: pp 50-62-66.

Radetsky, Peter; Garrick, James M.D. *Be Your Own Personal Trainer.* Crown, 1989.

Reese, Michael; Foote, Jennifer. "California: American Dream, American Nightmare." *Newsweek,* July 31, 1989: p 23.

Robbins, John. *Diet for a New America.* Stillpoint Press, 1987.

Schaeffer, Robert. "Car Sick: Automobiles Ad Nauseum." *Greenpeace,* Vol 15, No 3, May-June 1990: p 13.

Schlossberg, Nancy, M.D. *Overwhelmed: Coping with Life's Ups and Downs.* Lexington Books, 1990.

Schumacher, E. F. *Small is Beautiful: Economics as if People Mattered.* Abacus Press, 1974.

Siegel, Bernie S., M.D. *Love, Medicine and Miracles.* Harper & Row, 1986.

Silver, Marc. "Doing Your Bit to Save the Earth." *U.S. News,* April 2, 1990: p 61.

Tart, Charles. *Waking Up: Overcoming the Obstacles to Human Potential.* Shambhala—New Science Library, 1986.

Weber, Susan. "Curbing Planetary Woes Depends on Curbing Growth." *Zero Population Growth Reporter,* April 1990: p 1.; "In Troubled Waters: nation's water supplies being fast depleted by population growth." *Zero Population Growth Reporter,* June 1990: p 1.; *USA By Numbers—a statistical portrait of the U.S.* Zero Population Growth, 1988.

Williams, Redford, M.D. *The Trusting Heart: Great News About Type-A Behavior.* Random House, 1989.

Wolfe, Sidney M., M.D. et al. *Worst pills, Best Pills—the older adult's guide to avoiding drug-induced death or illness.* Public Citizen Health Research Group, 1988

Woods, B, Martin, L, Andrews, P. *Major Topics in Primate and Human Evolution.* Cambridge University Press, 1986.

# INDEX

lifestyle factor, 16
  mortality factor, 17
Nutritional awareness level in
  healthful cities, 77, 81

Obesity, a hazard to health, 84
Ornish, Dean, M.D., 2, 62
Osteoporosis, China vs. U.S., 64
Ott, John N., 54
Overeating, 80
Overpopulation, 21, 34
Ozone, poor air quality due to, 26

Paffenbarger, Ralph, Ph.D., 82
Paradise, CA, 202-204
Pelletier, Kenneth, Ph. D., 106
Pensacola, FL, 204-207
Pollution:
  from pesticides, 31
  most polluted cities, 28
  of coastal waters and shores, 31
Population size:
  effects on health, 39
  very small communities can be
  unhealthful, 40
Portland, OR, 207-209
Prescott, AZ, 210-212
Preventive medicine, 3, 60
Pritikin, program and centers, 61, 77
Primate ancestors of man, 68-70
Pro-health habits, see "Low-risk life-
  style"
Protein, dangers of excessive
  consumption, 64
Providence, RI, 212-214

Rand Corporation, study of surgical
  procedures, 59
Recycling:
  healthful cities have strong programs for, 31
  of garbage, 30
Redding, CA, 214-217
Retired Senior Volunteer Program,
  103-104

Rowing, as exercise, 88-89
Ruberman, William, M.D., 100

St. Petersburg, FL, 1, 217-220
San Antonio, TX, 220-223
San Diego, CA, 223-226
Santa Fe, NM, 52, 88, 226-229
Seasonal Affecting Disorder (SAD),
  48
Scherwitz, Larry, Ph.D., 62
Seattle, WA, 229-232
Second-tier city defined, 39-40
Sedentary living, hazardous to
  health, 84
Selenium, health benefits of, 56
Senior Companion Program, 104
Service Corps of Retired Executives
  (SCORE), 104
Seven Countries Study, 77
Silver City, NM, 232-234
Skiing, cross-country, 88
Smog, 26
  carbon monoxide, 27
  ozone, 26
Social contacts:
  beneficial to health, 99
  healthful cities offer more, 101
Spiritual growth, health benefits of,
  105-107
Stanford University School of Medi-
  cine, 82
State health statistics, 15-16
Statistics, unreliability of, 7-8
Strength-building exercises:
  health benefits for older people,
  85
  resources for, 86
Stress management resources, 93
  biofeedback, relaxation, 94
  most abundant in healthful
  cities, 95
  personality transformation, 94
Stretching and flexibility exercises,
  86
Sun Cities, AZ, 234-237

# Other Books Available From Mills and Sanderson

*Thirteen National Parks with Room to Roam,* by Ruthe and Walt Wolverton. Discover those under-utilized parks that lack the pressing crowds but have the beauty, charm, and facilities you want. $9.95

*Touring Europe by Motorhome,* by Helen Vander Male. A wonderful resource for the first time motorhome traveler in Europe. Answers your questions and tells you how to make the most of this special mode of travel. $9.95

*The World Up Close: A Cyclist's Adventures on Five Continents,* by Kameel B. Nasr. Discover the essence of humanity through various cultures by vicariously wandering the world by bicycle. $9.95

*The Alaska Traveler: Year 'Round Vacation Adventures for Everyone,* by Steven C. Levi. With maps and cartoons, this is a unique insider's guide to gold panning, stalking big game, windsurfing, dogsledding, etc. $9.95

*The Portugal Traveler: Great Sights and Hidden Treasures,* by Barbara Radcliffe Rogers and Stillman Rogers. A companion to fascinating places to eat and sleep, festivals and other events as well as insider tips to enrich your visit. Includes city maps. $9.95

*Sicilian Walks: Exploring the History and Culture of the Two Sicilies,* by William J. Bonville. Self-guided tours (with maps)of Sicily and the adjacent Italian mainland. $9.95

*Childbirth Choices in Mothers' Words,* by Kim Selbert, M.F.C.C.. Twenty-one mothers tell in their own words about their birth experiences—the highs and the lows—with the varied types of childbirth currently available in the U.S. $9.95.

*Bedtime Teaching Tales for Kids: A Parent's Storybook,* by Gary Ludvigson, Ph. D. Eighteen engrossing stories to help children 5-11 work through problems such as fear of failure, sibling rivalry, bullies, divorce, death, child abuse, handicaps,etc. $9.95

*Your Food-Allergic Child: A Parent's Guide,* by Janet E. Meizel. How to shop and cook for children with allergies, plus nutrient and chemical reference charts of common foods, medications, and grocery brands. $9.95

*Winning Tactics for Women Over Forty: How to Take Charge of Your Life and Have Fun Doing It,* by Anne De Sola Cardoza and Mavis B. Sutton. For women left alone through separation, divorce or death, "this title presents many positive, concrete options for change." — *The Midwest Book Review* $9.95

*Fifty and Fired: How to Prepare for It - What to Do When It Happens,* by Ed Brandt with Leonard Corwen. How to deal with getting forcefully "restructured" out of your job at the wrong time in your career. $9.95 / $16.95 (hardcover)

*Aquacises: Restoring and Maintaining Mobility with Water Excrcises,* by Miriam Study Giles. Despite age, obesity or physical handicaps, anyone can improve their fitness with this instructive illustrated handbook. $9.95

*60-Second Shiatzu: How to Energize, Erase Pain, and Conquer Tension in One Minute,* by Eva Shaw. A helpfully illustrated, quick-results introduction to do-it-yourself acupressure. $7.95

*Bachelor in the Kitchen: Beyond Bologna and Cheese*, by Gordon Haskett with Wendy Haskett. Fast and easy ways to make delectable meals, snacks, drinks from easily obtainable ingredients. $7.95

## Order Form

If you are unable to find our books in your local bookstore, you may order them directly from us. Please enclose check or money order for amount of purchase and add $1.00 per book handling charge.

( ) Bonville / *Sicilian Walks* $9.95 _____
( ) Levi / *The Alaska Traveler* $9.95 _____
( ) Nasr / *The World Up Close* $9.95 _____
( ) Rogers / *The Portugal Traveler* $9.95 _____
( ) Vander Male / *Touring Europe by Motorhome* $9.95 _____
( ) Wolverton / *Thirteen National Parks* $9.95 _____
( ) Ludvigson / *Bedtime Teaching Tales for Kids* $9.95 _____
( ) Meizel / *Your Food-Allergic Child* $9.95 _____
( ) Selbert / *Childbirth Choices in Mothers' Words* $9.95 _____
( ) Cardoza/Sutton / *Winning Tactics for Women* $9.95 _____
( ) Brandt/Corwen / *Fifty and Fired* $16.95 (cloth) _____
( ) Brandt/Corwen / *Fifty and Fired* $9.95 (paper) _____
( ) Giles / *Aquacises* $9.95 _____
( ) Shaw / *60-Second Shiatzu* $7.95 _____
( ) Haskett / *Bachelor in the Kitchen* $7.95 _____

$1.00 per book handling charge _____
5% sales tax for MA residents _____

Total amount enclosed _____

Name: _____

Address: _____

City: _____ State: _____ Zip code: _____

Mail to: **Mills & Sanderson, Publishers**
442 Marrett Road, Suite 6
Lexington, MA 02173
617-861-0992

*Our Toll-Free Order # is 1-800-441-6224*